First World War
and Army of Occupation
War Diary
France, Belgium and Germany

7 DIVISION
Divisional Troops
37 Brigade Royal Field Artillery,
Divisional Trench Mortar Batteries
and Divisional Ammunition Column
8 September 1914 - 30 November 1917

WO95/1644

The Naval & Military Press Ltd
www.nmarchive.com
Published in association with The National Archives

Published by

The Naval & Military Press Ltd

Unit 10 Ridgewood Industrial Park,

Uckfield, East Sussex,

TN22 5QE England

Tel: +44 (0) 1825 749494

www.naval-military-press.com

www.nmarchive.com

This diary has been reprinted in facsimile from the original. Any imperfections are inevitably reproduced and the quality may fall short of modern type and cartographic standards.

Contents

Document type	Place/Title	Date From	Date To
Heading	WO95/1644/1		
Heading	7th Division 37th Bde. R.F.A. Mar 1915-May 1916 Bde Broken Up May 1916		
Heading	7th Div R.F.A. 37th Brigade March-Dec 1915 May 1916		
Heading	7th Division 4th Corps (7th Division) Came From 4th Division 37th Bde R.F.A. Vol VIII 1-31.3.15		
War Diary	Riez Bailleul France	01/03/1915	31/03/1915
Heading	7th Division 37th Bde R.F.A. Vol IX 1-30.4.15		
War Diary	Laventie	01/04/1915	30/04/1915
Heading	7th Division 37th Bde. R.F.A. Vol X 1-31.5.15		
War Diary	Billets 1/2 N. Of Merries	01/05/1915	08/05/1915
War Diary	Bombardment	09/05/1915	31/05/1915
Heading	7th Division 37th Bde. R.F.A. Vol XI 1-30.6.15		
War Diary	Le Touret	01/06/1915	25/06/1915
War Diary	Gorre	26/06/1915	30/06/1915
Heading	7th Division 37th Bde R.F.A. Vol XII July 15		
War Diary	Gorre	01/07/1915	01/07/1915
War Diary	L'Ecleme	02/07/1915	31/07/1915
Heading	7th Division 37th Bde R.F.A. August 15 Vol XIII		
War Diary	L'Ecleme	02/08/1915	31/08/1915
Heading	Headquarters 37th Brigade R.F.A. (7th Division) September 1915		
War Diary		01/09/1915	25/09/1915
War Diary	Vermelles	25/09/1915	30/09/1915
Miscellaneous	Lieut. R.C. Reynolds (Now Captain) Adj. 2nd Training Brigade R.A. Depot	07/09/1917	07/09/1917
Heading	7th Division 37th Bde. R.F.A. Oct 15 Vol XV		
War Diary	Vermelles	01/10/1915	18/10/1915
War Diary	Mazinghem	23/10/1915	24/10/1915
War Diary	Gorre	25/10/1915	31/10/1915
War Diary	Vermelles	00/10/1915	00/10/1915
Heading	7th Division 37th Bde R.F.A. Nov Vol XVI		
War Diary	Gorre	01/11/1915	21/11/1915
War Diary	Loisnes	22/11/1915	30/11/1915
War Diary		11/11/1915	11/11/1915
War Diary	Gorre Loisnes	00/11/1915	00/11/1915
Heading	7th Div 37th Bde R.F.A. Dec Vol XVII		
War Diary	Loisnes	03/12/1915	06/12/1915
War Diary	Hangest	06/12/1915	31/12/1915
War Diary		11/12/1915	11/12/1915
Heading	37 Bde R.F.A. Jan Vol XVIII		
War Diary	Hangest	03/01/1916	21/01/1916
Heading	37 Bde R.F.A. Feb Vol XIX		
War Diary	Hangest	03/02/1916	09/02/1916
War Diary	Meaulte	10/02/1916	23/02/1916
War Diary		09/02/1916	12/02/1916
War Diary		11/02/1916	13/02/1916
Miscellaneous		00/02/1916	00/02/1916
Miscellaneous	Brought Forward		

War Diary	Meaulte	02/03/1916	30/04/1916
War Diary	Morlancourt	01/05/1916	19/05/1916
War Diary		30/05/1916	16/06/1916
Heading	WO95/1644/2		
Heading	7th Division Trench Mortar Batteries Feb 19156-1917 Nov To Italy		
Heading	2nd Trenches Mortar Battery Late 410 20th Inf. Bde. 7th. Division From February 25th To March 31st 1916 Vol I		
War Diary			
War Diary		14/04/1916	30/04/1916
Heading	War Diary Of X7 Trench Mortar Battery From 1st May 1916 To 31st May 1916 Volume 3		
Miscellaneous			
Heading	Confidential War Diary Of V7 Heavy Trench Mortar Battery From 1st August To 30th September 1916		
War Diary	Heilly	01/08/1916	20/08/1916
War Diary	Meaulte	20/08/1916	20/08/1916
War Diary	Montauban	21/08/1916	21/08/1916
War Diary	Devillewood	22/08/1916	31/08/1916
War Diary	Montanban	01/09/1916	30/09/1916
Heading	War Diary Of V 7 Heavy Trench Mortar Battery For Month of October 1916		
War Diary	Ploegsteert	01/10/1916	31/10/1916
Heading	7th Divisional Artillery "X" : "Y" : "Z" Trench Mortar Batteries August 1916		
Heading	Confidential War Diary Of X 7 Trenches Mortar Battery From 1st August To 30th September		
War Diary	Heilly	01/08/1916	20/08/1916
War Diary	Meaulte	20/08/1916	20/08/1916
War Diary	Fricourt	28/08/1916	30/09/1916
Heading	Confidential War Diary Of Y 7 Trenches Mortar Battery From 1st August To 30th Sept Vol 8+9		
War Diary	Heilly	01/08/1916	31/08/1916
War Diary		28/08/1916	28/08/1916
War Diary	Heilly	01/08/1916	18/08/1916
War Diary	Meaulte	20/08/1916	20/08/1916
War Diary	Delville Wd	21/08/1916	24/08/1916
War Diary	Mantanban	26/08/1916	29/08/1916
War Diary	Fricourt	01/09/1916	30/09/1916
Heading	War Diary Of X 7 Trench Mortar Battery For The Month Of October 1916		
War Diary	In The Field	31/10/1916	31/10/1916
War Diary	Montanban	01/09/1916	09/09/1916
War Diary	Tirancourt	11/09/1916	30/09/1916
Heading	War Diary For October 1916 Y 7 T.M.B		
War Diary	Ploegsteert	02/10/1916	31/10/1916
Heading	War Diary Of X 7 Trench Mortar Battery For Month Of November 1916		
War Diary			
Miscellaneous	Z 7 Trench Mortar Late 445 Bty Vol I		
Miscellaneous	Z 7 Trench Mot		
Miscellaneous	Nil (Not In Action)		
Heading	War Diary Of Z 7 Trench Mortar Battery From 1st August To 30th September 1916		
War Diary	In The Field	01/10/1916	01/10/1916

War Diary	Schaeken	02/10/1916	03/10/1916
War Diary	Ploegsteert	04/10/1916	28/10/1916
War Diary		00/02/1916	00/06/1916
War Diary	Picquigny	01/08/1916	12/08/1916
War Diary	Buire	13/08/1916	30/08/1916
Miscellaneous	22/2 T M Bty Vol I		
Heading	Confidential War Diary Of 22nd Trench Mortar Battery Volume I		
War Diary	Belloy. S. Somme (France)	01/08/1916	09/08/1916
War Diary	Belloy S Somme	10/08/1916	12/08/1916
War Diary	Dernancourt	13/08/1916	26/08/1916
War Diary	Montauban	27/08/1916	31/08/1916
War Diary	Ploegsteert	01/11/1916	30/11/1916
Heading	7th Div T.M. Brigade December 1916		
War Diary		01/12/1916	31/12/1916
Miscellaneous	To D A G	24/08/1916	24/08/1916
Heading	7th Division Trench Mortar Brigade January 1917		
Heading	Original 7th Trench Mortar Brigade War Diary For January 1917		
War Diary	In The Area	01/01/1917	24/01/1917
Heading	Original Trench Mortar Brigade 7th Division War Diary For February 1917		
War Diary	In The Field	01/02/1917	26/03/1917
War Diary		22/03/1917	31/03/1917
War Diary		24/03/1917	31/03/1917
War Diary		29/03/1917	31/03/1917
War Diary		27/03/1917	27/03/1917
War Diary	In The Field	28/03/1917	31/03/1917
War Diary	In The Field	01/03/1917	08/04/1917
War Diary	In The Field	01/04/1917	30/04/1917
Heading	7th Division Trench Mortar Battery May 1917		
War Diary	In The Field	01/05/1917	31/05/1917
War Diary	In The Field	17/05/1917	31/05/1917
Heading	7th Division Trench Mortar Battery June 1917		
War Diary	In The Field	01/06/1917	07/06/1917
War Diary		03/06/1917	04/06/1917
War Diary		15/06/1917	15/06/1917
War Diary	In The Field	13/06/1917	20/06/1917
War Diary		18/06/1917	18/06/1917
War Diary		11/06/1917	20/06/1917
War Diary		18/06/1917	23/06/1917
War Diary	In The Field	20/06/1917	22/06/1917
War Diary		01/06/1917	24/06/1917
War Diary	In The Field	26/06/1917	26/06/1917
War Diary		24/06/1917	28/06/1917
War Diary	In The Field	28/06/1917	30/06/1917
Heading	7th Division Trench Mortar Battery July 1917		
War Diary	In The Field	01/07/1917	31/07/1917
War Diary		29/07/1917	31/07/1917
War Diary	In The Field	31/07/1917	31/07/1917
Heading	7th Division Trench Battery August 1917		
War Diary	In The Field	01/08/1917	31/08/1917
War Diary		14/08/1917	30/08/1917
War Diary		28/08/1917	28/08/1917
Miscellaneous	7th Division Trench Mortar Battery September 1917		
War Diary		01/09/1917	30/09/1917

Heading	7th Division Trench Mortar Battery October 1917		
War Diary		01/10/1917	31/10/1917
Heading	7th Division Trench Mortar Battery October 1917		
War Diary	Dichebush	01/11/1917	10/11/1917
War Diary	Boeschepe	11/11/1917	14/11/1917
War Diary	Renescure	15/11/1917	18/11/1917
War Diary	Arques	19/11/1917	30/11/1917
War Diary	Italy	30/11/1917	30/11/1917
Heading	WO95/1644/3		
Heading	7th Division 7th Divl Ammn Column Sep 1914-1917 Nov		
Heading	7th Div Ammunition Column 1914 Sep-1915 Dec		
Heading	7th Divisional Artillery 7th Divisional Ammunition Column R.F.A. 8th September-9th December 1914 Mar 1919		
Heading	Original Confidential War Diary Of 7th Divisional Ammunition Column From 8th September 19147 To 9.12.14 (Volume I)		
War Diary	Southampton	08/09/1914	10/09/1914
War Diary	Portsmouth	12/09/1914	05/10/1914
War Diary	Southampton	05/10/1914	05/10/1914
War Diary	Ostend	07/10/1914	09/10/1914
War Diary	Southampton	05/10/1914	05/10/1914
War Diary	Zeebrugge	07/10/1914	07/10/1914
War Diary	Bruges	08/10/1914	08/10/1914
War Diary	Ostend	09/10/1914	09/10/1914
War Diary	Southampton	07/10/1914	07/10/1914
War Diary	Zeebrugge	08/10/1914	09/10/1914
War Diary	Bruges	10/10/1914	10/10/1914
War Diary	Akkerstraet	12/10/1914	12/10/1914
War Diary	Svevezeele	13/10/1914	13/10/1914
War Diary	Roulers	14/10/1914	14/10/1914
War Diary	Ypres	17/10/1914	31/10/1914
War Diary	Millekruis	02/11/1914	02/11/1914
War Diary	Westoutre	03/11/1914	04/11/1914
War Diary	Ouderdom	04/11/1914	13/11/1914
War Diary	Nr Bailleul	15/11/1914	15/11/1914
War Diary	Ouderdom	15/11/1914	15/11/1914
War Diary	Nr Bailleul	16/11/1914	16/11/1914
War Diary	Doulieu	17/11/1914	20/11/1914
War Diary	Nr Poperinghe	22/11/1914	22/11/1914
War Diary	Doulieu	24/11/1914	09/12/1914
Heading	7th Divisional Ammun Coln Vol II 16.12.14-26.1.15		
War Diary	Doulieu	16/12/1914	16/12/1914
War Diary	Nr Troubayard	17/12/1914	26/01/1915
Heading	7th Divisional Ammun Coln Vol III 3 2-4.3.15		
War Diary	Doulieu	03/02/1915	03/02/1915
War Diary	Trou Bayard	25/01/1915	25/01/1915
War Diary	Doulieu	03/02/1915	02/03/1915
War Diary	Vieux Berquin	03/03/1915	04/03/1915
Heading	7th Divl Ammun Coln Vol IV 4-30.3.15		
War Diary	Vieux Berquin	04/03/1915	06/03/1915
War Diary	Courant Metteren. Bec	08/03/1915	13/03/1915
War Diary	Metteren. Be.	11/03/1915	23/03/1915
War Diary	Le. Sart	23/03/1915	30/03/1915
Heading	Divl. Ammun Coln 7th Division Vol V 4-28.4.15		

War Diary	Le. Sart	04/04/1915	12/04/1915
War Diary	Meurillon	13/04/1915	27/04/1915
Heading	7th Divl. Ammun Coln Vol VI 4-22.5.15		
War Diary	Vieux Berquin	04/05/1915	04/05/1915
War Diary	Meurillon	05/05/1915	09/05/1915
War Diary	Nouveau Monde	10/05/1915	11/05/1915
War Diary	Annezin	11/05/1915	22/05/1915
Heading	7th Division 7th Divl Ammun Coln Vol VII 23.5-23.6.15		
War Diary	Annezin	23/05/1915	31/05/1915
War Diary	Les Choquaux	05/06/1915	25/06/1915
Heading	7th Division 7th Div A. Column Vol VIII 25-6-30.7.15		
War Diary	Les Choquaux	25/06/1915	02/07/1915
War Diary	Cantrainne	04/07/1915	30/07/1915
Heading	7th Division 7th Divl Ammun Coln Vol IX From 5-28.8.15		
War Diary	Cantrainne	05/08/1915	15/08/1915
War Diary	Riez Du Vinage	17/08/1915	18/08/1915
War Diary	Paradis	20/08/1915	27/08/1915
War Diary	Riez Du Vinage	27/08/1918	28/08/1918
Heading	War Diary Divisional Ammunition Coloumn 7th Division September 1915		
War Diary	Riez Du Vinage	02/09/1915	02/09/1915
War Diary	Fouquiers	03/09/1915	25/09/1915
War Diary	Labourse	26/09/1915	29/09/1915
War Diary	Bethune	30/09/1915	30/09/1915
Heading	7th Division 7th Divl Ammun Col Oct 15 Vol XI		
War Diary	Bethune	01/10/1915	16/10/1915
War Diary	Annezin	18/10/1915	19/10/1915
War Diary	Molinghem	20/10/1915	20/10/1915
War Diary	Vendin Lez Bethune	24/10/1915	30/10/1915
Heading	7th Div Ammun Col Nov Vol XII		
War Diary	Vendin-Lez Bethune	31/10/1915	26/11/1915
Heading	7th Divl Ammun Col Dec Vol XIII		
War Diary	Vendin	30/11/1915	03/12/1915
War Diary	Lagoulee	07/12/1915	07/12/1915
War Diary	Le Quesnoy	08/12/1915	31/12/1915
Heading	7 Div Ammn Col Jan Vol XIV		
War Diary	Le Luemot	01/01/1916	29/01/1916
War Diary	Le Qesnot	02/02/1916	06/02/1916
War Diary	Bonnay	06/02/1916	25/02/1916
Miscellaneous	Headquarters Office 7th Divisional Ammn Coln		
War Diary	Bonnay	02/03/1916	07/03/1916
War Diary	Buire	09/03/1916	31/03/1916
War Diary	Mericourt	23/04/1916	01/05/1916
War Diary	Bonnay	16/05/1916	25/05/1916
War Diary	Treux	26/05/1916	25/06/1916
War Diary	Morlancourt	30/06/1916	01/07/1916
War Diary	Meaulte	04/06/1916	09/06/1916
War Diary	Heilly	20/06/1916	20/06/1916
Heading	7th Divisional Artillery 7th Divisional Ammunition Column R.F.A. August 1916		
War Diary	Heilly	15/08/1916	15/08/1916
War Diary	Meaulte	20/08/1916	04/09/1916
War Diary	Montauban	17/09/1916	17/09/1916
War Diary	Becordel & Fricourt	18/09/1916	18/09/1916

War Diary	Bonnay	28/09/1916	28/09/1916
War Diary	Longeau	30/09/1916	01/10/1916
War Diary	Schaexken	02/10/1916	02/10/1916
War Diary	Nieppe	06/10/1916	23/10/1916
War Diary	Fletre	04/12/1916	05/12/1916
War Diary	Stern Becque	06/12/1916	06/12/1916
War Diary	Rely	07/12/1916	07/12/1916
War Diary	Monchy Cayeux	08/12/1916	09/12/1916
War Diary	Vacquerie	10/12/1916	10/12/1916
War Diary	Authieule	11/12/1916	11/12/1916
War Diary	Acheux	12/12/1916	31/12/1916
Heading	7th Division Divisional Ammunition Column January 1917		
War Diary	Acheux	01/01/1917	04/02/1917
War Diary	Amplier	05/02/1917	24/02/1917
War Diary	Arqueves	25/02/1917	25/02/1917
War Diary	Acheux	26/02/1917	03/03/1917
War Diary	Mailly	06/03/1917	20/03/1917
War Diary	Ablainzeville	26/03/1917	31/03/1917
Heading	7th Division Divisional Ammunition Column May 1917		
War Diary	Achiet-Le-Grand	01/05/1917	15/05/1917
War Diary	Behagnies	15/05/1917	31/05/1917
Heading	7th Division Divisional Ammunition Column June 1917		
Heading	Original 7 Divisional Ammunition Column War Diary For June 1917		
War Diary	Behagnies	21/06/1917	30/06/1917
Heading	7th Division Divisional Ammunition Column July 1917		
War Diary	Behagnies	05/07/1917	31/07/1917
Heading	7th Division Divisional Ammunition Column August 1917		
War Diary	Behagnies	01/08/1917	30/08/1917
Heading	7th Division Divisional Ammunition Column September 1917		
War Diary	Behagnies	01/09/1917	01/09/1917
War Diary	Meteren	02/09/1917	11/09/1917
War Diary	Strazeele	12/09/1917	21/09/1917
War Diary	Anestoutre	27/09/1917	27/09/1917
War Diary	Dickebusch	28/09/1917	30/09/1917
Heading	7th Division Divisional Ammunition Column October 1917		
War Diary	Dickebusch	01/10/1917	30/10/1917
Heading	7th Division Divisional Ammunition Column November 1917		
War Diary	Dickebusch	04/11/1917	08/11/1917
War Diary	Boscheppe	10/11/1917	12/11/1917
War Diary	Renescure	13/11/1917	19/11/1917
War Diary	Arques	20/11/1917	21/11/1917
War Diary	Cerea (Italy)	27/11/1917	27/11/1917
War Diary	Agugliar	29/11/1917	29/11/1917
War Diary	Cervaresse S. Croce	30/11/1917	30/11/1917
Heading	7 Division H.Q. Troops 37 Brigade. R.F.A. 1915 Mar To 1916 May 7 Division Trench Mortar Batteries (X,Y,& Z) 1916 Feb To 1917 Nov Division Ammunition Column 1914 Sept To 1917 Nov		

7TH DIVISION

37TH BDE R.F.A.

MAR 1915-MAY 1916

BDE Broken up May 1916

From 4 DIV TROOPS

Index

SUBJECT.

7TH DIV

No.	Contents.	Date.
	R.F.A. — 37TH BRIGADE — ~~JAN~~ MARCH - ~~DEC~~, 1915 — May 1916	

(56,425). Wt.24,741—161. 2000. 11/20. Gp.164. A.&E.W.

7th Division

181/4939

4th CORPS

[7th Division]

Came from 4th Division

37th Bde R.F.A.

Vol VIII 1 – 31. 3. 15.

B86

Instructions regarding War Diaries and Intelligence Summaries are contained in F. S. Regs., Part II. and the Staff Manual respectively. Title pages will be prepared in manuscript.

WAR DIARY
or
INTELLIGENCE SUMMARY.
(Erase heading not required.)

37th Brigade R.G.A.

Army Form C. 2118.

March 1915

Hour, Date, Place	Summary of Events and Information	Remarks and references to Appendices
1st RIEZ BAILLEUL FRANCE	35th Battery registering points about NEUVE CHAPELLE with Aeroplane	
2nd	31st and 35th Registering points about NEUVE CHAPELLE with aeroplane. [In morning wrong system used by Aeroplane observer result two shells into our own lines and registration useless.] In afternoon 31st Battery registered 8 points in ½ hour, correct system used & found satisfactory.	
7.pm	Four guns of 55th Battery rejoined the Brigade from the 7th Division and came into action 400 yards South of H.Q. near RIEZ BAILLEUL.	
	55th Section of Brig^d Am Col joined Am Col. H.Q. Section. and Am Col moved to Billets South of NEUF BERQUIN.	
3rd.	Remainder of 55th Battery under Lieut-Doake rejoin 55th Battery from 7th Division.	
	31. 35. 55 Batteries registering points about NEUVE CHAPELLE	

Army Form C. 2118.

WAR DIARY
or
INTELLIGENCE SUMMARY.
(Erase heading not required.)

Instructions regarding War Diaries and Intelligence Summaries are contained in F. S. Regs., Part II. and the Staff Manual respectively. Title pages will be prepared in manuscript.

Hour, Date, Place	Summary of Events and Information	Remarks and references to Appendices
4th 5 6 7	Batteries registering points about NEUVE CHAPELLE and improving observing stations.	
8th	Instructions received for bombardment of NEUVE CHAPELLE and an attack to be made on that place.	
9th	Preparations made by the brigade for the bombardment, final registrations carried out by batteries. Ammunition dumped at the guns, making each gun up to 120 rounds deposit.	

Army Form C. 2118.

WAR DIARY
or
INTELLIGENCE SUMMARY.
(Erase heading not required.)

Instructions regarding War Diaries and Intelligence Summaries are contained in F. S. Regs., Part II. and the Staff Manual respectively. Title pages will be prepared in manuscript.

Hour, Date, Place	Summary of Events and Information	Remarks and references to Appendices
10th 7.40 am. 8.5 am.	7.40 to 8.5 am Batteries bombarded German support trenches in front of NEUVE CHAPELLE (30 rounds per gun)	
	8.5 to 8.35 fire was directed on to support and communication trenches about the "triangle" NEUVE CHAPELLE and various fortified posts.	
	i.e. 35th Battery trench 47 to 22 & cross roads 18. 30 rounds per gun.	
	31st " point 6 & trenches 4 to 3. 30 " "	
	55th " trenches east of road 13 to 66 30 " "	
8.35 am.	At 8.35 am fire of Batteries lifted	
	35th Battery to point 94	
	55th " " " 66	
	31st " " A 3 A' } 30 rounds per gun.	
	31st was ordered to come under orders of 7th D.A. when 7th Division was ordered to attack. This Battery opened fire in support of 7th Div at 2.30 pm.	
~~9.40 am.~~	~~9.5 35 & 55 Batteries [illegible] of NEUVE CHAPELLE~~	

(9 26 6) W 257—976 100,000 4/12 H W V 79/3298

Instructions regarding War Diaries and Intelligence Summaries are contained in F. S. Regs., Part II. and the Staff Manual respectively. Title pages will be prepared in manuscript.

WAR DIARY
or
INTELLIGENCE SUMMARY.
(Erase heading not required.)

Army Form C. 2118.

Hour, Date, Place	Summary of Events and Information	Remarks and references to Appendices
8.10 Am	31st & 35th Batteries report front German trenches are taken (forwarded to 8th D.A.)	
8.20 Am	35th Battery report "right attack has gone beyond 'Cook houses'" (forwarded to 8th D.A.)	
8.35 Am.	35th Battery report "Our infantry have crossed the Pagoda (18)	
9-20 Am	35th " " Our infantry are right into NEUVE CHAPELLE and are now out of sight (to 8th D.A.	
9.40. Am	OCs 35th & 55th Batteries went off to NEUVE CHAPELLE leaving their Batteries temporarily in command of the Captains under Brigade orders, during the shifting of communication. Subalterns replacing them at PONT LOGY obs station.	
10.42 a ✱	31st Battery ordered to fire on trench 20 to 73) on orders recd from 8th D.A.	
9.45 Am.	Communication between PONT LOGY and obs Stns cut for a short time to 35th & 55th (till 10 Am.)	
10.43 Am.	Information received from 8th D.A. British hold pts 80. 19. 66. 48. 18. We are held up from 21 to 20. Indians hold 30 and line down South. Advance being pushed against 63. 91.	

Instructions regarding War Diaries and Intelligence Summaries are contained in F. S. Regs., Part II. and the Staff Manual respectively. Title pages will be prepared in manuscript.

WAR DIARY
or
INTELLIGENCE SUMMARY.

(Erase heading not required.)

Army Form C. 2118.

Hour, Date, Place	Summary of Events and Information	Remarks and references to Appendices
11.25 am.	35" Battery report 6" Shells dropping short of front of wood A B. It has stopped now. (to 8th D.C.)	
11 am	Major Steel (35") & Major Colvill (55") report establishment of observing stations in NEUVE CHAPELLE.	
11.55 am.	31st & 35" Batteries ordered to shell pt 6 till 12.15 pm. (from 8th D.A. a request of 23rd Inf Brig.)	
12.20 pm.	31st Report our own infantry in possession of pt 6 and are [illegible] [illegible] stalling it (report to 8th D.A.)	
12.27 pm.	8th D.A. said information pt 6 captured (Batteries + 6" Siege informed)	
1.10 pm	55" Battery report "We hold points 19. 55. 31. 50 [illegible] A"*	
1.45 pm	55" Battery asked to report on trench from pt 50 to 56. Answer received 2.1 pm "We hold it now."	
1.50 pm.	55" Battery report "The Royal Irish Rifles entrenching themselves along the line already reported* The Rifle Brigade are continuing the line on their right about 200 yards in front of the road running along the SE	* message 1.10 pm.

Army Form C. 2118.

Instructions regarding War Diaries and Intelligence Summaries are contained in F. S. Regs., Part II. and the Staff Manual respectively. Title pages will be prepared in manuscript.

WAR DIARY
or
INTELLIGENCE SUMMARY.

(Erase heading not required.)

Hour, Date, Place	Summary of Events and Information	Remarks and references to Appendices
	edge of NEUVE CHAPELLE with some men in old trench – Indians continue the line on their right	
2.5 pm.	55th Battery report Germans appear to be holding a line about 93–75–97 and edge of Bois du BIEZ — We now hold line 56–60 [illegible] and are entrenching it.	
	31st Battery report AUBERS CHURCH on fire (sent to 8th D.A.)	
2.45 pm	Orders from 8th D.A. No more fire for the present.	
	35th Battery report the enemy are in force from the Cross fire at the roads 36 – e – south to PIETRE (report to 8th D.A.)	
3. pm	31st Battery [illegible] under orders of 7th D.A.	
3.35 pm.	Confirmation [illegible] of previous report of line held by our own infantry, also request from O.C. Irish Rifles for enemy gun to be suppressed (NE of BOIS DU BIEZ) 55th ordered to engage this at 3.37 pm	
3.30 pm	Message received from 8th D.A. – there are indications of counter attack from direction of LA RUSSIE (Batteries informed)	
3.25	Message from 8th D.A. 7 Division ordered to advance 3.30 pm	

(9 26 6) W 257—976 100,000 4/12 H W V 79/3298

Army Form C. 2118.

Instructions regarding War Diaries and Intelligence Summaries are contained in F. S. Regs., Part II. and the Staff Manual respectively. Title pages will be prepared in manuscript.

WAR DIARY
or
INTELLIGENCE SUMMARY.
(Erase heading not required.)

Hour, Date, Place	Summary of Events and Information	Remarks and references to Appendices
3.32.	Message from 8th D.A. – 8th Division ordered to advance at 3.30 pm. 1st objective point 85-86-88. Second objective PIETRE	
	55th Battery to shell pts 85-86-88 } slow rate of fire 35th Battery " " pts 93 – }	
5.5 pm.	Message from 8th D.A. – 24 Inf Brigade commenced their advance from pt 14 on pt 85-86 [illegible] at 4.50 pm	
5.30 pm	55 Battery report – At 5.30 pm right of 24th Infantry Brigade were passing pt 18.	
6.25 pm.	55th Batt? report – left of 24th Inf Bde was passing pt 18 at 6.10 pm. their objective was pts 85-86-88	

(9 26 6) W 257—976 100,000 4/12 H W V 79/3298

Instructions regarding War Diaries and Intelligence Summaries are contained in F. S. Regs., Part II. and the Staff Manual respectively. Title pages will be prepared in manuscript.

WAR DIARY
or
INTELLIGENCE SUMMARY.
(Erase heading not required.)

Army Form C. 2118.

Hour, Date, Place	Summary of Events and Information	Remarks and references to Appendices
11th	Orders from 8th DA – 8th Division advances today on LA CLIQUETERIE FMe at 7am. 24th Inf Bde leading, 25th Inf Bde in support, 23rd Inf Bde will take over trenches now held by 24th & 25th Bdes.	
	35th & 55th [illegible] bombard points 56–93 and road 100 yds South of fork roads S.6.a.5.10 to farm M.36.d.	
8.37.	Report from F.O.O. – Welsh Fus[illegible] report enemy masses in TRIVELET and [illegible] road	
10.7 am	31st Battery F.O.O. reports – left front 21st Brigade is advancing at right angles to our front trench with the left along front of German trenches they have arrived about road running through M.23. M.30.a	not true
12.15.	55th Battery ask to be allowed to support attack by Rifle Brig. with whom they are in touch. Permission given, attack did not take place.	— This was to have been in conjunction with Indian Division

(9 26 6) W 257—976 100,000 4/12 H W V 79/3298

Army Form C. 2118.

Instructions regarding War Diaries and Intelligence Summaries are contained in F. S. Regs., Part II. and the Staff Manual respectively. Title pages will be prepared in manuscript.

WAR DIARY
or
INTELLIGENCE SUMMARY.
(Erase heading not required.)

Hour, Date, Place	Summary of Events and Information	Remarks and references to Appendices
11th		
1-28 pm	Orders from 8th D.A. – Bombardment of trench 85 to 86 to commence at 1.45 pm and to last until 2.15 pm. 4.5 How: 15 rounds per gun. Orders to this effect sent to 35–55 Batteries who bombardment carried out.	
3 pm	Report from 31st Battery F.O.O. – Right of 7th Division have reached the bend in road in M30A and are being held up by strongly defended orchard near MOULIN du PIETRE	
3.30 pm	35th Battery report – Left of Indian Division have not advanced beyond the line which is 400 yds beyond the Bois du BIEZ. They are apparently held up by a lot rifle and machine-gun fire from the edge of the wood.	
	Night line for 55 & 35 Batteries [illegible] [illegible] pt Cross Roads PIETRE point 98.	
12th	(at 12.7 pm) 35th Battery registered a few rounds on road from pt 85 to 86.	
	31st Cooperating with 7th Division & firing on [illegible] points during the day under orders of 7th D.A.	

Instructions regarding War Diaries and Intelligence Summaries are contained in F. S. Regs., Part II. and the Staff Manual respectively. Title pages will be prepared in manuscript.

WAR DIARY
or
INTELLIGENCE SUMMARY.
(Erase heading not required.)

Army Form C. 2118.

Hour, Date, Place	Summary of Events and Information	Remarks and references to Appendices
12th	Batteries registered various points in the morning	
10.25	Pt 94 reported in our hands – Bombardment postponed till 12 noon	
12 noon	Bombardment commenced 34 Battery firing on road and trenches to North of Eastern edge of Bois du Biez 55 Battery engaged points from 85 & 86.	
1.20 pm	35 Battery report – German counter attack from Bois du Biez repulsed with heavy loss to enemy. Information received from 4 Group HQ to 8th DA.	
2.50 pm	Brigade F.O.O. reports 25th Inf Brigade has reached old British trench and is held up by machine gun fire from points 93 & 95 and trench running NW of that line (to 8th DA)	
5.18 pm	55 Battery ordered to shell pt 86–85 till 6.15 pm at which time infantry will advance.	
5.30 pm	Report from North Hants Regt that Germans have brought guns on to road between 86–85. Orders from 8th DA to silence if fire is opened. (fire was not opened by these guns) Night time fired as for night of 11/12	

(9 26 6) W 257—976 100,000 4/12 H W V 79/3298

Army Form C. 2118.

Instructions regarding War Diaries and Intelligence Summaries are contained in F. S. Regs., Part II. and the Staff Manual respectively. Title pages will be prepared in manuscript.

WAR DIARY
or
INTELLIGENCE SUMMARY.
(Erase heading not required.)

Hour, Date, Place	Summary of Events and Information	Remarks and references to Appendices
13th	35th Battery registered.	
9.35	Brigade F.O.O. report - Rifle Brigade report that the guns on road running from 56 A.35 to 5.10 are bothering them (to 8th Div)	
11.5 am	Brig F.O.O. report - 24 Brigade report 15 machine guns in line 86-85 (to 8th Div)	
4.15 pm	Brigade F.O.O. reports - Houses in line 85-86 reported as [illegible] - Confirmed by report from 55th Battery at 4.2 pm [illegible] the effects of the Batteries fire.	
5.50 pm	Report sent to 8th D.A. - Mole (55th Battery) has [illegible] 86 to 85 and set it alight in several places.	
6.27 pm	Message from 8th Div Arty - [illegible] [illegible] by a signal point to massing of Germans out of Bois du Biez and their advance through the wood. Be prepared for an attack.	
8 pm	Night line laid on point 98-90	

Army Form C. 2118.

Instructions regarding War Diaries and Intelligence Summaries are contained in F. S. Regs., Part II. and the Staff Manual respectively. Title pages will be prepared in manuscript.

WAR DIARY
or
INTELLIGENCE SUMMARY.
(Erase heading not required.)

Hour, Date, Place	Summary of Events and Information	Remarks and references to Appendices
14th		
5-5pm	35" Battery report – I have engaged a battery in the open near the second M in POMMEREAU. has not fired since.	

(9 26 6) W 257—976 100,000 4/12 H W V 79/3298

Army Form C. 2118.

Instructions regarding War Diaries and Intelligence Summaries are contained in F. S. Regs., Part II. and the Staff Manual respectively. Title pages will be prepared in manuscript.

WAR DIARY or INTELLIGENCE SUMMARY.

(Erase heading not required.)

Hour, Date, Place	Summary of Events and Information	Remarks and references to Appendices
RIEZ BAILLEUL 15th	Some shelling by German on our trenches. 31, 35, 55 Batteries fired a few rounds during the day on various points behind German line.	
16	1 Section of 35th Battery ordered to move tonight to position near Cameron Lane.	
Night 16/17	Section of 35th Battery moves to new position (4 pm) under Lieut DEACON. This section ordered to cover front from RUE d'ENFER to BOIS du BIEZ.	
17th	No firing by 37 Brigade. Very little German shelling.	
18th	55th Battery registered BRICKFIELDS. TRIVELET and German front trenches	
19th	Quiet. Batteries registering. Section 35th Battery rejoin.	
20th	Batteries registering	
Night 20th/21st	55 moves to position at FORT D'ESQUIN.	
21st	55th Battery registering	
22nd	55 & 31 Batteries registering. Capt AGNEW (35th) slightly wounded while patrolling by shrapnel. Drew O.S. [illegible] LA CHAPELLE	

(9 26 6) W 257—976 100,000 4/12 H W V 79/3298

Instructions regarding War Diaries and Intelligence Summaries are contained in F. S. Regs., Part II. and the Staff Manual respectively. Title pages will be prepared in manuscript.

WAR DIARY
or
INTELLIGENCE SUMMARY.
(Erase heading not required.)

Army Form C. 2118.

Hour, Date, Place	Summary of Events and Information	Remarks and references to Appendices
23rd	Germans shelled LAVENTIE with 8" HOW in morning.	
24th	~~No firing~~ Batteries registering with aeroplane (31st 55th)	
25th	No firing. Orders received for Brigade to come under Col Sharp (III Corps Hows) on 27th inst. less 35th Battery who to be attached to LAHORE DIVISION.	
26th	31st 55 Batteries registering with aeroplane	
27th	31st Battery registering. 35th battery comes under LAHORE DIV	Brigade under III Corps
28th	Message from 7th DA [illegible] [illegible] [illegible] from [illegible] at point 215. Officers of 31-55 Batteries ordered to locate it personally. These officers were unable to see, or get any information as to gun reported. No firing.	
29th	31-55 Registering with aeroplane	
30th	31-55 Registering.	
31st	31-55 Batteries registering new German trenches near MIN du PIETRE	

2nd Division

121/5318

37th Bde R.F.A.

Vol IX 1—30.4.15

Army Form C. 2118.

Instructions regarding War Diaries and Intelligence Summaries are contained in F. S. Regs., Part II. and the Staff Manual respectively. Title pages will be prepared in manuscript.

WAR DIARY
or
INTELLIGENCE SUMMARY.
(Erase heading not required.)

Hour, Date, Place	Summary of Events and Information	Remarks and references to Appendices
April 1st	31st Battery registration.	
2nd LAVENTIE	31st Battery F.O.O. located Enemy Trench mortar (N.13.c.8.0) this information sent in reply to 43rd Brigade wire reporting Grenadier Guards being worried by mortar.	
7.20p	Order received from 7 Div. – No aeroplane of any kind is to be fired at between 3 am & 7 am tomorrow (this order was not cancelled.)	
7 pm	Report of Battalion groups effected at 7 pm. All Brigade came under direct orders of Div Arty.	
3rd	Orders received for 35th Battery to move to 7th Div area & come under 7 D.A.	
	Orders from 7th Div Arty to fire on Trench Mortar reported [illegible] if it opens fire.	
	H Q ordered to move on 5th to H.Q. vacated by 43rd Brigade R.F.A. near LAVENTIE	
	Am. col. and wagon lines to move into positions vacated by those of 43rd Brigade.	

Army Form C. 2118.

Instructions regarding War Diaries and Intelligence Summaries are contained in F. S. Regs., Part II. and the Staff Manual respectively. Title pages will be prepared in manuscript.

WAR DIARY
or
INTELLIGENCE SUMMARY.
(Erase heading not required.)

Hour, Date, Place	Summary of Events and Information	Remarks and references to Appendices
21st	Night of 4th/5th 35th Battery move to 40th Batteries position East of LAVENTIE [illegible] under 7th Division.	
6th	At 5 am H.Q. moved to Billet near LAVENTIE.	
	55th Battery firing during the ~~morning~~ afternoon (1.30pm) at French [illegible] at pt 520. No orders received from 7th Div 12.45pm. (This target was [illegible] but not hit)	
	35th Battery registering night lines.	
	Ammn Column & Wagon Lines moved after dark to new position	
6th	German observation Balloon reported up to S.E.	
	~~[illegible]~~ 31st Battery fired 6 rounds at German Barricade on RUE d'ENFER and hit it. (Time not reported).	
7th	~~[illegible]~~ Batteries registering.	

(9 26 6) W 257—976 100,000 4/12 H W V 79/3298

Instructions regarding War Diaries and Intelligence Summaries are contained in F. S. Regs., Part II. and the Staff Manual respectively. Title pages will be prepared in manuscript.

WAR DIARY
or
INTELLIGENCE SUMMARY.
(Erase heading not required.)

Army Form C. 2118.

Hour, Date, Place	Summary of Events and Information	Remarks and references to Appendices
8th	35th Battery registered pt 351 T cross roads 200x E of it (12 rounds)	
10-40am	31st Battery engaged trench mortar at Pt 275 (10 rds)	
11-27am	55th Battery fired 4 rounds into AUBERS in retaliation for shelling of RUE TILLELOY.	
9th 7.48am	55th Battery report at 7.48 am trench mortar firing from pt 313. Battery fired shrapnel at it. (Later report from 55th says — there is no doubt that the mortar reported firing from 316 is our own [illegible])	
10th 8.55am	Message from 7th Div. — Indian Corps expect to be attacked within the next 48 hours.	
11th 9am	55th Battery fired 2 shrapnel at house pt 300.	
6.40pm	35th " " 6 " " TRIVELET	
6.50pm	55th " " 6 " "	

Army Form C. 2118.

Instructions regarding War Diaries and Intelligence Summaries are contained in F. S. Regs., Part II. and the Staff Manual respectively. Title pages will be prepared in manuscript.

WAR DIARY
or
INTELLIGENCE SUMMARY.
(Erase heading not required.)

Hour, Date, Place	Summary of Events and Information	Remarks and references to Appendices
11th 10.15 pm	Message from 7 D.A. – Information received from 1st Div that enemy trenches in front of their left appear to be unusually strongly held tonight.	
12th 4.45 am	31st Battery fired [illegible] shrapnel at TRIVELET. (morning [illegible] observation)	
8.30 am	35th Battery fired 9 shrapnel at trench mortar between pts 324 – 323	
10.15 am	55th Battery registered on Bois du Biez, 12 shrapnel	
3 pm	" " fired [illegible] shrapnel into AUBERS in retaliation for shelling barricade on RUE TILLELOY	
	31st Battery reports enemy shelling road near Battery [illegible] at 3 pm with [illegible] this seemed to be the result of our Battery firing during the morning [illegible] [illegible] of 25th [illegible] [illegible] with [illegible] of 31 Battery.	
13th	Batteries registering	
14	"	
15	"	
16	"	
17		
18		
19 } 20	Night of 31st 55th Batteries move to positions [illegible] CROIX ? MESNIL 55th to position [illegible] of ROUGE DE BOUT. HQ to ROUGE DE BOUT	[illegible] LORRAIN?

(9 26 6) W 257—976 100,000 4/12 H W V 79/3298

Brigade [illegible] [illegible] 7th Division & joins 8th Div.

Army Form C. 2118.

Instructions regarding War Diaries and Intelligence Summaries are contained in F. S. Regs., Part II. and the Staff Manual respectively. Title pages will be prepared in manuscript.

WAR DIARY
or
INTELLIGENCE SUMMARY.
(*Erase heading not required.*)

Hour, Date, Place	Summary of Events and Information	Remarks and references to Appendices
	31st / 55th } each came into action under 7th Division in the position.	
21st	Orders issued for detached Batteries 31st and 55th to rejoin Brigade on evening 23rd	
22	Batteries registering	
23rd	" " Batteries 31st and 55th rejoin Brigade [illegible] at 8 pm	
24th	Batteries registering	
	31st Battery withdrawn from position at 10 pm to wagon line position [illegible] LAVENTIE and ordered to be ready to move at any time [illegible] orders of 7th Division. [illegible] 55 occupies position of 31st. At same time 1 section [illegible] Ammunition Column [illegible]	
	joins 22nd Brig [illegible] LAVENTIE.	
25	35th 55th Registering	
26	"	
27	Orders received for HQ and [illegible] Battery to withdraw and come under 7th Division. [illegible] Battery withdrawn at 10 pm to wagon line [illegible]. [illegible] Battery at 10 pm [illegible] to occupy position of 55th [illegible] CROIX MARECHAL.	
	HQ did not move	
	Brig[illegible] [illegible] Battery ready to move at 2 hours' notice.	

Instructions regarding War Diaries and Intelligence Summaries are contained in F. S. Regs., Part II. and the Staff Manual respectively. Title pages will be prepared in manuscript.

WAR DIARY
or
INTELLIGENCE SUMMARY.

(Erase heading not required.)

Army Form C. 2118.

Hour, Date, Place	Summary of Events and Information	Remarks and references to Appendices
28th.	Brigade less 35th Battery marched at 2.30pm with 7th Div Artillery from [illegible] via ESTAIRES [illegible] BERQUIN–MERRIS to billets ½ mile N of MERRIS arrived [illegible]pm.	
29th	Orders to be ready to move at 2 hours notice changed to 4 hours at [illegible]pm. [illegible] heavy fighting N of YPRES heard)	
30th	Brigade remained in billets [illegible] [illegible]	

(9 26 6) W 257—976 100,000 4/12 H W V 79/3298

7th Division

121/5576

37th Bde. R. F. A.

Vol X 1 — 31.5.15

Rv
RB

Instructions regarding War Diaries and Intelligence Summaries are contained in F. S. Regs., Part II. and the Staff Manual respectively. Title pages will be prepared in manuscript.

WAR DIARY
or
INTELLIGENCE SUMMARY.
(Erase heading not required.)

Army Form C. 2118.

[illegible] 37th Brigade R.F.A.

Hour, Date, Place	Summary of Events and Information	Remarks and references to Appendices
May 1st Billets ½ N of MERRIS	In Billets. Batteries [illegible]	
2	Brigade and Battery [illegible] Signalling scheme [illegible] Reported as [illegible] satisfactory.	
3rd	Brig [illegible] Battery [illegible] by [illegible]	[illegible] BREGIE de ROUTE
4th	[illegible] MARBECHOL [illegible] Batteries in action by 10 a.m. Battery [illegible] to Billets [illegible] BOUT [illegible] Battery wagon lines [illegible] (31.557) to Billets in SAILLY [illegible] at NAVMOYDE	
	Batteries registering	
5th	Batteries registering	
6.	Batteries registering	
7.	Orders received for bombardment, [illegible]	[illegible] support of 8th [illegible]
8th	Bombardment prepared [illegible] 9th	FROMELLES - AUBER

(9 26 6) W 257—976 100,000 4/12 H W V 79/3298

Instructions regarding War Diaries and Intelligence Summaries are contained in F. S. Regs., Part II. and the Staff Manual respectively. Title pages will be prepared in manuscript.

WAR DIARY
or
INTELLIGENCE SUMMARY.

(Erase heading not required.)

Army Form C. 2118.

Hour, Date, Place	Summary of Events and Information	Remarks and references to Appendices
Nr LAVENTIE (Rouge de Boot) 9th May 5 am	Bombardment of enemy's front [illegible] [illegible]	
5.20 am	[illegible]	
5.30 am	[illegible]	
6.5	[illegible] 6.20 a.m. 15 rounds per gun	
6.20.	[illegible]	

BOMBARDMENT

Army Form C. 2118.

Instructions regarding War Diaries and Intelligence Summaries are contained in F. S. Regs., Part II. and the Staff Manual respectively. Title pages will be prepared in manuscript.

WAR DIARY
or
INTELLIGENCE SUMMARY.
(Erase heading not required.)

Hour, Date, Place		Summary of Events and Information	Remarks and references to Appendices
9th Contd	6.16am	Message from Bde F.O.O.—attack held up behind salient by redoubt 366 to 368.	
	6.26am	35th Batty ordered to fire on pt 368. (two rounds. Colonel Tudor R.F.A. observing)	
	6.43am	On information from Col Tudor 35th Batty ordered to turn fire on to pt 366.	
	6.53am	Orders from 8th D.A. to fire slowly on points detailed in 2nd Phase of bombardment.	
	6.55am	Orders issued to Batteries to fire as detailed in 2nd phase.	
	7.3am	2 sections 75 Battery ordered to fire very slowly on 301.	
	7.5am	31st Ordered to engage machine gun between 882 & 879 with one gun.	
	7.20am	55th Ordered to turn fire again on to pt 351. slow continuous	
	7.24	8 D.A. orders, turn 31st Baty on to German trenches 882 to 883.	

(9 26 6) W 257—976 100,000 4/12 H W V 79/3298

Army Form C. 2118.

Instructions regarding War Diaries and Intelligence Summaries are contained in F. S. Regs., Part II. and the Staff Manual respectively. Title pages will be prepared in manuscript.

WAR DIARY
or
INTELLIGENCE SUMMARY.
(Erase heading not required.)

Hour, Date, Place	Summary of Events and Information	Remarks and references to Appendices
7.25.	35" Stop firing at 301.	
7.30	8" D.A. orders. Turn 35" Batty on to 356 & 361. Slow continuation	
"	31" Stop firing. and turn on to 832 " "	
8 am	35" fire section salvo at 356.	
8.5 am	8" D.A. order Turn 35" Battery on to Redoubt 363 at 8.15 am for 15 minutes bombardment. (done)	
8.21.	35" fire 3 round salvo at 363 Redoubt.	
8.37	8" D.A. order bombardment of 353 & 352 for 15 minutes from 9 am. (doubly ~~35~~" less one section)	
8.54 a	8" D.A. order 55" Batt to bombard 351 for 15 minutes from 9 am.	
9.8 am	31" ordered to fire on the line 828 827 one round per battery per minute.	

(9 26 6) W 257—976 100,000 4/12 H W V 79/3298

Army Form C. 2118.

Instructions regarding War Diaries and Intelligence Summaries are contained in F. S. Regs., Part II. and the Staff Manual respectively. Title pages will be prepared in manuscript.

WAR DIARY
or
INTELLIGENCE SUMMARY.
(Erase heading not required.)

Hour, Date, Place	Summary of Events and Information	Remarks and references to Appendices
9.17.	35th Batt. ordered to fire a salvo 2 rounds at pt 363.	
10.7 am.	8 D.A. order 35th to bombard slowly 355 & 356 & trench 357 - 360.	
	55th bombard slowly trench 352 - 354.	
10.35	O.C. Am Col reports no more lyddite.	
10.40.	55th Batt. Report Major Colville wounded.	
10.55 am.	8 D.A. order 35th to bombard trench 374 to R. LAYES.	
	55th " " " 376 to 374.	
12.31.	3 D.A. order 35th to bombard 374 to 375 & back to 351. commence 1 pm, cease 1.30 pm. 30 rounds per gun. 1 done.	
	55th BY. to fire slowly on trench 376 to 374. 1 pm to 1.30 pm	
	31st BY no firing.	

(9 26 6) W 257—976 100,000 4/12 H W V 79/3298

Instructions regarding War Diaries and Intelligence Summaries are contained in F. S. Regs., Part II. and the Staff Manual respectively. Title pages will be prepared in manuscript.

WAR DIARY
or
INTELLIGENCE SUMMARY.

(Erase heading not required.)

Army Form C. 2118.

Hour, Date, Place	Summary of Events and Information	Remarks and references to Appendices
1.25 pm.	35th By ordered to fire at redoubt, slowly.	
1.25 pm	8 D.G. – Germans reported to be counter attacking 576 to 579 31st Batt turn on to front trench 576 to 579 & bombard steadily for 15 minutes.	
2 pm	Arm Party report no [illegible] at Bridge Head.	
2.2 pm	35th ordered to stop firing at redoubt. (shooting reported by Col Tudor to have been very good)	
3.38.	8 D.G. message – Hostile reinforcements reported reaching FROMELLES from South. Keep look out & fire on them if they appear.	

(9 26 6) W 257—976 100,000 4/12 H W V 79/3298

Instructions regarding War Diaries and Intelligence Summaries are contained in F. S. Regs., Part II. and the Staff Manual respectively. Title pages will be prepared in manuscript.

WAR DIARY
or
INTELLIGENCE SUMMARY.
(*Erase heading not required.*)

Army Form C. 2118.

Hour, Date, Place	Summary of Events and Information	Remarks and references to Appendices
7.8 pm	Batteries ordered - no more shooting tonight.	
11.6 pm	8th DA. - Attack will not be renewed tomorrow morning.	
	Casualties in Brigade. R.g.	
	65826. Cpl LYDON. of 31st Batty. wounded.	
	90074 Gr KIRKPATRIC 31 " slight "	
	Major J. R COLVILLE 55 Battery wounded. and taken to hospital.	
	Capt Ferguson takes command of 55th Battery.	
10th	Batteries registering.	
	Orders received to move 31st + 35th + H.Q. + 2 section of Amn Col to vicinity of LA TOURET at 9.30 pm	

Instructions regarding War Diaries and Intelligence Summaries are contained in F. S. Regs., Part II. and the Staff Manual respectively. Title pages will be prepared in manuscript.

WAR DIARY
or
INTELLIGENCE SUMMARY.
(Erase heading not required.)

Army Form C. 2118.

Hour, Date, Place	Summary of Events and Information	Remarks and references to Appendices
9.30	31 - 35. 2 Sect. Am Col & H.Q. march to LA.TOURET Via X Roads near ROUGE de BOUT - LAVENTIE - LA GORGUE - LESTRIEM. - LOCON.	
	31st - 35th H.Q. & 2 Sect Am Col Join 7th D.A.	
11th 2.40 Am	Arrived at LA TOURET.	
	Batteries registering during the day and taking over positions of 5th London T Brigd.	
	Col. Spedding to take over 6 & 8th Siege Batteries in addition also 2 Batteries 8th London Brigd.	
12th -	6 & 8th Siege come under 7th Siege Bde	
	Batteries of 37th Bde & 8th London Registering.	

(9 26 6) W 257—976 100,000 4/12 H W V 79/3298

Instructions regarding War Diaries and Intelligence Summaries are contained in F. S. Regs., Part II. and the Staff Manual respectively. Title pages will be prepared in manuscript.

WAR DIARY
or
INTELLIGENCE SUMMARY.
(Erase heading not required.)

Army Form C. 2118.

Hour, Date, Place	Summary of Events and Information	Remarks and references to Appendices
13th.	Registration and enemys trenches bombarded for 3 periods of 2 hours each 7 am to 11 am, 1 pm to 3 pm, 6 pm to 8 pm (25 lyddite per gun for each period.)	
14th	Registration	
4th.	6th Siege Battery ~~[illegible]~~ come under 7 Siege Bde.	
15th	Bombardment of enemy position from 8.15 am to 10-15 am. Amn per gun {10 lyddite, 10 Shrapnel}	
	Bombardment repeated from 12 noon to 2 pm.	
	Bombardment repeated from 5 pm to 7 pm	
	Night firing 9 pm to 2.45 am.	

(9 26 6) W 257—976 100,000 4/12 H W V 79/3298

Instructions regarding War Diaries and Intelligence Summaries are contained in F. S. Regs., Part II. and the Staff Manual respectively. Title pages will be prepared in manuscript.

WAR DIARY
or
INTELLIGENCE SUMMARY.
(*Erase heading not required.*)

Army Form C. 2118.

Hour, Date, Place	Summary of Events and Information	Remarks and references to Appendices
16th	Battle near FESTUBERT. Most orders were given verbal to telephonists.	
17th 18th 19 20 21st	The Brigade fired a Carpets all over the country. F.O.O. were sent out to Advanced trenches and sent back important information. (EVELEGH, NEWMAN) Adjutant unable to keep record of battle as away for two days with Canadian Brigd. All messages referring to these operation are sent to Base records.	
	Casualties during the engagement.	
	21st 5.50a. Capt M.A. PHILLIPS 31st Battery killed while in advanced infantry trenches getting information.	
	16th Major STEEL 35th Batty. 2/Lt DEACON " " Gunner WILLIAMS E. 67673 killed.	

Army Form C. 2118.

Instructions regarding War Diaries and Intelligence Summaries are contained in F. S. Regs., Part II. and the Staff Manual respectively. Title pages will be prepared in manuscript.

WAR DIARY
or
INTELLIGENCE SUMMARY.
(Erase heading not required.)

Hour, Date, Place	Summary of Events and Information	Remarks and references to Appendices
	33681. Gnr WRIGHT, S 35th Batt Killed.	
	65715 Br R. TERRY 31st Batt wounded.	
	74903. Gr HITCH, W. " " wounded (accidental)	
	20th/ No 47744 3 Gr NASH. E 31st Batt wounded.	
22nd	22nd Br CHRISTMAS, A. No 13600 31st Batt wounded. Batteries registering	
23rd	Batteries registering. Order received to move at 9 pm on march to L'ECLEM to rest Bde marched via BETHUNE-CHOQUES.	
24th	Arrived 1.30 Am. at L'ECLEM.	
25th 26.	Batteries in rest overhauling.	

(9 26 6) W 257—976 100,000 4/12 H W V 79/3298

Instructions regarding War Diaries and Intelligence Summaries are contained in F. S. Regs., Part II. and the Staff Manual respectively. Title pages will be prepared in manuscript.

WAR DIARY
or
INTELLIGENCE SUMMARY.
(Erase heading not required.)

Army Form C. 2118.

Hour, Date, Place	Summary of Events and Information	Remarks and references to Appendices
27th	7th Division & Artillery inspected by General Joffre & Sir John French, near ECLAM.	
28th	H.Q. & Batteries resting.	
29th	" " "	
30th	" " "	
31st	7th Division Artillery march at 4.30pm to previous position East of LE TOURET arriving about 9pm. taking over from 118th Brigade.	

R. [illegible] Capt.

(9 26 6) W 257—976 100,000 4/12 H W V 79/3298

11th Division

181/5993

8th R.F.A.

Vol XL 1 — 30.6.15.

a2

a16

Instructions regarding War Diaries and Intelligence Summaries are contained in F. S. Regs., Part II. and the Staff Manual respectively. Title pages will be prepared in manuscript.

WAR DIARY
or
INTELLIGENCE SUMMARY.
(Erase heading not required.)

37th Bde RFA

Army Form C. 2118.

June 1915

Hour, Date, Place	Summary of Events and Information	Remarks and references to Appendices
LE TOURET		
1st	31st & 35th Batteries registering.	
2nd	" " " "	
3rd	" " " " on the morning	
4/pm	Bombardment commenced of enemy trenches East of GIVENCHY 1st Bombardment ~~[illegible]~~ 4/pm to 6/pm — 2nd Bombardment 8 pm to 9.40 pm 3rd Bombardment 9.40 pm to 9.50 pm	
	At 9.40 pm Infantry (6th Gordons) assault I.4 to I.2	
	35th Battery from 9.50 pm to 3 am (4th) firing 10 rounds shrapnel per hour on trench J14 to J15.	
4th	Nothing doing. 6th Gordons were driven back early in the morning –	
5th	Captain R.C. Dodgson left the Bde to take charge of a trench mortar school.	
5th – 12th	No records. batteries registering –	
	12th Captain P.H. Ferguson took over the duties of Adjutant	

(9 26 6) W 257—976 100,000 4/12 H W V 79/3298

Instructions regarding War Diaries and Intelligence Summaries are contained in F. S. Regs., Part II. and the Staff Manual respectively. Title pages will be prepared in manuscript.

WAR DIARY
or
INTELLIGENCE SUMMARY.
(Erase heading not required.)

Army Form C. 2118.

June 1915

Hour, Date, Place	Summary of Events and Information	Remarks and references to Appendices
June 13th LE TOURET	Both batteries registering J10 - K6	
14th	Bombardment. Both batteries fired. 12 noon - 1 pm 5 pm - 6 pm 8 pm - 9 pm 31st Battery. Front trench M10 - North of L12 35th Battery - Communication Trenches running South from M10 Ammunition allotted 90 rounds shrapnel per battery -	
15th	~~Bombardment was as follows~~. Object of operations to establish a new line H2 - J18 - K7 - M9 - ~~[illegible]~~ Canadian Divn attack H2-H3 to I16 & I17 7th Divn I7 & I4. objective I.18 - Chaple St Roche - K8 Highland Divn (154th Bde) attack from L8 - Z redoubt thence L11 - L13 - Join hands with 7th Divn towards K7 & eventually dig in on a line K7 - Nsw Ho. Attacks take place simultaneously at 6 pm. 152nd Bde attack opposite M6 about 3/4 hour ~~later~~ after the 154th providing that the latter are successful.	

Instructions regarding War Diaries and Intelligence Summaries are contained in F. S. Regs., Part II. and the Staff Manual respectively. Title pages will be prepared in manuscript.

WAR DIARY
or
INTELLIGENCE SUMMARY.
(Erase heading not required.)

Army Form C. 2118.

Hour, Date, Place	Summary of Events and Information	Remarks and references to Appendices
LE TOURET. June 15th	Bombardments as follows	

37th Bde

Time	31st Batty SHRAP	31st Batty LYD	35th Batty SHRAP	35th Batty LYD	Targets
2pm - 4pm	60				K12 - L17 - M11
2 - 4pm			70		RUE MARAIS
4 - 4.30pm				30	L13 L11
4.30 - 5pm		60			Front trench K6 & 200x North -
5 - 6pm		120			Z - L11
5 - 6pm				120	100x south of Z - L13
6 - 6.30pm		60		60	L11 - L12 - L13
6.50 - 7.30		40			J12 - K7.

37th Bde support the Highland Divn -
Infantry lost all the ground they took during the night.

Army Form C. 2118.

WAR DIARY
or
INTELLIGENCE SUMMARY.
(Erase heading not required.)

Instructions regarding War Diaries and Intelligence Summaries are contained in F. S. Regs., Part II. and the Staff Manual respectively. Title pages will be prepared in manuscript.

Hour, Date, Place	Summary of Events and Information	Remarks and references to Appendices
LE TOURET		
June 16.	Lt. W. P. M. Newman was wounded slightly. and left for the base.	
	Operations were continued from the 15th with the same object.	
	The 154th Bde attack at 4.45 pm. on both sides of the salient (Z). If this attack succeeded the 152nd Bde attack from M6 at 9pm.	
	Bombardment ~~[illegible]~~ commences 3.15 pm.	
	Break. 4.18 – 4.25. pm	
	1st Lift 4.45 pm	
	2nd Lift 5 pm.	
	3rd Lift 5.30 pm.	
	Target. 1st bombardment. 31st Z – L 11	
	35th Trench 100x South of Z redoubt towards L13.	
	1st Lift. K7 – K8	
	2nd Lift. RUE MARAIS not to fire unless ordered	
	Ammunition allowed 20 rounds per gun Lyddite for each bombardment	

(9 26 6) W 257—976 100,000 4/12 H W V 79/3298

Instructions regarding War Diaries and Intelligence Summaries are contained in F. S. Regs., Part II. and the Staff Manual respectively. Title pages will be prepared in manuscript.

WAR DIARY
or
INTELLIGENCE SUMMARY.
(Erase heading not required.)

Army Form C. 2118.

Hour, Date, Place	Summary of Events and Information	Remarks and references to Appendices
LE TOURET.		
June 16th.	The Bde did not fire after 5 pm.	
17th	Nothing doing	
18th	Nothing doing. An attack ordered for 2.45 am. postponed -	
19th	Nothing doing -	
20th	— do —	
21st	— do — . 35th Battery wagon lines were shelled - [Casualties 3 men killed - 8 wounded 17 horses killed - 12 wounded]	
22nd	— do —	
23rd	— do —	
24th	— do —	
25th	Brigade moved at 8.45 pm - 31 horses arrived.	
GORRE	Bde HQ. in ~~[illegible]~~. GORRE.	
	31st Battery to a position close to the canal among the woods. F.11.c.5.9. vacated the 57 Battery -	
	35th Battery to a position 1000x North of the 31st previously occupied by the 118th Bde.	
26th	Batteries registered -	

(9 26 6) W 257—976 100,000 4/12 H W V 79/3298

Army Form C. 2118.

Instructions regarding War Diaries and Intelligence Summaries are contained in F. S. Regs., Part II. and the Staff Manual respectively. Title pages will be prepared in manuscript.

WAR DIARY
or
INTELLIGENCE SUMMARY.
(Erase heading not required.)

Hour, Date, Place	Summary of Events and Information	Remarks and references to Appendices
GORRE. June. 27th	Batteries registering. [illegible, struck through]	
28th	— do —	
29th.	35th Battery fired 13 shrapnel at a working party and 13 lyddite at a mine crater opposite H2 which was supposed to contain the entrance to the shaft of a German mine –	
30th	No shooting –	

(9 26 6) W 257—976 100,000 4/12 H W V 79/3298

7th Division

J

121/7429

37th Bde R.F.A.

Vol XII

July 15

Brit Em

Army Form C. 2118.

Instructions regarding War Diaries and Intelligence Summaries are contained in F. S. Regs., Part II. and the Staff Manual respectively. Title pages will be prepared in manuscript.

WAR DIARY

or

~~INTELLIGENCE SUMMARY.~~

(*Erase heading not required.*)

37th Bde R.F.A.

July 1915

Hour, Date, Place	Summary of Events and Information	Remarks and references to Appendices
GORRE July 1st	No shooting.	
	35th Battery on relief by 47th How. Bty. [2nd Div.]	
9.30 p.m.	marched to L'ECLÈME (near BUSNES) in reserve.	
L'ECLÈME 4.a.m.	Brigade headquarters marched from GORRE to L'ECLÈME.	
July 2nd 9. p.m.	31st Battery and ammunition column came out of action and joined remainder of Brigade at L'ECLÈME in reserve.	
July 3rd to July 31st	Bde in Reserve at L'ECLEME.	
July 25th	31st Battery ~~R.F.A.~~ went into action to assist the MEERUT D.A ½ mile S.W of RICHEBOURG ST VAAST.	
		[signature] Capt R.F.A. Adjt 37 Bde R.F.A.

(9 26 6) W 257—976 100,000 4/12 H W V 79/3298

7th Division

121/7437

37th Bde R.F.A.

August '15

Vol XIII.

Army Form C. 2118.

Instructions regarding War Diaries and Intelligence Summaries are contained in F. S. Regs., Part II. and the Staff Manual respectively. Title pages will be prepared in manuscript.

WAR DIARY
or
INTELLIGENCE SUMMARY.
(Erase heading not required.)

37th Bde RFA –

Hour, Date, Place	Summary of Events and Information 1915	Remarks and references to Appendices
August 2nd L'ECLEME	31st Battery RFA rejoined the Brigade at L'ECLEME.	
11	Lieut J.P Knight DSO joined the 35th Battery from 'F' Battery RHA for duty as Captain –	
14.	(Temp) Capt G. Beveridge attached to 31st Battery RFA – 2 sections 31st Battery RFA (X 18 a 3.1 / X 24 a 7 5) 1 section 35th Battery RFA (X 17 d. 9.8.) went into action –	
15th	The Bde went into action in the same positions it was in in June (except one sectn 31st Batty detached RUE L'EPINETTE) taking over from the 53rd Bde (IXth Divn)	
16th	Registering & checking telephone lines –	
17th 18th 19th 20th 21 22nd 23rd	A telephone line was layed along the front line trench the whole length of the Division and connected up to Batteries & Bde HQ Qrs.	[illegible]

(9 26 6) W 257–976 100,000 4/12 H W V 79/3298

Instructions regarding War Diaries and Intelligence Summaries are contained in F. S. Regs., Part II. and the Staff Manual respectively. Title pages will be prepared in manuscript.

WAR DIARY.
or
~~INTELLIGENCE SUMMARY.~~
(Erase heading not required.)

Army Form C. 2118.

37th Bde R.F.A.

Hour, Date, Place	Summary of Events and Information	Remarks and references to Appendices
August. 1915		
24th 9 pm.	one section per battery moved out on relief by sections of 89th Bde	(1st Div)
25th 26th 27th 9 pm.	Remainder of Bde moved out on relief by 89th Bde RFA and marched to PACAUT.	
25th.	Major Steel D.S.O. left for England to report to the War office.	
28.29.30.31.	Digging parties from 31st went to VERMELLES to prepare new posns.	
31st	1 section of 35th Battery went into action at VERMELLES.	
8th August.	Major Mahon proceeded to England to report to W.O.	
	Capt. G.E.A. Granet took over Command of 31st Battery	

[signature]
ADJT. 37th. BDE. R.F.A.
CAPT. R.F.A.

(9 26 6) W 257—976 100,000 4/12 H W V 79/3298

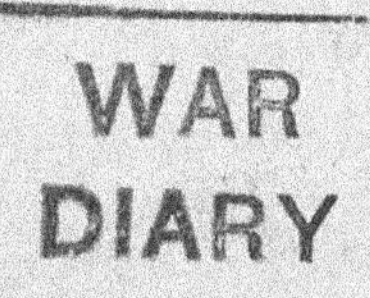

Headquarters,

37th BRIGADE, R.F.A.

(7th Division)

S E P T E M B E R

1 9 1 5

Army Form C. 2118.

Instructions regarding War Diaries and Intelligence Summaries are contained in F. S. Regs., Part II. and the Staff Manual respectively. Title pages will be prepared in manuscript.

WAR DIARY
or
~~INTELLIGENCE SUMMARY.~~

(Erase heading not required.) All references to Trench Map 1/10.000. 37th Bde RFA.

Hour, Date, Place	Summary of Events and Information	Remarks and references to Appendices
Sept. 1st 1915. Sept 2nd	Remainder of 35th Battery and Bde A.C. went into action. H.Qrs. 37th Bde RFA (To VERQUIGNEUL) & 31st Battery RFA went into action.	2nd Lieut G.W. Milne from 37th Bde A.C. joined Bde H.Qrs as Orderly Officer.
	35th Battery registered.	
Sept. 3rd. 4th	Both batteries registered by aeroplane.	
	Arcs of fire were roughly. 35th Battery LOOS – AUCHY 31st Battery BOIS CARRÉ – Railway Triangle	
	O.Ps. 31st. House in VERMELLES (G.8c98) No 3 Siding (HULLUCH Alley) Dugout on the Railway (G.9a15) 35th VERMELLES Church Machine House	
	Telephones. 31st to No 3 siding through Railway Dug out. 35th to Chapel Keep. down Rutoire Alley. Bde line to DA. batteries & FOSSE 9. Batteries connected by direct line.	
5th 6th 7th 8th &c	Registration continued. (Visual & by Aeroplane)	

[illegible]

WAR DIARY

or

INTELLIGENCE SUMMARY.

(*Erase heading not required.*)

Instructions regarding War Diaries and Intelligence Summaries are contained in F. S. Regs., Part II. and the Staff Manual respectively. Title pages will be prepared in manuscript.

Hour, Date, Place	Summary of Events and Information	Remarks and references to Appendices
~~August~~ 1915. September 18th	Ammunition is allotted as follows	

Rounds per Gun.

Situation at Dawn	with Btys.	with BAC.	with DAC.	with Park
1st Day	168	48	44	80
2nd Day	168	32	/	80
3rd Day	168	32	/	80
4th Day	168	32	/	80
5th Day	138	48	14	80

21st 1st day of bombardment.

Targets allotted 37th Bde. No firing by day night firing only

31st Battery. Communication trenches N.W of the QUARRY about G 5 d 1 0 1

Top of the DUMP G 5 a 8 8
Trench Junction G 5 b 3 7

35th Battery Cross roads G 11 d 9 3
Trench Junction G 11 b 8 2
Trench Junction G 11 b 1 7.

Night firing begins at 6 pm each night & continue until the opening of the next Day's bombardment. Ammunition allotted 60 rds per gun HE.

PWS

(9 26 6) W 257—976 100,000 4/12 H W V 79/3298

Instructions regarding War Diaries and Intelligence Summaries are contained in F. S. Regs., Part II. and the Staff Manual respectively. Title pages will be prepared in manuscript.

WAR DIARY
or
INTELLIGENCE SUMMARY.
(Erase heading not required.)

Hour, Date, Place	Summary of Events and Information	Remarks and references to Appendices
September –		
22. 23 – 24.	Bombardment continued	
	37th Bde firing by night	
24th	Bde HQrs moved into dugouts L6a82 (Ref. 1/40.000 Comb. Sheet)	
3.45am. 25th	Time of 0.0 O'clock notified as 5.50am 25/9/15.	
	Bde O.O. joined FOO 35th Battery at Chapel Keep.	
5.50am	31st Battery opened fire on G12a28, G5d101, G6c15 } 1 round per gun per minute HE.	
	35th — do — G12c5½2 – 84	
6. am	Rate of fire one round per gun every 5 minutes.	For more detailed information see notes attached.
6.5 am	31st Battery changed target to CITÉ TRENCH G6d4½5½ along new trench to the road at G6b5½1.	
6.~~35~~ am	35th Battery changed target to Trench G12d60 – 10.1.	
6.35am	35th Battery changed target to H7d26 – H7a60.	
7.5 am	Batteries stopped firing – 7.15 am opened fire again on the last Barrage.	
8.8am	Batteries stopped firing	
8.20am	35th Battery opened fire 6 guns on far end of comm. trenches leading to HULLUCH trench at H13b66 – 7.10 & H8c24. ~~[illegible]~~	
?	3 rds per minute and search into HULLUCH. 10% Shrapnel.	
8.57.	35th Battery stopped firing.	
9.10	35th Battery commenced firing again on the last target.	PWS

(9 26 6) W 257—976 100,000 4/12 H W V 79/3298

Instructions regarding War Diaries and Intelligence Summaries are contained in F. S. Regs., Part II. and the Staff Manual respectively. Title pages will be prepared in manuscript.

WAR DIARY
or
~~INTELLIGENCE SUMMARY.~~

(Erase heading not required.)

37th Bde RFA -

Hour, Date, Place		Summary of Events and Information	Remarks and references to Appendices
September 1915. 25th. VERMELLES	9.55.	35th Battery stopped firing -	
	10.10.	IV Corps about to attack HULLUCH. Fire 3 rounds per minute at far end of HULLUCH. Stop at 10.30 am. Sent to 31st Battery H8d01 - 63 - 28 - 17.	
	10.30.	31st Battery stopped firing -	
	10.40.	31st to continue firing	
	10.55	31st Battery stopped firing -	
	11.7.	31st Battery continued firing -	
	10.20.	35th Battery sent for their teams.	
	1 pm.	31st Battery ordered to fire on CITE TRENCH + PUITS 13	
	1.30 pm.	31st stopped firing -	
	2.15 pm.	Orders from 7 DA to fire as follows - Houses H7a64 35th Battery; G6d71, H7a18 } 31st Battery. 3 rounds per battery per minute.	
	2.40 pm.	35th Battery to put one gun to shell wire H7a23 - H7a61	
	3.11. p.m	6 guns to shell ~~[illegible]~~ wire. 4 guns into houses in St ELIE.	
	4 pm.	Both batteries stopped firing -	
	5.50 pm.	Night Firing to start at once. Target. St ELIE. { 2 sections 31st Battery, 1 section 35th Battery } 1 round per section per minute.	PMB

(9 26 6) W 257—976 100,000 4/12 H W V 79/3298

Instructions regarding War Diaries and Intelligence Summaries are contained in F. S. Regs., Part II. and the Staff Manual respectively. Title pages will be prepared in manuscript.

WAR DIARY
or
INTELLIGENCE SUMMARY.
(Erase heading not required.)

37th Bde RFA.

Hour, Date, Place	Summary of Events and Information 1915.	Remarks and references to Appendices
VERMELLES Sept. 25th 6.40 pm.	Rate of fire ~~fire~~ increased to one round per gun every two minutes.	
6.50 pm.	Rate of fire one round per section every 5 minutes.	
7.15 pm.	Rate of fire 1 round per battery every 10 minutes.	
11.18 pm.	Lay the guns that are not firing on H1c87	
Sept. 26th 12.30 am	Enemy reported to be attacking (from 7th DA) rate of fire increased	
About 12.45 am.	Information from DA that a hostile counter attack had captured the QUARRY	
12.50 am.	Message from 35th Battery that Germans had captured gun trench and 2nd Lieut Scott has been badly wounded and that gun trench has been retaken by us.	Casualties 25th/26th Sept.
1.30 am.	Turn all your guns onto the East edge of the QUARRY. Section fire one minute (from 7th D.A.)	2nd Lieut K W POWER. 31st Batty missing. Later reported (Prisoner of War)
3.10 am	FOO (31st Battery) reports the Quarries are in German hands but we are shortly going to counter attack. We still hold the trench to the right. 2nd Lieut Power is still missing.	WOUNDED 2nd Lieut. T.D. SCOTT. 35th Batty. KILLED No 72712 Gr VIVASH 35th Batty.
3.30 am	35th advanced section rejoined the battery.	MISSING aBr Huncombe 31st Batty. Gr Wiseman. Bde H.Q. Ams.
9.30 am.	31st Battery report all quiet. very misty.	WOUNDED Gr Wale 35th Batty.

[illegible initials]

(9 26 6) W 257—976 100,000 4/12 H W V 79/3298

Instructions regarding War Diaries and Intelligence Summaries are contained in F. S. Regs., Part II. and the Staff Manual respectively. Title pages will be prepared in manuscript.

~~WAR DIARY~~ or ~~INTELLIGENCE~~ SUMMARY.
(Erase heading not required.)

37th Bde RFA

Place	Date	Hour	Summary of Events and Information 1915.	Remarks and references to Appendices
VERMELLES	Sept. 26th.	morning	Both batteries re-registered the QUARRIES	
		1.20pm	35th Battery retaliated on PUITS TRENCH for shelling of HULLUCH road	
		1.30pm	Bombardment of the QUARRIES to commence at 2.30pm.	
		1.47.	Bombardment postponed to 3.30pm.	
		2.55	31st Battery fired 6 rounds per gun on St ELIE (H1c & G6d)	
		3 –	35th Battery —— do ——	
		3.8.	Orders for bombardment of the QUARRIES as follows:—	

TIME.	31st Battery	35th Battery
3.30 – 4.30pm.	line G12a 28 – G6c01 – 15 – 45	G6a42 – G6c45 – 82 – G6d23 ~~[illegible]~~
4.30 onwards.	H7d14 – 34.	H7d45 – 07 – H7a61 –

Ammunition allowed.

31st Battery		35th Battery	
3.30 – 4.30pm.	120 rds.	3.30 – 4.27	60 rds.
4.30 – 4.40	one rd per gun every two minutes	4.27 – 4.40	one round per gun every 2 minutes
4.40 onwards	one round per gun every 5 minutes	4.40 onwards	one round per gun every 5 minutes

Place	Date	Hour	Summary of Events and Information	Remarks
		3.7	Hostile infantry advancing in a westerly direction from BILLY BERCLAU I have opened fire on them. (From 35th Battery)	

T2134. Wt. W708—776. 500000. 4/15. Sir J. C. & S.

Instructions regarding War Diaries and Intelligence Summaries are contained in F. S. Regs., Part II. and the Staff Manual respectively. Title pages will be prepared in manuscript.

or

INTELLIGENCE SUMMARY.

(Erase heading not required.)

37th Bde RFA –

Place	Date	Hour	Summary of Events and Information 1915.	Remarks and references to Appendices
	SEPT			—
VERMELLES	~~25~~ 26th	3.30pm.	CARTER'S FORCE (3 Battns 2nd Divn) will attack at the QUARRY from roughly the line G11b34 – G5d12. Assault at 4.30p.m. 9th Divn will assist by a movement from FOSSE 8. 7th Divn line runs as follows:—	2nd Lieut T. Taylor 31st Battery RFA wounded (slight)
			20th Inf. Bde G12d44 – 39 – b22	
			22nd Inf. Bde G12a54 – 51 – 22 – G11b41 – G5d12	
		5.25	31st Baty FOO reported 4TH Worcesters attacked and took the wrong direction they did not go near the QUARRY.	
		6.30.	Night line:— 31st Baty. G6b90 – G12b79. G6d96.	
			35th Baty. H1c77. H7a17. H7a66.	
	27th	AM. 5.50	Worcesters report Germans appear to be preparing an attack from the QUARRY.	
		6.	31st Battery opened fire on QUARRY. one round every 2 minutes.	
		6.30.	31st Baty stopped firing –	
		6.30.	31st Baty. FOO. reports. Our infantry are holding the line approximately G12a54 – G5d10.0 – G5d5.3. The Battns are Norfolks. KRR. Middlesex. Northants 12th Welsh. On the right our infantry are supposed to be in STONE ALLEY.	
		9.40.	31st Baty FOO reports. Our infantry are retiring about G5b55 – G5d88	

T2134. Wt. W708—776. 500000. 4/15. Sir J. C. & S.

Instructions regarding War Diaries and Intelligence Summaries are contained in F. S. Regs., Part II. and the Staff Manual respectively. Title pages will be prepared in manuscript.

or

~~INTELLIGENCE~~ SUMMARY.

(Erase heading not required.)

37th Bde RFA –

Place	Date	Hour	Summary of Events and Information	Remarks and references to Appendices
VERMELLES	27th	1pm.	German attack east of FOSSE ALLEY (FOO 31st)	
			31st Battery fired at G6c42	
		2.12	31st Battery opened fire (shrapnel) on square A29d on a line parallel to the East face of the DUMP and about 200 yards over it – 1 RD per minute.	
		2.15	35th Battery FOO reports :– R.S.F. Camerons and Wilts are in GUN trench G12d55 – G12a54. Battn H.Q. Qrs G12c54. 21st Bde H.Q. Qrs Chapel Keep. Infantry report chief trouble coming from G12c70 – (12 noon delayed)	
		2.27.	Enemy are retiring from East face of the DUMP and our men are advancing. [31st F.O.O.]	
		2.40.	31st Battery stopped firing.	
		5.29	7th DA report gas attack repulsed on the front HULLUCH – St ELIE.	
		6pm.	31st FOO reports. our front line runs as follows – From old German front line near POPE'S NOSE up St ELIE AVENUE to G11b69 – G11b81½ – G12a22 – 54 – G12b22.	
		6.45	Foo 31st Baty reports. Enemy bombing party ~~[illegible]~~ at G12a54 – 46 was forced to retire	
		8.12pm	from 7th DA. The situation of our line between G12a54 and G11b78 is as follows G12a41½ BRESLAU AVENUE G11b78 with a bombing party at G5d7½.½.	

T2134. Wt. W708—776. 500000. 4/15. Sir J. C. & S.

Instructions regarding War Diaries and Intelligence Summaries are contained in F. S. Regs., Part II. and the Staff Manual respectively. Title pages will be prepared in manuscript.

WAR DIARY
or
~~INTELLIGENCE SUMMARY.~~
(Erase heading not required.)

37th Bde RFA.

Place	Date	Hour	Summary of Events and Information 1915	Remarks and references to Appendices
VERMELLES	28th	P.M. 3.12	35th Battery fired on PUITS TRENCH in retaliation	2nd Lieut. STROYAN - joined 35th Battery from D.A.C.
		5 -	31st Battery fired at QUARRIES in retaliation	
		6.6.	Night lines :- 31st. G5b39 - G6a42 - G6C45-15 - G6d24 - G12b57 (one gun on each)	
			35th H7a04 - H7C47 - H7C44	
	29th	AM. 7.54.	From 7th D.A. Germans are trying to bomb along St. ELIE AVENUE.	
			31st battery fired one section at the QUARRY. 1 round a minute.	
		7.20	35th Battery opened fire on PUITS Trench	
		9.10.	31st Battery opened fire on SLAG ALLEY.	
		10 am	35th opened fire East of the DUMP	
		10.40.	35th fired 20 rds rapid at PUITS TRENCH in retaliation for enemy shelling GUN trench	
		11.40.	Posn at St. ELIE AVUE is now the same as last night. 60th Rifles made a bayonet charge and recovered the lost ground. (FOO 31st)	
		12.35	31st Battery fired 36 rounds at CITÉ TRENCH in retaliation.	
		3.5.	F.O.O 31st reports enemy digging in SLAG ALLEY. 31st Batty fired 6 rds and they stopped.	
		3.15	35th Battery retaliated on PUITS trench	
		6.24	FOO 35th reports enemy observed entrenching from point H7C14 towards CITÉ St. ELIE (They fired on them)	

RW

T2134. Wt. W708-776. 500000. 4/15. Sir J. C. & S.

Instructions regarding War Diaries and Intelligence Summaries are contained in F. S. Regs., Part II. and the Staff Manual respectively. Title pages will be prepared in manuscript.

~~WAR DIARY~~ or ~~INTELLIGENCE~~ SUMMARY.

(Erase heading not required.)

37 Bde RFA.

1915

Place	Date	Hour	Summary of Events and Information	Remarks and references to Appendices
	SEPT	PM.		
VERMELLES	29th	6.25	31st Battery to fire at G5b39 and behind the DUMP up to A29d26. one rd per minute	
		6.55.	35th Battery to fire at the QUARRIES 10 rds HE rapidly.	
		7.8.	31st Battery stopped firing.	
	30th	AM. 11.10	31st Battery fired 6 rds at the QUARRY in retaliation	
		PM. 6.18	Night lines :— 31st G5b39. G6a15 G6a42 - G6c45. G6c70. G12b57	
			35th H7a23 H7a61 H7c44 H13b17 H13a94 H13b19.	
		6.55	From 7th D A. Germans reported to be massing at G12a29. Open fire on the further edge of the QUARRY one round every 2 minutes. (To 31st Battery)	
		7.45	35th Battery to open with a slow rate on H7a13	
		8.15	31st Battery stopped firing. 35th Battery slow rate of fire. (10 rds an hour)	
		9.23	FOO 35th Battery reports :– (Report delayed) – Germans attacked GUN TRENCH at 6 pm. They were repulsed south of the HULLUCH road but north of the road have gained a footing.	

Instructions regarding War Diaries and Intelligence Summaries are contained in F. S. Regs., Part II. and the Staff Manual respectively. Title pages will be prepared in manuscript.

~~WAR DIARY~~
or
~~INTELLIGENCE SUMMARY~~.
(Erase heading not required.)

37th Bde RFA.

Place	Date	Hour	Summary of Events and Information	Remarks and references to Appendices
VERMELLES	September		1915. Ammunition expended – (6pm – 6pm daily)	

Date	31st Battery HE	31st Battery Shrapnel	35th Battery HE	35th Battery Shrapnel	Total HE	Total Shrapnel	TOTAL Rounds
21st/22nd	344	—	351	—	695	—	695
22nd/23rd	360	—	349	—	709	—	709
23rd/24th	372	—	375	—	747	—	747
24th/25th	1021	131	960	15	1981	146	2127
25th/26th	778	—	110	—	888	—	888
26th/27th	56	11	35	38	91	49	140
27th/28th	27	33	79	15	106	48	154
28th/29th	250	98	84	16	334	114	448
29th/30th	62	12	44	21	106	33	139
TOTAL. 21st/30th	3270	285	2387	105	5657	390	6047

[signature] Capt RFA
Adjt 37th Bde RFA

T2134. Wt. W708—776. 500000. 4/15. Sir J. C. & S.

Lieut. R.C. Reynolds (Now Captain)
Adj. 2nd Training Brigade, R.A. Depôt.

At Loos
F.O.O. 35th (How.) Battery R.F.A.,
XXXVII Brigade R.F.A.
7th Division.

R.A. Mess, Woolwich,
7th Sept. 1927.

Dear Major,

I have just seen in my copy of the R.A. Regimental News, which I received to-day that you want some information re some 6" hows. which went forward on the first day of the battle of Loos into action in No Man's Land north of the Vermelles - Hulluch road and on the left of T Battery R.H.A. I think that I can elucidate the problem. It was <u>not</u> 6" hows. but one section of 4.5" hows.

Colin Jardine took his section of T Bty. R.H.A. up the Hulluch road from Vermelles at about 8 a.m. on the 25th. It was a very gallant display. They galloped up the road, being heavily fired on by rifles and machine guns from a point about 300 yards south of the Hulluch road in the old German front line, which was still held by an isolated party of Germans who were holding out against the 1st Division. I think it was the London Scottish who were preparing to drive them out at that time.

About 12 noon when these Huns had been captured and all was quiet, I, who was acting as F.O.O. was called to take my section of the 35th How. Battery, 37th Brigade R.F.A. up the Hulluch Road and to come into action in the old No Man's Land on the left of T Battery. We proceeded at a sedate walk without any rifle or gunfire and came into action, I think, about 1 p.m. about 100 yards to the left of T Battery We spent most of our time firing at the towers of Cité St. Elie, over open sights and on Cité St. Elie itself in preparation of the infantry attack on that place.

No other guns, 6" or otherwise, came up there. *

About 5 p.m. the Germans opened fire on us with gas shell, the first the battery had met up till then, and we had a few casualties from gas.

We observed fire from Gun Trench and Stone Alley.

Some time about midnight an infantry officer told Jardine and I that we had ~~took~~ the Quarries and that our infantry had come back to their old front line there, so that our guns were between the opposing front lines. We informed our respective brigades and were ordered to retire. The teams came up to the guns about 2 a.m. on the 26th and without any molestation from the Huns we hooked in, pull out on to the Hulluch road and walked back to our battery positions in Vermelles. Our F.O.O. during the night was a young subaltern called Scott who was badly wounded during the night when the Germans recaptured the Quarries, he was, however, brought in by the telephonist and so escape, but the Brigade F.O.O. in the Quarries, a Lieut. Power, was captured with the infantry Bn. H.Q. at that place.

I hope this will be of some use to you, and if there is anything else I can tell you that you will write and ask me.

Yours sincerely,

R.C. Reynolds, Capt. R.A.

* But see Diary of VII Bde., R.G.A. for 25th Sept. 1915, with reference to move of R. Sec. of 59th Battery, R.G.A.
A.F.B. 8.IX.27

7th Division

37th Bde. R.F.A.

121/7435

Oct 15 31 & 35 H batteries

Vol XV

Instructions regarding War Diaries and Intelligence Summaries are contained in F. S. Regs., Part II. and the Staff Manual respectively. Title pages will be prepared in manuscript.

WAR DIARY
or
~~INTELLIGENCE SUMMARY.~~
(Erase heading not required.)

Army Form C. 2118.

37th Bde RFA.

Place	Date	Hour	Summary of Events and Information	Remarks and references to Appendices
	Oct.	AM.	1915.	
VERMELLES	1st	1.8	Order from DA. Open fire at once on the line H7a61 – B3. Section fire 30 secs (Passed to 35th Battery)	
		1.10	31st Battery to open fire at 1.15 am on the line G12a28 – G6c01 1 round every 2 mins. Stop firing at 1.35 am –	
		1.40	At 1.45 reduce rate of fire on trench H7a13 – H7a61 & continue till 2.30 am –	
		3.	Fight is still going on at Gun trench	
		6.4	Situation in GUN trench is as follows. Germans hold from G12d39 – 57. Our infantry hold trench south of the road	
		6.35	Please register trench from H7a13 to the portion of our own front line now occupied by the Germans. Refer to GOC 21st Inf Bde before firing from 7th D.A –	
		10.25	Open fire at once on the new Redoubt G5a84. one round a minute (To 31st)	
		P.M. 1.35	To 31st :– have a section ready to shoot at the cross roads H7c44	
		~~1.55~~ 3.20.	35th Battery firing at GUN trench.	
		6 pm.	Night firing – 35th { one section G12d39 – H7a44 ; one section H7c0½ – H7c44 } 12 rds per target per hour –	

[signature]

T2134. Wt. W708–776. 500000. 4/15. Sir J. C. & S.

Instructions regarding War Diaries and Intelligence Summaries are contained in F. S. Regs., Part II. and the Staff Manual respectively. Title pages will be prepared in manuscript.

WAR DIARY
or
~~INTELLIGENCE SUMMARY.~~
(Erase heading not required.)

Army Form C. 2118.

37th Bde RFA

Place	Date	Hour	Summary of Events and Information 1915	Remarks and references to Appendices
	Oct.			
VERMELLES	2nd	AM. 8.15	From 7th D.A. :- A new british trench has been dug from about G18b95 to about G12d60	
			The right of the 2nd Divn is about G18b95.	
		~~8.15~~	35th Battery firing on Gun trench	
			31st Battery checked registration on Gun trench in the afternoon.	
		PM. 6.0	one section of 35th on trench G12d39 – H7a04 }	
			one section — — H7c0½ – 44 } 12 rounds per hour all night per target	
		8.0 to 8.30	31st battery to fire 6 special shell at each of the following G12b78½ H7a16	
			35th Battery —— ditto —— —— do —— H7a64 – H7a44	
		8.30	35th Battery to concentrate fire on the North commn trench at H7a13	
		8.30 to 8.40.	Sectn Fire 20 secs	
		8.40	onwards Sectn Fire 30 secs	
		9.25	1 round a minute –	
		10.45	35th to carry on same arrangements as last night. Attack having failed –	
			The above firing was in support of an attack made on Gun trench.	
				PM

T2134. Wt. W708—776. 500000. 4/15. Sir J. C. & S.

Army Form C. 2118.

WAR DIARY
or
~~INTELLIGENCE SUMMARY.~~
(Erase heading not required.)

Instructions regarding War Diaries and Intelligence Summaries are contained in F. S. Regs., Part II. and the Staff Manual respectively. Title pages will be prepared in manuscript.

37th Bde RFA – 1915.

Place	Date	Hour	Summary of Events and Information	Remarks and references to Appendices
	Oct			
VERMELLES	3rd	10.30am.	Everything is quiet now round the HOHENZOLLERN except for a few rounds shrapnel from our artillery round LITTLE WILLIE –	
		10.33	From 7th DA. Enemy have dug a trench from G6c70 – G6c82 – TUDOR trench.	
		4.9pm.	To 35th. Retaliate on German trench from G6d41 – G12b85 about 20 rds [?]	
		4.10pm.	Heavy shelling on the north end of GUN trench (Col Spedding)	
		~~4.35~~ 4.50.	To 31st Batty. Germans bombing down St ELIE AVENUE fire on G5d82 49.0.	
		5.27.	FOO. 31st Battery reports. Heavy bombing about G12a54 –	
		6pm.	KRRs are holding their own they are very pleased with artillery support (FOO 31st) –	
		7.25	31st FOO reports heavy rifle fire from direction of HOHENZOLLERN	
		8.5pm.	31st reports Bomb attack in HOHENZOLLERN. 31st fired one rd shrapnel per minute on West end of SLAG ALLEY.	

PBO [?]

Instructions regarding War Diaries and Intelligence Summaries are contained in F. S. Regs., Part II. and the Staff Manual respectively. Title pages will be prepared in manuscript.

WAR DIARY

or

~~INTELLIGENCE SUMMARY~~.

(Erase heading not required.)

Army Form C. 2118.

37th Bde RFA — 1915.

Place	Date	Hour	Summary of Events and Information	Remarks and references to Appendices
	Oct	AM.		
VERMELLES.	4th	11.45	King's Own were unsuccessful in bombing attack at G4b60 this morning – we hold BIG WILLIE to G4d98 – (FOO 31st Battery) –	
		PM. 12.35	To 31st Battery RFA. Retaliate on German trench running South East from G6c70 as soon as possible. Your FOO should observe this.	
		1pm.	31st retaliated on trench running SE from G6c70.	
		2.50	35th retaliated opposite Gun Trench.	
		6pm	35th Battery reports – The wire in front of the trench running from A30c96 to A30d30 appears to be very strong. Working parties were at work on the trench and also on the communication trench from about G5b58 – d18.	
	5th	AM 8.39.	35th Battery FOO reports German shelling GUN Trench & HAY alley very heavily with 4.2 Hows. Have retaliated on PUITS trench with 36 rds Lyd	
		10.16	Turn a Gun onto SLAG ALLEY G5a95 – G5b28. One rd every 5 mins. The infantry say there is a gun near there. (From 7th DA passed to 31st)	
		~~10.40~~	To ~~31st from 7th DA Inf~~	
		10.47	Enemy are shelling our trenches with 5.9 N of the HULLUCH road – 35th Battery retaliated (Information from DA	[initials]

T2134. Wt. W708—776. 500000. 4/15. Sir J. C. & S.

Instructions regarding War Diaries and Intelligence Summaries are contained in F. S. Regs., Part II. and the Staff Manual respectively. Title pages will be prepared in manuscript.

WAR DIARY
or
~~INTELLIGENCE SUMMARY~~.
(Erase heading not required.)

Army Form C. 211

37 Bde RFA.
1915.

Place	Date	Hour	Summary of Events and Information	Remarks and references to Appendices
VERMELLES	Oct 5th	PM. 12.20	From 35th FOO 3rd Guards Bde report that Germans have blown in a portion of front trench about G12a54	
		12.30	To 31st Batty. Be ready to fire on the following pts G6c90 – G12a28 and TUDOR TRENCH.	
		1.20	35th Battery retaliated for shelling of GUN Trench –	
		1.45	Enemy have stopped shelling GUN trench. (FOO 35th Batty) –	
		5.15	35th reports Enemy has been shelling STONE ALLEY have retaliated on GUN trench	
		7.5.	Orders to 31st Batty. Fire 5 rounds Lyddite per hour all night – Stop firing when it gets light.	
	6th	12.45 pm.	35th Retaliated for the shelling of GUN Trench	
		2.45	31st ——— ditto ———	
		12.30	31st Battery firing one Gun on SLAG ALLEY (Request of Infantry)	
		5.8	35th Battery report. 8 guns firing from Railway cutting B26c88 and trying to	
		5.30	35th Battery report. at 4 pm enemy's working party was seen at Trench then H1a15 and was fired on and dispersed.	

[signature]

T2134. Wt. W708—776. 500000. 4/15. Sir J. C. & S.

Instructions regarding War Diaries and Intelligence Summaries are contained in F. S. Regs., Part. II. and the Staff Manual respectively. Title pages will be prepared in manuscript.

WAR DIARY
or
~~INTELLIGENCE SUMMARY.~~
(Erase heading not required.)

Army Form C. 2118

37th Bde RFA

1915

Place	Date	Hour	Summary of Events and Information	Remarks and references to Appendices
	Oct			
VERMELLES	6th	PM 6.35	To 31st Batty. Fire 3 rds an hour into the Quarry all night.	
	7th	AM 8.23	To 31st. Retaliate opposite STONE ALLEY 12 rounds and also on the QUARRY.	
		PM 2.25	From 31st. Germans working in the QUARRY am firing shrapnel –	
		7.22	To 3rd. Fire on the QUARRIES same as last night –	
	8th	AM 9.9.	31st Retaliated in front of G12a54.	
		10.25.	From 31st. Enemy shelling GOEBEN ALLEY have retaliated.	
		PM 2.55.	Enemy are firing bombs from direction of SLAG ALLEY. I am firing battery fire 30 secs (From 31st)	
		4.55pm	35th Batty Report. Enemy are shelling GUN Trench from direction of HULLUCH.	
		5.20pm	31st Batty Report. Bomb attack about G5c87. Aerial torpedoes firing from direction of QUARRY.	
		~~7.30~~	Orders for attack of GUN Trench 8.10.15.	
			Assault by R.W. Kent Regt at 6.15 pm.	
			3.15 p.m – 3.45 pm. Both batteries fire at Commn Trench G12d89–981 2 rounds per batty per min. (50% Shrap)	
			3.45 pm Both batteries STOP.	
			4.30–6.15 Batteries continue as before –	
			6.15. 31st Battery. one sectn on H7a03	
			35th Battery one sectn on G12b81 one sectn on H7c44 One round per target per minute for one hour after that one round per target every 2 minutes.	PBH

T2134. Wt. W708—776. 500000. 4/15. Sir J. C. & S.

Army Form C. 2118.

Instructions regarding War Diaries and Intelligence Summaries are contained in F. S. Regs., Part II. and the Staff Manual respectively. Title pages will be prepared in manuscript.

WAR DIARY
or
~~INTELLIGENCE SUMMARY.~~
(Erase heading not required.)

37th Bde RFA
1915

Place	Date	Hour	Summary of Events and Information	Remarks and references to Appendices
	Oct.			
VERMELLES	8th		The above orders were modified. The 31st battery only using one section throughout and having one section on the QUARRY and one on SLAG ALLEY. to assist the 3rd Coldstreams who were being attacked.	
		P.M. 5.25	Firing has practically ceased (i.e in front of the Guards) but a German Maxim is still firing about G 5 c 8 7 (F.O.O 31st)	
		5.45	31st stopped firing on SLAG ALLEY. All reported quiet except slight rifle and artillery fire. (F.O.O 31st at SPURN HEAD)	
		6.50.	F.O.O 35th Battery. (HAY ALLEY) reports attack (on GUN TRENCH) appears to be held up. Germans are still holding their trenches. German artillery has not opened fire.	
		7.20	F.O.O 35th Reports the bomb attack appears to proceed only on the Right of GUN Trench. The enemy's machine guns are very active. German artillery has ceased fire.	
		8.45.	F.O.O 35th Battery reports that we captured part of GUN Trench but have now been bombed out again	
		9.45	Both batteries to reduce rate of fire to 12 rds per battery per hour.	

[illegible]

T2134. Wt. W708—776. 500000. 4/15. Sir J. C. & S.

Instructions regarding War Diaries and Intelligence Summaries are contained in F. S. Regs., Part II. and the Staff Manual respectively. Title pages will be prepared in manuscript.

WAR DIARY or INTELLIGENCE SUMMARY.

(*Erase heading not required.*)

Army Form C. 2118.

37th Bde RFA.

Place	Date	Hour	Summary of Events and Information 1915.	Remarks and references to Appendices
VERMELLES.	8th	PM. 10.15	FOO. 35th Batty reports the situation is as it was before the attack.	
		10.30	To 31st. Fire 12 rds an hour into the QUARRIES – Stop firing on all other targets.	
	9th	AM 8.50	To 35th Stop Firing –	
		PM 3.0	31st fired 6 HE at the QUARRIES.	
		8.5	Rifle fire & bombing in the direction of the QUARRIES.	
		8.45.	31st Batty retaliated on SLAG ALLEY (For trench mortars)	
		10.58	31st Batty — do — QUARRY (— do —)	
	10th	morning	Batteries registering & retaliating –	
		5.30PM.	(Instructions received from D.A.) 31st Batty open fire at once on the following Gun Targets H13b96 fire 30 rounds in Salvos of 3 wait 15 mins and fire another 9 wait 15 minutes & fire another 9 (48 rds HE) search & sweep.	
		PM. 5.35	35th Battery same orders to fire on guns at H13b93 H14a28	
		6	31st Battery reports enemy shelling QUARRY TRENCH Aerial Torpedoes retaliated on SLAG ALLEY.	F.00

T2134. Wt. W708—776. 500000. 4/15. Sir J. C. & S.

Instructions regarding War Diaries and Intelligence Summaries are contained in F. S. Regs., Part II. and the Staff Manual respectively. Title pages will be prepared in manuscript.

WAR DIARY
or
~~INTELLIGENCE SUMMARY.~~
(Erase heading not required.)

Army Form C. 2118.

37th Bde RFA.
1915

Place	Date	Hour	Summary of Events and Information	Remarks and references to Appendices
	Oct	PM.		
VERMELLES	10.	7.5	31st Baty FOO reports. 2nd Grenadier Guards are going to attack at 8.30pm starting at H5c87. They hope to advance a little along SLAG ALLEY to about G5a7.2. He would like us to bombard SLAG ALLEY from 8.30pm onwards (Permission given)	
		9.15	We are progressing slowly have taken 70 trench. (FOO 31st)	
		11.	31st report they have reduced rate to 12 rds an hour. (They starting firing 30 secs slackened to 1 min)	
	11.	AM. 7.30	31st Baty fired 4 rounds at trench Mortar West of the Dump.	
		11.9am	35th F.O.O. reports that enemy has been shelling HAY ALLEY for over. 35th retaliated [twice]	
		11.40.	Enemy shelling head of SPURN HEAD with 4.2s they have fired 5 rds —	
		PM. 12.35pm	FOO 31st Reports. Enemy shelling old German frontline near the WINDOW have retaliated on SLAG ALLEY.	
		4.55	Enemy shelling SPURN HEAD & front line near it with 4.2 (4 a minute) True bearing of sound from G5d12 is 59° (FOO 31st Baty)	
		5.5	Enemy's fire has slackened to about 2 rounds a minute. Have retaliated one Salvo on SLAG ALLEY.	
		5.55	FOO. 35th Baty reports a lot of work was done on PUITS trench and commt trench H7c44–11. The latter appears to have been deepened. The trench H13a26 to G12b80 has been completed.	PDR

T2134. Wt. W708—776. 500000. 4/15. Sir J. C. & S.

Instructions regarding War Diaries and Intelligence Summaries are contained in F. S. Regs., Part II. and the Staff Manual respectively. Title pages will be prepared in manuscript.

WAR DIARY or INTELLIGENCE SUMMARY.

(Erase heading not required.)

Army Form C. 2118.

37th Bde RFA.

1915.

Place	Date	Hour	Summary of Events and Information	Remarks and references to Appendices
VERMELLES	Oct 11th	PM 6.20	31st Retaliated on trench in front of QUARRY (for shelling of SPURN HEAD)	
	12th	PM.	Batteries registering SLAG ALLEY, CITE TRENCH & QUARRIES.	
		12.55	31st Batty Siding No 3 – Enemy shelling Spurnhead and old German front line with 4.2s direction unknown am retaliating on SLAG ALLEY – A German field gun battery is also shelling in salvos of 3 from direction of DOUVRIN CH.	
		3.30	FOO 31st. report. There appears to be a bomb attack about G5C89 (from SIDING 3)	
		5pm	Grenadiers are being heavily attacked. Trench mortars are doing most of the damage. Trench mortar appears to be in the trenches near the DUMP. From FOO 31st at SPURN HEAD This wire was cut from 1pm – 5pm –	
		6.	FOO 35th Battery reports Germans working on their new trench H7C44–11 last night. An emplacement is visible at H7C11 – There is a trench G5a96 – G5b40 visible from G5C87.	
		7.	FOO 35th reports hostile batteries visible firing at 6.15 as follows – All observed by flashes seen from G18a96 True bearings. 28° apparently just behind St ELIE houses (Field guns) 36° neighbourhood of DOUVRIN CH. Field guns firing repeatedly 45° railway cutting field guns – 53° & 55° one of the latter was a field How.r	

T2134. Wt. W708—776. 500000. 4/15. Sir J. C. & S.

Instructions regarding War Diaries and Intelligence Summaries are contained in F. S. Regs., Part II. and the Staff Manual respectively. Title pages will be prepared in manuscript.

WAR DIARY
or
INTELLIGENCE SUMMARY.
(Erase heading not required.)

Army Form C. 2118.

37th Bde RFA.

1915

Place	Date	Hour	Summary of Events and Information	Remarks and references to Appendices
	Oct.			
VERMELLES	13		XIth Corps will attack the DUMP the QUARRIES and GUN trench The 35th Infantry Bde will attack the QUARRIE - Batteries 37th Bde fire as follows:—	

Time	31st Battery.	35th Battery.
12 noon - 1pm	SLAG ALLEY G5a73 - G5a96	SLAG ALLEY G5a96 - G5b39
1pm - 1.45pm 31st Batty do not fire from 1.45 - 2pm.	Ends of commn trenches at G5d9½ and G5d10½	
1pm - 2pm -		Trench from G6c½5 to G6c34
2pm - 4pm & onwards	CITE Trench (Both Batteries) G6d89 to G6d42 (both inclusive)	

Rate of fire

12 - 2p.m. 45 rounds per gun per hour
2 - 4pm 30 — do —
4 - 6pm 15 — do —
6pm onwards 10 rounds per battery per hour

50 Rounds HE per gun surplus was allowed for the operation.

Officers disposed as follows:— Colonel Spedding FOSSE No 9
Capt. Agnew - Machine House VERMELLES
Capt Granet.
F.O.O 31st Batty } In the neighbourhood of the POPE'S
F.O.O. 35th Batty } NOSE and the CUPOLA -

RAF

T2134. Wt. W708-776. 500000. 4/15. Sir J. C. & S.

Instructions regarding War Diaries and Intelligence Summaries are contained in F. S. Regs., Part II. and the Staff Manual respectively. Title pages will be prepared in manuscript.

WAR DIARY
or
INTELLIGENCE SUMMARY.
(Erase heading not required.)

Army Form C. 2118.

37th Bde RFA.

1915

Place	Date	Hour	Summary of Events and Information	Remarks and references to Appendices
	October			
VERMELLES.	13.		Bde O.O. CHAPEL KEEP	
			A line was layed from CHAPEL KEEP to the POPE'S NOSE as an alternative to the 31st Battery line. The former worked up till about 5.30pm. The latter was cut practically all day until about 2am on the 14th	
		P.M.	Assault at 2p.m.	
		2.10	46th Divn appear to have taken HOHENZOLLERN (Capt Agnew)	
		2.30	Our infy appeared to take the HOHENZOLLERN but we have just seen about 100 running back. Nothing can be seen at the QUARRIES except bombing. Our infantry advanced against GUN Trench and disappeared (Col Spedding)	
		3.12	Our infantry are retiring from the HOHENZOLLERN (Capt. Agnew)	
		3.55	A bomb fight is in progress along the North face of the HOHENZOLLERN. The germans can be distinctly seen throwing bombs. (Col Spedding)	
		3.20	SUFFOLKS progressing slowly on the right but held up on the left. (F.O.O 31st)	
		3.25	12th Divn Flag seen flying at G 6 c 70 (F.O.O 35th Battery).	
		3.45	Suffolks have overcome the difficulty on the right and are progressing well on the left (31st)	
		5.20	~~Brocheataske~~ ~~appears~~ & Battery active at A 24 b 12. Please turn onto (31st) (Passed to 31st Batty)	

T2134. Wt. W708—776. 500000. 4/15. Sir J. C. & S.

Instructions regarding War Diaries and Intelligence Summaries are contained in F. S. Regs., Part II. and the Staff Manual respectively. Title pages will be prepared in manuscript.

WAR DIARY
or
INTELLIGENCE SUMMARY.
(Erase heading not required.)

Army Form C. 2118.

37th Bde RFA.

1915.

Place	Date	Hour	Summary of Events and Information	Remarks and references to Appendices
	Oct.			
VERMELLES	13th	7pm.	To 35th Battery - Turn your fire onto trench G6d24 - G12b85 - 6 rounds a minute.	
		7.20	31st Battery stopped firing -	
		7.25	35th Battery original rate -	
		9.30	35th Battery stopped firing	
	14th	A.M. 12.20	Bombing SIELIE AVENUE & HOHENZOLLERN otherwise quiet.	
	15th		Retaliation.	
	16th			
	17th		one section ~~two~~ each Battery moved to wagon lines on ~~two~~ relief by XIIth Divn Hows.	
	18th		Bde marched to MAZINGHEM near FONTES arriving early on the 19th.	
MAZINGHEM.			In Reserve -	
	23rd		35th Battery (less one section) relieved the 61st Battery RFA on the TUNING FORK (F5C48)	
	24th		37th Bde (less H.Qrs) moved to new divnl area - section 35th Battery rejoined the battery in action - 31st Battery W30b91 (near ESSARS - 37th Bde A.C. BELZAGE Fme (W22d66)	
GORRE.	25th		Bde Head quarters moved to GORRE (F3d53)	
	29th		31st Battery ~~[illegible]~~ was one of the units representing 7th Divn which was reviewed by H.M. the King near HESDIGNEUL.	

PTO

T2134. Wt. W708—776. 500000. 4/15. Sir J. C. & S.

Instructions regarding War Diaries and Intelligence Summaries are contained in F. S. Regs., Part II. and the Staff Manual respectively. Title pages will be prepared in manuscript.

WAR DIARY
or
~~INTELLIGENCE SUMMARY.~~
(Erase heading not required.)

Army Form C. 2118.

37th Bde RFA

1915

Place	Date	Hour	Summary of Events and Information	Remarks and references to Appendices
	October			
GORRE.	30th		35th Battery registered.	
	31st		31st Battery brought 4 guns into action 200 yards behind the 35th Battery RFA.	
			The following officers joined the Bde during October.	
			2nd Lieut Beckett posted to Bde A.C. 1.10.15.	
			2nd Lieut. H. Bonney attached 35th Battery. 8.10.15.	
			Lieut Braid A.V.C joined the Bde as veterinary officer 22.10.15.	
			Capt Knight posted from 35th Battery to 14th Bde RHA 26.10.15.	
			~~Lt Braid AVC~~	
				PNO

T2134. Wt. W708—776. 500000. 4/15. Sir J. C. & S.

Instructions regarding War Diaries and Intelligence Summaries are contained in F. S. Regs., Part II. and the Staff Manual respectively. Title pages will be prepared in manuscript.

WAR DIARY
or
INTELLIGENCE SUMMARY.
(Erase heading not required.)

Army Form C. 2118.

37 Bde RFA

Place	Date	Hour	Summary of Events and Information 1915	Remarks and references to Appendices
VERMELLES	Oct.		Ammn Expenditure – 6pm – 6pm daily	

Date	31st Battery HE	31st Battery Shrapnel	35th Battery HE	35th Battery Shrapnel	TOTAL HE	TOTAL Shrapnel	TOTAL
30th/1st	73	2	94	—	167	2	169
1st/2nd	19	6	154	2	173	8	181
2nd/3rd	111	—	179	192	290	192	482
3rd/4th	2	44	87	9	89	53	142
4th/5th	50	16	117	—	167	16	183
5th/6th	86	—	65	2	151	2	153
6th/7th	71	5	10	1	81	6	87
7/8	417	223	135	135	552	358	910
8th/9th	168	95	279	197	447	292	739
9th/10th	10	7	72	—	82	7	89
10th/11th	224	108	80	40	304	148	452
11th/12th	182	1	198	—	380	1	381
12th/13th	857	20	907	52	1764	72	1836
	2270	527	2377	630	4647	1157	5804

[illegible] Capt RFA
Adj. 37 Bde RFA

T2134. Wt. W708—776. 500000. 4/15. Sir J. C. & S.

7th Division

37th Bde R.F.A.

Nov.

Vol XVI

121
7418

Instructions regarding War Diaries and Intelligence Summaries are contained in F. S. Regs., Part II. and the Staff Manual respectively. Title pages will be prepared in manuscript.

WAR DIARY
or
~~INTELLIGENCE SUMMARY.~~
(Erase heading not required.)

Army Form C. 2118.

31st Bde R.F.A.
1915.

Place	Date	Hour	Summary of Events and Information	Remarks and references to Appendices
November				
Gorre	1		Light very bad all day. Enemy fired about a dozen 77 mm at GIVENCHY during the afternoon.	
	4		31st battery registering.	
		3.15pm	Enemy fired 12 rounds 4.2 H.E over POINT FIXE.	
	6	4.15pm	We exploded a mine at DUCKS BILL. The mine was successful & the crater was occupied by our troops.	
	7		31st Battery registering.	
	8.		Enemy fired 14 rounds 4.2 H.E at our front trenches East of GIVENCHY. The 20th Infantry Brigade relieved the 22nd Brigade in the trenches.	
	9		Enemy shelled POINT 6 with 4.2 How. 31st Battery registering. 35th " retaliated on CANTELEUX, TOWPATH ALLEY & LA BASSEE	
	10		Enemy shelled railway line by GUINCHY STATION, PONT FIXE & front trenches from direction of CANTELEUX. The 2nd Bat Royal Scots Fusiliers & the 2nd Bat Bedfordshire Regts relieved the 2nd Bat Wilts & the 2nd Bat Yorks in the trenches	

T2134. Wt. W708—776. 500000. 4/15. Sir J. C. & S.

Instructions regarding War Diaries and Intelligence Summaries are contained in F. S. Regs., Part II. and the Staff Manual respectively. Title pages will be prepared in manuscript.

WAR DIARY
or
~~INTELLIGENCE SUMMARY.~~
(Erase heading not required.)

Army Form C. 2118.

34th Bde R F A

1915

Place	Date	Hour	Summary of Events and Information	Remarks and references to Appendices
GORRE	11	12.30pm	Enemy shelled PONT FIXE & our front line trenches, the 35th Battery retaliated on VIOLAINES, CANTELOUX & LA BASSEE	
	12		Enemy shelled our 2nd line trenches & round LONE FARM also west side of GIVENCHY 35th Battery retaliated on CHAPEL ST ROCHE	
			The 7th Bat Kings Liverpool Regt & the 6th Gordons relieved the 2nd R.S.F. & the 2nd Bat Bedfords in the trenches.	
	14	4.15pm	Enemy shelled our front trenches (hitting their own as well) opposite B.3 with 4.2 How.	
		5.40pm	Enemy shelled PONT FIXE with 4.2 Hows	
			" aeroplanes were active this morning.	
	15	11 am	" shelled ground in front of LE PLANTIN & our front line trenches with field guns from direction of LA BASSEE	
			31st Battery registering	
	16	3pm	Enemy shelled 105th Battery on Canal Bank with 4.2 hows, very little damage was done	
		3.55pm	A German observation balloon was observed at a magnetic bearing of 82°	[initials]

T2134. Wt. W708—776. 500000. 4/15. Sir J. C. & S.

Instructions regarding War Diaries and Intelligence Summaries are contained in F. S. Regs., Part II. and the Staff Manual respectively. Title pages will be prepared in manuscript.

WAR DIARY
or
~~INTELLIGENCE SUMMARY.~~
(Erase heading not required.)

Army Form C. 2118.

37th Bde R.F.A.

Place	Date	Hour	Summary of Events and Information 1915.	Remarks and references to Appendices
GORRE	16		from WINDY CORNER. 21st Infantry Bde relieved the 20th Bde in the trenches	
	17		Weather cold & wet, snowed about 12 noon	
		12 noon	20 rounds of ammunition were fired by 35th Battery to test 'Amatol' for detonation	
		10.45am	The Enemy shelled the Canal bank E of PONT FIXE with 4.2 Hows & continued till 12.45 pm	
		2 pm	The enemy shelled GIVENCHY CHURCH with 5.9	
			31st Battery retaliates.	
	18		Very cold night, heavy frost. Cold & wet day.	
			The trenches were ~~inspected by 2 officers & were found~~ found to be in very bad condition, half full of mud & water. Capt P H Ferguson while going ~~inspecting~~ round the right half trenches was twice arrested as a spy. This was caused by a new relief having just come into the trenches. 2/Lt J Taylor went round the left half of the trenches.	
			Guns are beginning to shoot short owing to the colder weather	
		11.5am	Enemy shelled our front trenches with 5.9 from direction of LA BASSEE	

T2134. Wt. W708—776. 500000. 4/15. Sir J. C. & S.

Instructions regarding War Diaries and Intelligence Summaries are contained in F. S. Regs., Part II. and the Staff Manual respectively. Title pages will be prepared in manuscript.

WAR DIARY
or
~~INTELLIGENCE SUMMARY~~
(Erase heading not required.)

Army Form C. 2118.

37th Bde R.F.A.

Place	Date	Hour	Summary of Events and Information 1915.	Remarks and references to Appendices
GORRE	18	2.30pm	Enemy shelled GIVENCHY with 77 field guns. 35th Battery retaliated.	
	19		Cold & fine day	
		3.30pm	Enemy shelled PONT FIXE from direction of CANTELOUX with 77 mm field guns [10 rounds]	
		4.15pm	" " position on Canal bank recently evacuated by 105th Battery with 5.9 from direction of VIOLAINES, 6 rounds at 5 mins interval.	
		10.30am	The Bedfords reported that Germans were using gas, but it turned out to be gas shells fired at trenches East of GIVENCHY, 31st Battery retaliated with gas shells on enemys front line trenches.	
	20		Cold & fine day. Enemy shelled Canal Bank East of PONT FIXE at intervals during day with 5.9 from direction of LA BASSEE, 35th Battery retaliated on point B1. 4 on CANTELOUX.	
	21		Cold & fine day. Batteries registered.	
LOISNE	22		Headquarters of Brigade moved to LOISNE, taking over from the	WW

T2134. Wt. W708—776. 500000. 4/15. Sir J. C. & S.

Instructions regarding War Diaries and Intelligence Summaries are contained in F. S. Regs., Part II. and the Staff Manual respectively. Title pages will be prepared in manuscript.

WAR DIARY
or
~~INTELLIGENCE SUMMARY~~.
(Erase heading not required.)

Army Form C. 2118.

37th Brigade R.F.A.

Place	Date	Hour	Summary of Events and Information 1915.	Remarks and references to Appendices
LOISNE	22nd		87th Brigade, 19th Division, forming 'B' Group of Artillery under C.O. of this Brigade, consisting of :- 105th Battery R.F.A. 106th Battery, 12th Battery 1 section 25th Battery R.F.A. & 35th Battery R.F.A. covering 20th Infantry Brigade.	
	23rd		Batteries registered.	
	24th		- idem -	
	26th	5pm	Enemy shelled RUE CAILLOUX with 77 m/m guns. 12th Battery retaliated on RUE D'OUVERT.	
	27th	1pm 2 20pm.	Enemy shelled RUE DU BOIS & GOLDNEY'S KEEP with 77 m/m guns, 12th Battery retaliated.	
		8 20pm	Enemy shelled Support trenches in A3C. with 15 cm how	
		9.30pm	Field gun flashes were seen 13½° left of VOILAINES from CAILLOUX BREWERY	
	28th		Enemy shelled PRINCES ROAD during the morning with 77 m/m guns	
			106th Battery registered.	
			Infantry report trench mortar active from support trenches about S. 22. c. 31st Battery have arranged to engage this.	

WK

T2134. Wt. W708—776. 500000. 4/15. Sir J. C. & S.

Instructions regarding War Diaries and Intelligence Summaries are contained in F. S. Regs., Part II. and the Staff Manual respectively. Title pages will be prepared in manuscript.

WAR DIARY
or
~~INTELLIGENCE SUMMARY~~.
(Erase heading not required.)

Army Form C. 2118.

37th Brigade R.F.A.

Place	Date	Hour	Summary of Events and Information 1915.	Remarks and references to Appendices
LOISNES.	29th	9.37am	Enemy shelled North of FIFE ROAD with 77 mm guns	
		2.30pm	" fired 7 rounds at X.22.d. with 5.9 Hows from direction of VIOLAINES.	
		4pm	" " 19 " at GIVENCHY with 4.2.	
			12th & 106th retaliated & registered.	
	30th	7.30pm	Enemy shelled our trenches at A3.a with 77 mm	
		9.48am	" " " " , Barnton Rd.	
			Retaliation by all batteries against Trench Mortar opposite the orchard	
			12th Battery engaged a working party.	
			Flashes of a hostile field battery were observed from the Brewery one degree right of the Distillery (S.17. central) True bearing 68° from Brewery.	
		The	following Officers joined the Brigade during ~~October~~ November.	
5/11/15			2/Lieut J. Perry attached to 31st Battery.	
11/11/15			2/Lieut J R H C Probert. attached to 35th Battery.	
5/11/15			2/Lieut H. Romney Posted to Headquarters (from attached 35th Battery)	

W.A.

T2134. Wt. W708—776. 500000. 4/15. Sir J. C. & S.

Instructions regarding War Diaries and Intelligence Summaries are contained in F. S. Regs., Part II. and the Staff Manual respectively. Title pages will be prepared in manuscript.

WAR DIARY
or
~~INTELLIGENCE SUMMARY.~~
(Erase heading not required.)

Army Form C. 2118.

37th Brigade R.F.A.

1915.

Place	Date	Hour	Summary of Events and Information	Remarks and references to Appendices
			The following transfers took place during November.	
	6/11/15		Capt D. H. Ferguson to 35th Battery vice Capt Knight (Posted 14th Bde R.H.A.)	
	"	"	2/Lieut G. W. Milne as Adjutant vice Capt Ferguson.	
	"	"	2/Lieut H. Romney as Brigade Orderly Officer vice 2/Lieut Milne.	
				Wy

T2134. Wt. W708—776. 500000. 4/15. Sir J. C. & S.

Instructions regarding War Diaries and Intelligence Summaries are contained in F. S. Regs., Part II. and the Staff Manual respectively. Title pages will be prepared in manuscript.

WAR DIARY
or
~~INTELLIGENCE SUMMARY.~~
(Erase heading not required.)

Army Form C. 2118.

37th Brigade R.F.A.

1915.

Place	Date	Hour	Summary of Events and Information	Remarks and references to Appendices
GORRE & LOISNES	Nov		Amm! Expenditure 12 noon – 12 noon daily	

Date	31st Battery HE	31st Battery Shrapnel	35th Battery HE	35th Battery Shrapnel	Total HE	Total Shrapnel	Total
31st/1st	12	14	6		18	14	32
1st/2nd	4	5			4	5	9
2nd/3rd			14		14		14
3rd/4th	2	10			2	10	12
4th/5th	2	15	10		12	15	27
5th/6th	19		41		60		60
6th/7th			7		7		7
7th/8th	3	3	13		16	3	19
8th/9th			49	14	49	14	63
9th/10th	35	9	19		54	9	63
10th/11th	4		41		45		45
11th/12th	49	10	41		90	10	100
12th/13th			43		43		43
14th/15th			30		30		30
Carried forward	130	66	314	14	444	80	524

[illegible initials]

Army Form C. 2118.

Instructions regarding War Diaries and Intelligence Summaries are contained in F. S. Regs., Part II. and the Staff Manual respectively. Title pages will be prepared in manuscript.

WAR DIARY
or
INTELLIGENCE SUMMARY.
(Erase heading not required.)

37th Brigade R.F.A.

1915.

Place	Date	Hour	Summary of Events and Information	Remarks and references to Appendices
GORRE + LOISNES	Nov		Ammt Expenditure. 12 noon – 12 noon daily	

Date	31st Battery HE	31st Battery Shrapnel	35th Battery HE	35th Battery Shrapnel	Total HE	Total Shrapnel	Total
Brought forward	130	66	314	14	444	80	524
15th/16th	32		1		33		33
16th/17th	14	3			14	3	17
17th/18th			38		38		38
18th/19th	20		10		30		30
19th/20th	4	4			4	4	8
20th/21st		8	33	2	33	10	43
21st/22nd	8		40	1	48	1	49
22nd/23rd	6				6		6
23rd/24th	16	19			16	19	35
25th/26th	7	15			7	15	22
26th/27th	11		13	9	24	9	33
27th/28th	2		24		26		26
28th/29th	36		20		56		56
29th/30th	24		22		46		46
	310	115	515	26	~~[illegible]~~ 825	~~[illegible]~~ 141	966

[illegible] Adj 37th Bde R.F.A.

T2134. Wt. W708—776. 500000. 4/15. Sir J. C. & S.

7th Div

7

37th Bde R.F.A.

Dec

Vol. XVII

121
7929

Instructions regarding War Diaries and Intelligence Summaries are contained in F. S. Regs., Part II. and the Staff Manual respectively. Title pages will be prepared in manuscript.

WAR DIARY
or
~~INTELLIGENCE SUMMARY.~~
(Erase heading not required.)

Army Form C. 2118.

37th Brigade R. F.A.

1915.

Place	Date	Hour	Summary of Events and Information	Remarks and references to Appendices
	December			
LOISNES	3		Light very bad all day.	
			31st Battery fired 72 rounds HE at the mound A.4.c.8½.6½ & appeared to get several direct hits.	
			Brigade moved to MAZINGHEIM to prepare for entraining	
	5/6		Brigade entrained for PONT REMY. & moved to billeting area at HANGEST.	
HANGEST	6/31		Brigade resting.	
			The following transfers took place during December.	
	11/12/15		Capt. [illegible] H. FERGUSON to England.	
	December		Ammunition expended (12 noon to 12 noon daily)	

Date	31st Battery HE	31st Battery Shrapnel	35th Battery HE	35th Battery Shrapnel	Total HE	Total Shrapnel	Total Rounds
30/1st	70		51		121		121
1st/2nd	86	6	6		92	6	98
2nd/3rd	78		3		81		81
	234	6	60		294	6	300

[illegible] 2/1
Adj 37th Bde R.F.A.

T2134. Wt. W708—776. 500000. 4/15. Sir J. C. & S.

78

34 Bde R.F.A

Jan

Vol XVIII

Army Form C. 2118.

Instructions regarding War Diaries and Intelligence Summaries are contained in F. S. Regs., Part II. and the Staff Manual respectively. Title pages will be prepared in manuscript.

WAR DIARY
or
~~INTELLIGENCE SUMMARY.~~

(Erase heading not required.)

37th Bde R.F.A.

1916

Place	Date	Hour	Summary of Events and Information	Remarks and references to Appendices
HANGEST	January		Brigade resting at HANGEST.	
			Officers joined during month.	
	Jan 3rd		Capt D. R. C. HARTLEY from 86th Battery 4th Division posted to 35th Battery	
	" 20th		2/Lieut F. L. V. POPE attached to 35th Battery	
	" 21st		2/Lieut J. GILLESPIE " " 31st "	

[signature] Lt. R.F.A.
Adj 37th Bde R.F.A.

T2134. Wt. W708—776. 500000. 4/15. Sir J. C. & S.

7

37 Bde R F A

Feb

Vol XIX

Instructions regarding War Diaries and Intelligence Summaries are contained in F. S. Regs., Part II. and the Staff Manual respectively. Title pages will be prepared in manuscript.

WAR DIARY
or
~~INTELLIGENCE SUMMARY.~~
(Erase heading not required.)

Army Form C. 2118.

37th Brigade R F A
1916.

Place	Date	Hour	Summary of Events and Information	Remarks and references to Appendices
	Febuary.			
HANGEST.	3		Brigade marched from HANGEST to LA CHAUSSEE	
	5		" " " LA CHAUSSEE to CONTAY.	
	6/7		One section 31st Battery R F A moves into action at F.13.c.9.9. (Ref ALBERT combined sheet 1/40000) in relief of C. Battery, 85th Brigade.	
			One section 35th Battery R F A. moves into action at F.26 d 7 6 in relief of B. battery 85th Brigade.	
	7/8		Brigade H.Qrs moves to BONNEY.	
			One section 31st Battery completes relief of C/85	
			" " 31st " " " B/85 forming a composite Bty.	
			One section 35th Battery into action at F.38.c 7 6 in relief of C Battery 151st Brigade R F A.	
	8/9		One section 35th Battery completes relief of C/151	
			The 31st Battery (2 sections) grouped with 14th Bde R.H.A. forming left group, under the command of Lt Col H.C.S. CLARKE D.S.O.	
			The Composite (How) battery, composed of 1 section 31st Battery & 1 section 35th Battery, grouped with 35th Brigade R F A. forming Centre group	

T2134. Wt. W708—776. 500000. 4/15. Sir J. C. & S.

Instructions regarding War Diaries and Intelligence Summaries are contained in F. S. Regs., Part II. and the Staff Manual respectively. Title pages will be prepared in manuscript.

WAR DIARY
or
~~INTELLIGENCE SUMMARY.~~
(Erase heading not required.)

Army Form C. 2118.

37th Brigade R.F.A.

1916.

Place	Date	Hour	Summary of Events and Information	Remarks and references to Appendices
	February			
	9		under the command of Lt Col O. C. Du PORT	
			The 35th Battery (2 sections) grouped with 22nd Brigade R.F.A.	Lt. Col. J. W. Spedding left Bde to join 4?th Div as C.R.A.
			forming left group, under the command of Lt Col A. S. BUCKLE	Lt. Col. W. G. Kirke joined Bde
MEAULTE.	10		Brigade moves to MEAULTE	
	11/14		Batteries registering.	
	13	5.10 pm	Composite battery retaliates on F.9.b.9.1 (ref 1/20,000 Sheet 52? N.E.)	
	15	10.30 am	Enemy fires 4 rounds 4.2 in direction of F.19.b. from front edge of MAMETZ WOOD	
	16/17		Batteries registering.	
	18		A working party was seen at F.5.a.4.1. & were fired on by Composite Battery	
	19	8 am	We exploded a mine	
			Small parties of Germans were seen during the day by FRICOURT WOOD & BUNNY WOOD	
	20	2.50 pm	What appeared to be gas was seen issuing from the enemy trenches N of LA BOISELLE	

Instructions regarding War Diaries and Intelligence Summaries are contained in F. S. Regs., Part II. and the Staff Manual respectively. Title pages will be prepared in manuscript.

WAR DIARY
or
~~INTELLIGENCE SUMMARY.~~
(Erase heading not required.)

Army Form C. 2118.

37th Bde R.F.A.

Place	Date	Hour	Summary of Events and Information 1916	Remarks and references to Appendices
MEAULTE	21		Enemy bombarded our front trenches during the day	
	22	5.15 pm	" " " trenches in sector D.1 every sort of shell up to 5.9" being used. Our artillery retaliated on enemy's trenches	
		×6.5 pm	opposite sectors D.2 & D.3. ×An enemy infantry attack was made on our trenches in F.3.C but were repulsed by our M.G. & rifle fire.	
		7.15 pm	Artillery fire dies down.	
	23/9		Batteries registering	
			The following Officers joined the Brigade during February	
	9/2/16		Lt Col. H G KIRKE. vice Lt Col. E W Spedding to 47th Division	
	12/2/16.		2/Lieut T. BELL. attached to 31st Battery R.F.A.	
	11/2/16		Capt JARDINE. D.S.O. to 31st Battery R.F.A. from 25th Battery R.F.A.	
	13/2/16		2/Lieut V. POPE. from 35th Battery R.F.A. transferred to 114th Brigade R.F.A.	

T2134. Wt. W708—776. 500000. 4/15. Sir J. C. & S.

Instructions regarding War Diaries and Intelligence Summaries are contained in F. S. Regs., Part II. and the Staff Manual respectively. Title pages will be prepared in manuscript.

WAR DIARY
or
~~INTELLIGENCE~~ SUMMARY.
(Erase heading not required.)

Army Form C. 2118.

37th Brigade R.F.A.

1916

Place	Date	Hour	Summary of Events and Information	Remarks and references to Appendices
February			Ammunition Expended (12 noon to 12 noon daily)	

Date	31st Battery HE	31st Battery Shrapnel	35th Battery HE	35th Battery Shrapnel	Total HE	Total Shrapnel	Total rounds
8/9			15		15		15
9/10	98		21		119		119
10/11	20		33		53		53
11/12	6		53		59		59
12/13	18		44		62		62
13/14	109		88		197		197
14/15	6				6		6
15/16			40		40		40
16/17	2			2	2	2	4
17/18	15	2	40		55	2	57
18/19	19				19		19
19/20	15		7	5	22	5	27
20/21	225	1	48		273	1	274
21/22	78		93		171		171
Carried forward	611	3	482	7	1093	10	1103

Wrz[?]

T2134. Wt. W708—776. 500000. 4/15. Sir J. C. & S.

Instructions regarding War Diaries and Intelligence Summaries are contained in F. S. Regs., Part II. and the Staff Manual respectively. Title pages will be prepared in manuscript.

WAR DIARY

or

~~INTELLIGENCE SUMMARY~~.

(Erase heading not required.)

Army Form C. 2118.

34th Brigade RFA

1916

Place	Date	Hour	Summary of Events and Information							Remarks and references to Appendices
				31st Battery		25th Battery		Total		Total
			Brought forward.	HE	Shrapnel	HE	Shrapnel	HE	Shrapnel	Rounds
				611	3	482	7	1093	10	1103
			22/23	239		81	6	320	6	326
			23/24			54		54		54
			24/25	13		18		31		31
			25/26			9		9		9
			26/27	22		33		55		55
			27/28	27		3		30		30
			28/29	9		10		19		19
				921	3	690	13	1611	16	1627

[signature] Lt. RFA
Adj 34th Bde RFA

T2134. Wt. W708—776. 500000. 4/15. Sir J. C. & S.

WAR DIARY
or
~~INTELLIGENCE~~ SUMMARY.
(*Erase heading not required.*)

Army Form C. 2118.

Instructions regarding War Diaries and Intelligence Summaries are contained in F. S. Regs., Part II. and the Staff Manual respectively. Title pages will be prepared in manuscript.

37th Bde R.F.A.

1916

Place	Date	Hour	Summary of Events and Information	Remarks and references to Appendices
March				
MEAULTE	2	5.25pm	The 31st Battery shot at F 3 a 50 25 in retaliation for German canisters falling on PURFLEET. At the first shot a large column of dense white smoke was seen to rise from the German trench exactly as if a canister had burst. No more canisters fell on PURFLEET.	
			Hostile Trench Mortars very active all day firing on D.1.	
	5	12.50	The Composite Battery fired at ROSE COTTAGE, where an observer was seen using a periscope. Two direct hits were obtained.	
		12.30	Enemy shelled the CEMETERY for about one hour.	
	6/8		Batteries retaliated.	
	10		Hostile Trench Mortars were fairly active during the night but were stopped by our retaliation	
	11	2.30pm	Enemy shelled the CEMETERY with Field guns. composite battery retaliated on AEROPLANE TRENCH.	
	13		Enemy's artillery were fairly active during the day shelling our front & support trenches. Field guns were mostly used.	
	15	12.30	Enemy shelled our front line from station to cemetery with 5.9 hows.	

T2134. Wt. W708—776. 500000. 4/15. Sir J. C. & S.

Instructions regarding War Diaries and Intelligence Summaries are contained in F. S. Regs., Part II. and the Staff Manual respectively. Title pages will be prepared in manuscript.

WAR DIARY
or
~~INTELLIGENCE SUMMARY~~
(Erase heading not required.)

Army Form C. 2118.

37th Brigade R.F.A.

1916.

Place	Date	Hour	Summary of Events and Information	Remarks and references to Appendices
MEAULTE.			firing from direction of CONTALMAISON. 23 shots were fired.	
	18		Usual hostile shelling of CEMETERY during day & by Field guns	
			& 4.2 hows. Composite battery retaliated on F.3.a.8.0 & HIDDEN WOOD.	
	19		Quiet day with the exception of 4 hostile shells from 4.2 hows	
			which fell in MEAULTE killing 5 & wounding 8 men of the Gordons	
			also cutting all telephone lines, thereby delaying retaliation	
	20		Lt Col. S. G. KIRKE took over command of the Centre Group during	
			Lt Col. O. C. DU PORT's absence on leave.	
	23/24		Batteries retaliating.	
	25		Hostile trench mortars were active during the day against	
			the TAMBOUR & the STATION.	
	26	8 am	Hostile working parties were active about X 29 b. 3.3.	
	27/31		Very little firing went on, on either side.	
			The following Officers joined the Brigade during March.	
	12-3-16		Capt. J. P. KNIGHT. DSO to 35th Battery R.F.A. vice Capt. JARDINE to 14th Bde R.H.A.	
	29-3-16		2Lieut. H. W. WOOLLEY from 14th Bde R.H.A. to 31st Battery R.F.A.	
	30-3-16		2Lieut. P. G. POPE. to Composite Battery.	[signature]

Instructions regarding War Diaries and Intelligence Summaries are contained in F. S. Regs., Part II. and the Staff Manual respectively. Title pages will be prepared in manuscript.

WAR DIARY
or
~~INTELLIGENCE~~ SUMMARY.
(Erase heading not required.)

Army Form C. 2118.

37th Brigade R.F.A.

1916

Place	Date	Hour	Summary of Events and Information	Remarks and references to Appendices
MEAULTE			The following transfers took place during March ~~February~~.	
	1/3/16		2/Lieut J GILLESPIE to Trench Mortars.	
	5/3/16		2/Lieut J TAYLOR. to from 31st Battery to Bde HQ. R.F.A. as Orderly Officer vice 2/Lt H BONNEY to 35th Battery R.F.A.	
	" "		2/Lieut J PERRY from 31st Battery to Bde Ammn Column.	
	12/3/16		Capt JARDINE from 35th Battery to 14th Bde R.H.A.	
	20/3/16		Lt F. R. JAMES from 31st Battery to 4th Field Survey Co. R.E.	

Ammunition Expended (12 noon to 12 noon daily)

March	31st Battery HE	31st Battery Shrapnel	35th Battery HE	35th Battery Shrapnel	Composite Bty HE	Composite Bty Shrapnel	Total HE	Total Shrapnel	Total Rounds
29/1	146	/	20	/	65	/	231		231
1/2	6	/	29	/	73	/	108		108
2/3	49	/	62	4	43	/	154	4	158
3/4	52	/	13	4	21	/	86	4	90
4/5	9	/	4	/	6	/	19	/	19
5/6	49	/	28	/	56	/	133	/	133
Carried forward	311	/	156	8	264	/	731	8	739

T2134. Wt. W708—776. 500000. 4/15. Sir J. C. & S.

Instructions regarding War Diaries and Intelligence Summaries are contained in F. S. Regs., Part II. and the Staff Manual respectively. Title pages will be prepared in manuscript.

WAR DIARY
or
~~INTELLIGENCE~~ SUMMARY.
(Erase heading not required.)

Army Form C. 2118.

37th Brigade R.F.A.

1916.

Place	Date	Hour	Summary of Events and Information								Remarks and references to Appendices
	March		31st Battery		35th Battery		Composite Bty		Total Rounds		Total
MEAULTE			H.E.	Shrapnel	H.E.	Shrapnel	H.E.	Shrapnel	H.E.	Shrapnel	Rounds
Bght forward			311	✓	156	8	264	✓	731	8	739
	6/7		53	✓	1	5	46	✓	100	5	105
	7/8		55	3	6	5	130	✓	191	8	199
	8/9		119	18	2	8	69	✓	190	26	216
	9/10		78	✓	53	33	74	✓	205	33	238
	10/11		✓	✓	6	6	30	✓	36	6	42
	11/12		11	✓	✓		52	✓	63	✓	63
	12/13		11	✓	✓	✓	25	✓	36	✓	36
	13/14		68	32	7	3	60	4	135	39	174
	14/15		117	6	3	✓	71	✓	191	6	197
	15/16		96	✓	43	✓	138	✓	277	✓	277
	16/17		20	✓	33	✓	44	✓	97	✓	97
	17/18		86	✓	21	✓	84	✓	191	✓	191
	18/19		34	✓	28	✓	90	✓	152	✓	152
	19/20		14	✓	11	✓	44	4	69	4	73
Carried forward			1073	59	370	68	1221	8	2664	135	2799

T2134. Wt. W708—776. 500000. 4/15. Sir J. C. & S.

Instructions regarding War Diaries and Intelligence Summaries are contained in F. S. Regs., Part II. and the Staff Manual respectively. Title pages will be prepared in manuscript.

WAR DIARY
or
~~INTELLIGENCE SUMMARY.~~
(Erase heading not required.)

Army Form C. 2118.

37th Brigade RFA

1916.

Place	Date	Hour	31st Battery HE	31st Battery Shrapnel	35th Battery HE	35th Battery Shrapnel	Composite Bty HE	Composite Bty Shrapnel	Total Rounds HE	Total Rounds Shrapnel	Total Rounds
MEAULTE	March										
Brought	Forward		1073	59	370	68	1221	8	2664	135	2799
	20/21		32	–	35	–	40	–	107	–	107
	21/22		32	–	62	–	46	–	140	–	140
	22/23		33	–	13	–	40	–	86	–	86
	23/24		5	5	2	19	6	–	13	24	37
	24/25		2	–	–	–	4	–	6	–	6
	25/26		8	11	3	–	–	–	11	11	22
	26/27		1	7	8	–	–	–	9	7	16
	27/28		–	–	11	–	4	–	15	–	15
	28/29		8	3	18	–	10	–	36	3	39
	29/30		8	63	2	–	4	–	14	63	77
	30/31		8	18	2	–	8	–	18	18	36
			1207	166	526	87	1384	8	3119	261	3380

[illegible] RFA
Adj 37th Bde RFA

Instructions regarding War Diaries and Intelligence Summaries are contained in F. S. Regs., Part II. and the Staff Manual respectively. Title pages will be prepared in manuscript.

WAR DIARY
or
~~INTELLIGENCE SUMMARY.~~
(Erase heading not required.)

Army Form C. 2118.

37th Brigade R.F.A.

1916

Place	Date	Hour	Summary of Events and Information	Remarks and references to Appendices
MEAULTE	1st	11am	Enemy shelled Composite battery, about 110 5.9 how shells were fired from direction of CONTALMAISON. One direct hit was obtained on gun pit which was knocked in. No damage to gun & no casualties.	
	2	9am	Enemy shelled HAPPY VALLEY, about 110 5.9 shells were fired. One dugout belonging to the Composite battery was wrecked by a direct hit & the water cart ruined. No casualties.	
	3/6		Nothing happened worth recording, only the usual desultory shelling of trenches	
	8		Brigade Headquarters moved to CORBIE.	
	29.		" " " " MORLANCOURT.	
			The following Officers joined the Brigade during April	
	5/4/16		Capt JARDINE D.S.O. to Composite battery vice Capt BEVERIDGE to 155th Bde	
	22/4/16		2/Lieut. S. BAINES " " " "	

[illegible signature]
Adj 37th Bde R.F.A.

T2134. Wt. W708—776. 500000. 4/15. Sir J. C. & S.

Army Form C. 2118.

Instructions regarding War Diaries and Intelligence Summaries are contained in F. S. Regs., Part II. and the Staff Manual respectively. Title pages will be prepared in manuscript.

WAR DIARY
or
~~INTELLIGENCE SUMMARY.~~
(*Erase heading not required.*)

37th Brigade R.F.A.

Place	Date	Hour	Summary of Events and Information	Remarks and references to Appendices
			1916	

Ammunition expended from (12 noon to 12 noon daily)

April	31st Battery H.E.	31st Battery Shrapnel	35th Battery H.E.	35th Battery Shrapnel	Composite Battery H.E.	Composite Battery Shrapnel	Total H.E.	Total Shrapnel	Total Rounds
31/1	8	45	3	-	10	13	21	58	79
1/2	8	27	4	-	25	-	37	27	64
2/3	25	.	5	11	25	-	55	11	66
3/4	25	20	14	-	25	-	64	20	87
4/5	25	3	8	-	25	-	58	3	61
5/6	25	.	84	-	29	-	138	-	138
6/7	20	13	38	-	16	-	74	13	87
7/8	20	.	12	-	8	-	40	-	40
8/9	20	12	14	-	39	-	73	12	85
9/10	20	4	19	-	30	-	69	4	73
10/11	20	6	12	-	35	-	67	6	73
11/12	20	2	66	-	35	-	121	2	123
12/13	20	-	10	-	17	-	47	-	47
13/14	-	-	67	1	23	-	90	1	91
14/15	-	-	-	-	36	-	36	-	36
15/16	-	20	15	-	46	-	61	20	81
16/17	55	-	44	-	63	-	162	-	162
17/18	25	-	95	-	6	-	126	-	126
18/19	16	-	54	-	9	1	79	1	80
19/20	80	-	209	46	49	5	338	51	389
20/21	32	-	295	2	.	-	327	2	329
21/22	12	-	53	6	50	-	115	6	121
22/3	130	4	133	-	34	1	297	5	302
23/4	24	-	34	-	9	12	67	12	79
24/5	22	-	68	-	66	17	156	17	173
25/6	55	-	-	-	12	-	67	-	67
26/7	122	-	-	-	96	4	218	4	222
27/8	183	-	26	-	40	-	248	-	248
28/9	162	-	-	-	98	4	260	4	264
29/30	55	10	-	-	154	-	209	10	219
	1228	166	1385	66	1110	57	3723	289	4012

Instructions regarding War Diaries and Intelligence Summaries are contained in F. S. Regs., Part II. and the Staff Manual respectively. Title pages will be prepared in manuscript.

WAR DIARY
or
~~INTELLIGENCE SUMMARY.~~
(Erase heading not required.)

Army Form C. 2118.

34th Bde R.F.A.

Place	Date	Hour	Summary of Events and Information 1916	Remarks and references to Appendices
	MAY			
MORLANCOURT	1/3		Batteries retaliating for hostile fire	
	5	12.45pm	Enemy shelled BECORDEL & MEAULTE with 5.9 hows from direction of CONTALMAISON	Capt W.H. Oliver posted to 8th Div
		8pm	Composite battery bombarded FRICOURT WOOD.	
	7	12.30pm	The Survey Post reported a hostile working party at the S. end of RAILWAY TRENCH. They were fired on & dispersed	
	8	12.30pm	Composite battery fired a few rounds into HIDDEN WOOD in retaliation for enemy fire on our front line.	
	10		The detached sections of the 31st & 35th Batteries, known as the Composite battery, was today formed into a seperate battery & will be known as D/14 Battery R.F.A. under the command of Lieut (Temp Capt) JARDINE D.S.O thus making 3 four gun batteries	
	11	9.35pm – 1.20am	D/14 battery shelled enemys trenches at F.10.b.6.5 in retaliation for heavy Trench Mortar fire on our front trenches.	
	13	4.30pm	D/14 battery shelled enemys trenches at F.10.b.6.5 & F.9.b.8.3 in retaliation for enemy fire on BECORDEL	

[initials]

T2134. Wt. W708—776. 500000. 4/15. Sir J. C. & S.

Instructions regarding War Diaries and Intelligence Summaries are contained in F. S. Regs., Part II. and the Staff Manual respectively. Title pages will be prepared in manuscript.

WAR DIARY
or
~~INTELLIGENCE SUMMARY.~~
(Erase heading not required.)

Army Form C. 2118.

37th Brigade RFA
1916

Place	Date	Hour	Summary of Events and Information	Remarks and references to Appendices
MORLANCOURT	17		The 37th Brigade ceases to exist as a unit, the three batteries being transfered as follows -	
			Composite battery as D/14 to 14th Brigade R.F.A	
			31st Battery to 35th " R.F.A	
			35th " " 22nd " R.F.A	
			The Brigade ammunition column transfers to Divisional ammunition column	
	19		The Brigade Hd Qrs transfers to D.A.C	
				Ly

T2134. Wt. W708—776. 500000. 4/15. Sir J. C. & S.

Instructions regarding War Diaries and Intelligence Summaries are contained in F. S. Regs., Part II. and the Staff Manual respectively. Title pages will be prepared in manuscript.

WAR DIARY
or
~~INTELLIGENCE SUMMARY~~.

(Erase heading not required.)

Army Form C. 2118.

37th Brigade R.F.A.

1916

Place	Date	Hour	Summary of Events and Information								Remarks and references to Appendices
			Ammunition expended from (12 noon to 12 noon daily).								
			31st Battery		35th Battery		Composite Battery		Total		Total Rounds
	May		HE	Shrapnel	HE	Shrapnel	HE	Shrapnel	HE	Shrapnel	
	30/1		269	-	179	-	243		691	-	691
	1/2		66	10	6	-	4	-	76	10	86
	2/3		92	-	20	-	41	6	153	6	159
	3/4		70	-	40	-	42	14	152	14	166
	4/5		113	-	87	-	44	28	244	28	272
	5/6		48	-	76	-	23	-	147	-	147
	6/7		20	-	102	-	71	7	193	7	200
	7/8		4	-	4	-	7	-	15	-	15
	8/9		46	-	25	-	97	-	168	-	168
	9/10		156	1	68	-	43	-	267	1	268
	10/11		176	-	30	-	12	-	218	-	218
	11/12		34	-	27	4	36	-	97	4	101
	12/13		19	-	10	-	12	-	50	-	50
	13/14		63	-	26	-	52	-	141	-	141
	14/15		-	-	1	-	-	-	1	-	1
	15/16		20	7	44	-	9	7	73	14	87
			1196	18	754	4	736	62	2686	84	2770

[illegible]
Adj, 37th Bde R.F.A.

7TH DIVISION

TRENCH MORTAR BATTERIES

FEB 1916 - ~~JAN 1919~~ 1917 NOV

TO ITALY

Army Form C. 2118.

7

Instructions regarding War Diaries and Intelligence Summaries are contained in F. S. Regs., Part II. and the Staff Manual respectively. Title Pages will be prepared in manuscript.

WAR DIARY
or
INTELLIGENCE SUMMARY
(Erase heading not required.)

Place	Date	Hour	Summary of Events and Information	Remarks and references to Appendices
			X 7 2" Trench Howitzer Battery WE H12 20th. INF. BDE. 7th. DIVISION From February 25th. to March 31st 1916. Vol I	

2449 Wt. W14957/M90 750,000 1/16 J.B.C. & A. Forms/C.2118/12.

Army Form C. 2118.

Instructions regarding War Diaries and Intelligence Summaries are contained in F. S. Regs., Part II. and the Staff Manual respectively. Title Pages will be prepared in manuscript.

WAR DIARY
or
INTELLIGENCE SUMMARY

(Erase heading not required.)

Place	Date	Hour	Summary of Events and Information	Remarks and references to Appendices
			This newly formed unit of Officers and [illegible] of the Division arrived from 3rd. Army Trench Mortar School on 25th. February 1916 and relieved the 90th B Trench Mortar Battery on 29th. and fired that afternoon its first shots. Up till the 31st. March 300 rounds were fired, which included 10 [illegible]. One gun position was destroyed by enemy without casualty to the unit. Positions in front of supports & behind front line in some disused trenches have had the effect of taking fire from our front line on to themselves which was desirable as enemy mortars frequently damaged our parapets. Alternative positions it is found are necessary & each gun should apparently have its alternative position, though this is sometimes a laborious work in unadaptable trenches. Considerable damage can be done unaided with the 2" Howitzer with well observed fire & with at present lack of telephone communication makes this difficult. Telephones were proved on important occasions, however. The gun is not such a powerful weapon as the larger enemy mortars which also have [illegible] the annoying (for troops) occurrence of a 60lb. steel ball returning through the air to the point from where it was "thrown". This Battery is on 20th. INF. BDE. front in front of FRICOURT. It works in half Batteries which are relieved at INF. BATT. relief times. Its H.Q. are at MEALTE. During the month parapets have been blown in & one enemy post of strength demolished. Direct hits have been obtained blowing up enemy dugouts, debris, &c on several occasions.	

R. L. [illegible]
Lieut. R.G.A. Comdg. X7 T.M. Bty.

2449 Wt. W14957/M90 750,000 1/16 J.B.C. & A. Forms/C.2118/12.

Army Form C. 2118.

WAR DIARY
or
INTELLIGENCE SUMMARY
(Erase heading not required.)

Instructions regarding War Diaries and Intelligence Summaries are contained in F. S. Regs., Part II. and the Staff Manual respectively. Title Pages will be prepared in manuscript.

App 13 Vol I

Place	Date	Hour	Summary of Events and Information	Remarks and references to Appendices
			During the month 31 rounds only have been fired by the 9.45" Howitzer Bty. On the 7th it was relieved from Fricourt District by the 21st Div Trench Mortars & moved by 2 Motor Lorries to 91st Inf. Bde area with Billets & H.Q. at Bray-sur-Somme. One section of guns was put into action at (Sheet 62D N.E.) F12 c 5.4 & the unit has been mostly occupied in constructing 4 gun positions with trench & dugout for men; mine & ammunition gallery being in course of construction under R.E. supervision. The main ammunition store is in a cellar in Carnoy and B.C. store is at Bray.	
			Of the firing done 18 rounds were fired by one gun during bombardment (the other not being in action) on [illegible] and had fortunate results, two enemy dugouts having been reported as being destroyed.	
			(Signed) L. T. [illegible] Capt R.A.	
			30th April 1916 Comdg. [illegible] T.M.B.	

2449 Wt. W14957/M90 750,000 1/16 J.B.C. & A. Forms/C.2118/12.

Army Form C. 2118.

Instructions regarding War Diaries and Intelligence Summaries are contained in F. S. Regs., Part II. and the Staff Manual respectively. Title Pages will be prepared in manuscript.

WAR DIARY
or
~~INTELLIGENCE SUMMARY~~
(Erase heading not required.)

Place	Date	Hour	Summary of Events and Information	Remarks and references to Appendices
	12-4-16		22/2 Trench Mortar Battery formed. guns 4 3" Stokes.	
	15-4-16		Battery allotted C1 right of 22nd Infantry Bde chose positions.	
	16-4-16 } 17-4-16 }		Digging positions.	
	18-4-16		Ranging on various points in German front & support lines	
	19-4-16		Quiet	
	20-4-16		Blew in a sniper's post	
	22-4-16		Quiet	
	24-4-16		Under fire from aerial Torpedo, retaliated but gun was beyond my range (with present cartridge).	
	29-4-16		Blew in an [illegible] post	
	30-4-16		Enemy bombarded Front line. retaliated.	
			[illegible signature] Lieut O.C. 22/2 T.M.B.	

2449 Wt. W14957/M90 750,000 1/16 J.B.C. & A. Forms/C.2118/12.

Army Form C. 2118.

VII

Instructions regarding War Diaries and Intelligence Summaries are contained in F. S. Regs., Part II. and the Staff Manual respectively. Title Pages will be prepared in manuscript.

WAR DIARY
or
INTELLIGENCE SUMMARY

(Erase heading not required.)

Place	Date	Hour	Summary of Events and Information	Remarks and references to Appendices
			Confidential.	Vol 2
			War Diary	
			of	
			X7 Trench Mortar Battery	
			from 18 May 1916 to 31st May 1916.	
			Volume 3.	

2449 Wt. W14957/M90 750,000 1/16 J.B.C. & A. Forms/C.2118/12.

Instructions regarding War Diaries and Intelligence Summaries are contained in F. S. Regs., Part II. and the Staff Manual respectively. Title Pages will be prepared in manuscript.

WAR DIARY
or
INTELLIGENCE SUMMARY
(Erase heading not required.)

Army Form C. 2118.

Place	Date	Hour	Summary of Events and Information	Remarks and references to Appendices
			During the month 136 rounds have been fired by this unit, mostly in "retaliation" as instructed by BDE. HQS. 91st. INF. BDE. The Battery is still located in action at F.12. C. 5.H. (SHEET 62D N.E.) but billets have been moved from BRAY to BOIS DES TAILLES. Further gun positions have been constructed, at F.12.C.5.7, and 6 positions are now available in B1 SUBSECTOR.	
			Of the rounds fired the majority were used in night firing, it being an Enemy habit to open fire at 12 midnight or 1 or 2 o/c a.m. Our bombs were also used to "retaliate" for Rifle Grenades fired from a greater range than could be used by our Rifle Grenades, who could not thus "retaliate" on that particular point of Enemy lines.	
			[signature] Lieut. R.A. Comdg. X7 T.M. Battery.	

2449 Wt. W14957/M90 750,000 1/16 J.B.C. & A. Forms/C.2118/12.

Army Form C. 2118.

Instructions regarding War Diaries and Intelligence Summaries are contained in F. S. Regs., Part II. and the Staff Manual respectively. Title Pages will be prepared in manuscript.

WAR DIARY
or
INTELLIGENCE SUMMARY
(Erase heading not required.)

May 1916

App 6 Vol 2

Place	Date	Hour	Summary of Events and Information	Remarks and references to Appendices
			During this month 145 rounds of ammunition were expended firing on Bulgar Point. Two guns were in action at the junction of Pall Mall Street & Pioneer Avenue in B 2 sub sector. Towards the end of the month Headquarters of Unit [illegible] moved to F 22 c 5.6, Bois des Tailles.	
			31-5-16 W. S. Lebin 2nd Lt. Cmdg. 87 T.M.B.	

2449 Wt. W14957/M90 750,000 1/16 J.B.C. & A. Forms/C.2118/12.

Instructions regarding War Diaries and Intelligence Summaries are contained in F. S. Regs., Part II. and the Staff Manual respectively. Title Pages will be prepared in manuscript.

WAR DIARY
or
INTELLIGENCE SUMMARY
(Erase heading not required.)

Army Form C. 2118.

Place	Date	Hour	Summary of Events and Information	Remarks and references to Appendices
			During the month 247 rounds of ammunition were fired by the 2" Trench How. Battery. The Battery was in action near Bray, until the 20th of June when it moved into the Bois de Tailles, where it was in action until the first of July.	
			W. J. Lecken 2nd Lt. R.A. Cmdg X 7 T.M.B.	
			July 31st 1916.	

2449 Wt. W14957/M90 750,000 1/16 J.B.C. & A. Forms/C.2118/12.

Army Form C. 2118.

WAR DIARY
or
INTELLIGENCE SUMMARY

(Erase heading not required.)

X7 T M Bty 1916

Vol 4

Instructions regarding War Diaries and Intelligence Summaries are contained in F. S. Regs., Part II. and the Staff Manual respectively. Title Pages will be prepared in manuscript.

Place	Date	Hour	Summary of Events and Information	Remarks and references to Appendices
			On the 1st July this Battery came out of Action in BOIS de TAILLES and proceeded to Méaulte where it stayed until the 11th. It then moved in motor lorries to a rest camp at Heilly.	
			31-8-16 W.J. Lesker 2nd Lt. Cmdg. X7 T.M.B	

2449 Wt. W14957/M90 750,000 1/16 J.B.C. & A. Forms/C.2118/12.

7

Vol I & II

CONFIDENTIAL

War Diary
of
V 7 Heavy Trench Mortar Battery
from 1st August to 30th September 1916.

Instructions regarding War Diaries and Intelligence Summaries are contained in F. S. Regs., Part II. and the Staff Manual respectively. Title Pages will be prepared in manuscript.

WAR DIARY

or

~~INTELLIGENCE SUMMARY~~

(Erase heading not required.)

Army Form C. 2118.

August

V7. T.M.B

Place	Date	Hour	Summary of Events and Information	Remarks and references to Appendices
HEILLY	1/8/1916 to 20/8/1916		Rest Camp	
MEAULTE	20-8-16		Moved by road to MEAULTE	
MONTAUBAN	21-8-16		Moved to position in Valley rear of MONTAUBAN	
DELVILLE WOOD	22-8-16		Epaulment in rear of DELVILLE WOOD & Gun fixed in position	
	23-8-16 } 24 " " }		Battery in Camp in Valley to rear of MONTAUBAN awaiting orders	
	25-8-16		In action at 850 yds No of Rounds fired 25. 3.45 PM to 5.45 PM	
	26-8-16		As above for 23rd	
	27 " "		Gun moved to fresh position Casualty No 34120 Pte Sterri[?] G.S. Wounded	
	28th to 31st		As above for 23rd. Casualties 29-8-16 30-8-16 { No 82750 " Harrison[?] } Killed; " 127679 " Ferrer[?] T. } Killed; " 545 " Frost[?] W. Cpl Shell shock	

Instructions regarding War Diaries and Intelligence Summaries are contained in F. S. Regs., Part II. and the Staff Manual respectively. Title Pages will be prepared in manuscript.

September

WAR DIARY
or
~~INTELLIGENCE SUMMARY~~
(Erase heading not required.)

Army Form C. 2118.

V7. T.M.B.

Place	Date	Hour	Summary of Events and Information	Remarks and references to Appendices
MONTANBAN	1/9/16 to 15/9/16		Valley in rear of MONTANBAN awaiting orders	
			Casualties { 1/c 56556 Bombr Cooper. H.A Gas. / " 113195 " Andrews G Gas / " 60421 Gr Beresford J Sick / " 53947 " Clark J Gas } 1-9-16	2-9-1916 LT. TAYLOR 2/LT McNEIL Gas.
			Casualties { " 55145 BSM Allett W.W. Gas / " 12372 Gr Stout A Gas / " 64323 " Lauksbi G Gas } 2-9-16	
			60206 Gr Collins J. Sick } 3-9-16	
			20265 " Jordan V G Wound } 5-9-16	
			74187 " Breeze. A. Shellshock } 6-9-16	
			5589 " Holleborn T. Wound / 4111 " Saylor C.S. " " / 136329 " Godfrey W.A " " } 10-9-16	
	16/9/16		left MONTANBAN for FRICOURT await orders	
	27/9/16		left FRICOURT proceeded to BINNAY	
	28/9/16		arrived at LONGEAU entrained 3-30 AM	
	29/9/16		By train to CAESTRE	
	30/9/16		Rest at SHAEKHEN	

2449 Wt. W14957/M90 750,000 1/16 J.B.C. & A. Forms/C.2118/12.

Vol III.

CONFIDENTIAL

War Diary of V 7 Heavy Trench Mortar Battery
for month of October 1916

Instructions regarding War Diaries and Intelligence Summaries are contained in F. S. Regs., Part II. and the Staff Manual respectively. Title Pages will be prepared in manuscript.

WAR DIARY
or
~~INTELLIGENCE SUMMARY~~

(Erase heading not required.)

Army Form C. 2118.

V. 7. T.M.B.

Place	Date	Hour	Summary of Events and Information	Remarks and references to Appendices
Ploegsteert	1.10.16		By road from Schaexken to Ploegsteert	
	2.10.16 to 5.10.16		Taking over and inspecting positions. Fixing guns and telephones.	
	6.10.16		Received new gun from Ordnance, Bailleul	
	8.10.16		2/Lt Parker joined the battery from 7th D.A.C. Escort sent to 4th Army H.Q. guardroom to bring Gnr Williams X7 Bty	
	7.10.16		G.O.C. 36th Div inspected gun pits.	
	9.10.16		Fired two rounds.	
	10.10.16		do ten do Bdr Jones & Gunner Price awarded Military Medals.	
	11.10.16	4.45am	do three do. Escort returned from 4th Army Guardroom with Gnr Williams X7 Bty	
	12.10.16	7.30pm	do five do. Barrage during raid	
	13.10.16		do three do. Gun disabled through rifle mechanism being blown out	
	14.10.16	3 pm	do nine do — do — do — do —	
	15.10.16		Retaliation. Enemy fire silenced. do ten do — do — do — Telephone communication established with Right Batt. H.Q. Rifle House.	
	17.10.16		do three do Second round fell behind our own line but did no damage.	
	18.10.16		do fourteen do. Gun moved from No 1 pit to No 4 pit.	
	21.10.16		do ten do Silenced enemy mortars. Rifle mech. blown out gun temp. disabled	
	22.10.16	3.30pm	do three do	
	23.10.16		do ten do	
	24.10.16	12.30pm	do two do Rifle mech. blown out. Gun temporarily out of action	
	25.10.16		Guns out of action disabled.	
	26.10.16		— do — do —	
	27.10.16		Guns returned from ordnance and fixed in positions	
	28.10.16		Rifle mechanism blown out gun temporarily disabled. New pattern gas masks received and tested by M.O. 36th Brigade R.F.A. (Sgt Riley commenced Course)	

2449 Wt. W14957/M90 750,000 1/16 J.B.C. & A. Forms/C.2118/12.

2

Army Form C. 2118.

Instructions regarding War Diaries and Intelligence Summaries are contained in F. S. Regs., Part II. and the Staff Manual respectively. Title Pages will be prepared in manuscript.

WAR DIARY
or
INTELLIGENCE SUMMARY

(Erase heading not required.)

V. 7. T.M.B. (Continued)

Place	Date	Hour	Summary of Events and Information	Remarks and references to Appendices
Ploegsteert	29.10.16	3 pm to 3.41 pm	Fired seven rounds. Rifle mechanism blown out of one gun at fifth round. Gun changed and firing continued until end of time for scheme.	
	30.10.16		[illegible] gun out of action	
	31.10.16		Do [illegible]	

[illegible]
O.C. V.7. T.M.B.

2449 Wt. W14957/M90 750,000 1/16 J.B.C. & A. Forms/C.2118/12.

Vol 8 + 9

CONFIDENTIAL

War Diary

of

X7 Trench Mortar Battery

from 1st August to ~~[illegible]~~ 1916

Instructions regarding War Diaries and Intelligence Summaries are contained in F. S. Regs., Part II. and the Staff Manual respectively. Title Pages will be prepared in manuscript.

or

~~INTELLIGENCE SUMMARY~~

(Erase heading not required.)

August — Y 7 T.M. Battery.

Place	Date	Hour	Summary of Events and Information	Remarks and references to Appendices
HEILLY	1.8.16 to 19.8.16		In rest at HEILLY. Gun drill daily.	
	20.8.16		Battery moved by G.S. waggons to BERNAFAY WOOD. Took over 6 guns from Medium T.M. Battery of 5th Division. 4 guns in DELVILLE WOOD, 2 guns (not in action) near BERNAFAY WOOD.	
	21.8.16	4-25 pm	Fired 12 rounds during a short intense Artillery bombardment on German trench.	
	22.8.16	12-30 pm	Fired 6 rounds on German strong point.	
	24.8.16		Completed 2 new emplacements in LONGUEVAL ALLEY.	
		3-45 pm to 5-45 pm	Fired 75 rounds (during 2 hours Artillery preparation for attack) into German front & support trenches.	
		5-45 pm	Moved up with Infantry attacking to gun position in our front line. Fired 18 rounds into COCOA LANE while Infantry were attacking through the wood to EDGE TRENCH.	
	25.8.16		Ordered to bring battery out of action, got guns out of wood. 2nd Lieut Robson wounded, evacuated to England.	

2449 Wt. W14957/M90 750,000 1/16 J.B.C. & A. Forms/C.2118/12.

Instructions regarding War Diaries and Intelligence Summaries are contained in F. S. Regs., Part II. and the Staff Manual respectively. Title pages will be prepared in manuscript.

or

INTELLIGENCE SUMMARY.

(Erase heading not required.)

August — Y 7 Tn Battery

Place	Date	Hour	Summary of Events and Information	Remarks and references to Appendices
~~26/70~~	26.8.16		Battery came back to T.M. Camp near MEAULTE	
	27.8.16 – 31.8.16		Battery out of action.	
	28.8.16		Battery moved to near FRICOURT to be nearer the line (guarded).	

T2134. Wt. W708–776. 500000. 4/15. Sir J. C. & S.

Instructions regarding War Diaries and Intelligence Summaries are contained in F. S. Regs., Part II. and the Staff Manual respectively. Title Pages will be prepared in manuscript.

August.

~~INTELLIGENCE SUMMARY~~

(Erase heading not required.)

Z 7 T M B.

Place	Date	Hour	Summary of Events and Information	Remarks and references to Appendices
Heilly	Aug 1st		Went back towards the end of July with 7th D.A from MANSEL COPSE	
"	Aug 5th		2Lt B.M. BAUER left the battery. 2Lt T. ADDIS posted from Y7 T.M.B	
"	- 18th		2Lt H.C. ATKINSON posted from 7th D.A.C	
Meaulte	- 20th		Left Heilly and went to Meaulte by Motor Lorry.	
Delville Wd	- 21st		Went up to Delville Wood, spent the night just outside Montauban	
"	- 22nd		At 3 A.M. went up to Delville Wood with Heavy T.M. Battery. met Y7 T.M.B there. Got two positions started on the left of Delville Wood.	
"	- 23rd	6.30 pm	Gr. SKINNER and Gr MALLET buried by a shell, Gr SKINNER killed, Gr MALLET shell shock. ~~[illegible]~~	
"	- 24th	12 noon	Two gun to be dug on right of wood, no time for it to be done as positions on left not yet completed	
"	"	4 pm	Fired 20 rounds from rear gun position	
"	"	5 pm	" 10 " " " " " had no time to bring up more ammunition	
"	"	6.10 "	Did not fire from ~~forward~~ gun in the wounded state they have advanced beyond our range. Cpl LOVE wounded	
"	"	9 pm	The slackening of the German barrage enabled us to leave Delville Wood	

2449 Wt. W14957/M90 750,000 1/16 J.B.C. & A. Forms/C.2118/12.

Instructions regarding War Diaries and Intelligence Summaries are contained in F. S. Regs., Part II. and the Staff Manual respectively. Title Pages will be prepared in manuscript.

August

INTELLIGENCE SUMMARY

(Erase heading not required.)

27 T.M.B

Place	Date	Hour	Summary of Events and Information	Remarks and references to Appendices
Montauban	Aug 26th		begin digging two gun positions on right of Delville Wood opposite ALE ALLEY	
	-28th		" " " " fifty yds in front of former positions	
	-29th		two guns in action in original two right hand positions	

2449 Wt. W14957/M90 750,000 1/16 J.B.C. & A. Forms/C.2118/12.

Army Form C. 2118. 7

X 7 TMBG

Vol 5

Instructions regarding War Diaries and Intelligence Summaries are contained in F. S. Regs., Part II. and the Staff Manual respectively. Title Pages will be prepared in manuscript.

WAR DIARY
or
INTELLIGENCE SUMMARY

(Erase heading not required.)

Place	Date	Hour	Summary of Events and Information	Remarks and references to Appendices
			This Battery was in rest at [illegible] until the 20-8-16 when we moved up to Meaulte. On the same date a portion of the Battery went into action with Y 7 T.M.B for a week in Delville Wood. On the 27-8-16 we moved up to Fricourt.	
			31-8-16 W. G. [illegible] 2nd Lt. Comdg. X 7 T.M.B.	

2449 Wt. W14957/M90 750,000 1/16 J.B.C. & A. Forms/C.2118/12.

Instructions regarding War Diaries and Intelligence Summaries are contained in F. S. Regs., Part II. and the Staff Manual respectively. Title pages will be prepared in manuscript.

September

WAR DIARY
or
INTELLIGENCE SUMMARY.
(Erase heading not required.)

Army Form C. 2118.

Y7 T.M. Battery

Place	Date	Hour	Summary of Events and Information	Remarks and references to Appendices
FRICOURT	1.9.16 to 27.9.16		Battery out of action, gun drill etc daily. Reliefs of men sent to Z7 & X7 T.M. Batteries who were in action.	
	28.9.16		Battery moved in G.S. waggons to BONNAY. Billeted for night.	
	29.9.16		" " " " " LONGEAU.	
	30.9.16		Battery entrained for 2nd Army Area.	

T2134. Wt. W708–776. 500000. 4/15. Sir J. C. & S.

Vol 7

CONFIDENTIAL.

War Diary of X7 Trench Mortar Battery
for the month of October 1916.

Instructions regarding War Diaries and Intelligence Summaries are contained in F. S. Regs., Part II. and the Staff Manual respectively. Title Pages will be prepared in manuscript.

WAR DIARY
or
~~INTELLIGENCE SUMMARY~~
(Erase heading not required.)

Army Form C. 2118.

For the month of ~~Sept~~ October 1916

Place	Date	Hour	Summary of Events and Information	Remarks and references to Appendices
In the Field	31/10/16		On Sept. 30th this battery detrained at CAESTRE. It spent one night at METTERIN on line of march and on Oct. 2nd arrived at its billet in PONT DE NIEPPE. After a 3 day's wait pending the receipt of instructions 2 guns were placed in action on 6th in LE TOUQUET sector. Nothing of importance occurred till the night of 12th, when in preparation for a raid which was carried out on the enemy trenches at U.28 c. 7.5 a 3rd gun was moved into the line to cut wire beforehand and fire during the raid. Altogether on this occasion the battery fired 147 RDS. On 13th two new officers were posted to the battery, those relieved being transferred to D.A.C and Y7 TMB respectively. Apart from retaliation nothing of importance took place till 26th, when wire cutting was commenced with all 3 guns at noon 54 RDS being fired. On 27th however fresh instructions were received. All 4 guns was placed in position close together for the object of flattening a small section of German front line trench. The bombardment was carried out on afternoon of 29th in conjunction with batteries. During the 30 MINS allotted we fired 146 RDS. On 30th 2 guns were transferred to Z7 TMB, and on 31st the remaining section were reinstated in their former positions, and wire cutting was commenced with one gun. Towards the end of the month the front has become considerably livelier the enemy proving to have an abundance of trench mortars of every size, but few batteries of field and heavy guns. The total of rounds expended during the month is 398.	

A M P Wilson 2Lt RFA
Comdg. X7 TMB

2449 Wt. W14957/M90 750,000 1/16 J.B.C. & A. Forms/C.2118/12.

Army Form C. 2118.

Instructions regarding War Diaries and Intelligence Summaries are contained in F. S. Regs., Part II. and the Staff Manual respectively. Title Pages will be prepared in manuscript.

WAR DIARY
or
INTELLIGENCE SUMMARY
(Erase heading not required.)

September

Z.I. T.M.B.

Place	Date	Hour	Summary of Events and Information	Remarks and references to Appendices
Montauban	Sept 5th	11.55 to 12 noon	Fired 5 rounds on ALE ALLEY	
"	– 7th	3 am	" 7 " " " "	
"	– 8th		2LT ATKINSON left for a T.M. course	
"	– 9th		Fired 30 rounds on ALE ALLEY	
Fricourt	– 11th		Battery came back to FRICOURT	
"	– 27th		Went to BONNAY	
"	– 28th		Marched to LONGEAU	
"	– 30th	4 AM	entrained for CAESTRE. Marched to SCHAEXKEN	
~~"~~	~~– 31st~~			

2449 Wt. W14957/M90 750,000 1/16 J.B.C. & A. Forms/C.2118/12.

Instructions regarding War Diaries and Intelligence Summaries are contained in F. S. Regs., Part II. and the Staff Manual respectively. Title Pages will be prepared in manuscript.

WAR DIARY
or
INTELLIGENCE SUMMARY
(Erase heading not required.)

Army Form C. 2118.

Vol 10

Place	Date	Hour	Summary of Events and Information	Remarks and references to Appendices
			War Diary for October 1916 Y 7 T M B.	

2449 Wt. W14957/M90 750,000 1/16 J.B.C. & A. Forms/C.2118/12.

Instructions regarding War Diaries and Intelligence Summaries are contained in F. S. Regs., Part II. and the Staff Manual respectively. Title Pages will be prepared in manuscript.

WAR DIARY
or
INTELLIGENCE SUMMARY
(Erase heading not required.)

October 1916

Army Form C. 2118.

Place	Date	Hour	Summary of Events and Information	Remarks and references to Appendices
Ploegsteert	2nd	–	On this date we arrived in the Ploegsteert Area & on the following day proceeded to get the guns into action, digging emplacements & carrying	
	8th		up Ammunition. On the 8th We fired 14 rounds on the enemy's barbed wire & front line from our positions at Rutters Lodge. On the	
	10th		10th 3 rounds were fired from a gun at [illegible] (German House)	
	11th		We fired 15 rounds from German House gun.	
	12th		Next day we cut wire in front of Rutters Lodge preparatory to a Bombing attack which came off in the evening. 34 rounds were expended.	
	14th		10 rounds were fired from a position at the Post Office in retaliation for damage done by a German Heavy T.M. in this area.	
	16th		We fired 24 rounds from Rutters Lodge on the enemy front line.	
	17th		Some damage was done to the enemy's trenches known as the "Bird Cage" in front of German House. [illegible] rounds were expended on this day.	
	20th		14 rounds were fired from Rutters Lodge.	

2449 Wt. W14957/M90 750,000 1/16 J.B.C. & A. Forms/C.2118/12.

Instructions regarding War Diaries and Intelligence Summaries are contained in F. S. Regs., Part II. and the Staff Manual respectively. Title Pages will be prepared in manuscript.

WAR DIARY
or
INTELLIGENCE SUMMARY

(Erase heading not required.)

Army Form C. 2118.

October 1916

Place	Date	Hour	Summary of Events and Information	Remarks and references to Appendices
Ploegsteert	24th		On this day the Enemy Trench Mortars were very active on the left edge of Ploegsteert Wood. 76 rounds were fired in order to silence them from 4th positions at the Post Office & German House.	
	25th		29 rounds were expended in retaliation from the same positions as were fired from the previous day	
	27th		We fired 4 rounds from [illegible] Lodge.	
	28th to 29th		The next two days were employed in making two new positions at Halls Burnt Farm & one position at Lone house Farm.	
	30th		On this day we had a big bombardment of the enemy lines, firing 164 rounds from three guns in 30 minutes. The guns were fired from Halls Burnt Farm & Lone house Farm	
	31st		No rounds were fired on this day.	

W Gordon Leslie 2nd Lt
for O.C. y ?T.M.B.

2449 Wt. W14957/M90 750,000 1/16 J.B.C. & A. Forms/C.2118/12.

Army Form C. 2118. 7

Instructions regarding War Diaries and Intelligence Summaries are contained in F. S. Regs., Part II. and the Staff Manual respectively. Title Pages will be prepared in manuscript.

WAR DIARY
or
INTELLIGENCE SUMMARY
(Erase heading not required.)

Vol 8

Place	Date	Hour	Summary of Events and Information	Remarks and references to Appendices
			War Diary of X7 Trench Mortar Battery for month of November 1916.	

2449 Wt. W14957/M90 750,000 1/16 J.B.C. & A. Forms/C.2118/12.

Instructions regarding War Diaries and Intelligence Summaries are contained in F. S. Regs., Part II. and the Staff Manual respectively. Title Pages will be prepared in manuscript.

WAR DIARY
or
~~INTELLIGENCE SUMMARY~~
(Erase heading not required.)

Army Form C. 2118.

Place	Date	Hour	Summary of Events and Information	Remarks and references to Appendices

On the 1st of the month wirecutting which had been temporarily suspended, was continued with one gun, in accordance with the proposed scheme of last month of destroying the enemy's wire on as large a front as possible. The same was carried out on the 3rd, but after this date no more was done. The retaliation of enemy mortars was intense; one of our positions was accurately located and rendered useless by direct hits, while two others were isolated and inundated by the destruction of the communication trenches leading to them. On the 26th a small bombardment was carried out on enemy trenches in front of PLOEGSTEERT WOOD one mortar only of this battery taking part, while on the 24th a similar bombardment was executed further South opposite RUTTER LODGE on a larger scale. Three of our guns were put in position with 35 ROUNDS per gun, 4 mortars of other batteries being in the vicinity. Unfortunately all three were put out of action during the bombardment by slight accidents, and only 78 ROUNDS were fired. The effect of it, however, was most marked; the enemy front and probably support lines were levelled and wire buried or destroyed on a front of about 40 yards. Nothing much of importance occurred till the 29th when X 25 relieved us. This was complete by 7 pm. and the battery was accommodated in huts at PONT de NIEPPE.

We were unfortunate at the beginning in having 3 of our positions rendered useless, but handed over 2 guns in action with 3 other emplacements, two of which were being reconstructed by the R.E. Altogether throughout the month 180 ROUNDS were fired.

AmP Wilson 2Lt RFA
OC X7 TMB 1/12/16

2449 Wt. W14957/M90 750,000 1/16 J.B.C. & A. Forms/C.2118/12.

7

VII

L Y Trench Mortar
late 445 Bty

Vol I

Z. Y Trench Mot

Instructions regarding War Diaries and Intelligence Summaries are contained in F. S. Regs., Part II. and the Staff Manual respectively. Title pages will be prepared in manuscript.

WAR DIARY
or
INTELLIGENCE SUMMARY.
(Erase heading not required.)

Z 7
TRENCH MORTAR
BATTERY.
No. ....
Date 31. 3. 16.

Army Form C. 2118.

Place	Date	Hour	Summary of Events and Information	Remarks and references to Appendices
			Nil (Not in Action)	
			[illegible] Capt R.F.A. O.C. Z.7 T.M. Bty	

2353 Wt. W2544/1454 700,000 5/15 D. D. & L. A.D.S.S./Forms/C. 2118.

7

Vol 5.6

CONFIDENTIAL

War Diary

of

Z 7 Trench Mortar Battery

from 1st August to 30th September 1916

Z. 7 T.M. Batty

Army Form C. 2118.

Vol 10

Instructions regarding War Diaries and Intelligence Summaries are contained in F. S. Regs., Part II. and the Staff Manual respectively. Title Pages will be prepared in manuscript.

WAR DIARY
or
INTELLIGENCE SUMMARY
(Erase heading not required.)

Place	Date	Hour	Summary of Events and Information	Remarks and references to Appendices
In the Field	1916 Oct. 1	—	Disembarked at CAESTRE for SCHAEXKEN prior to going into action at PLOEGSTRETE.	
SCHAEKEN	2		Stayed one day at SCHAEXKEN marching next	
"	3		morning through BAILLEUL to our Headquarters at PLOEGSTRETE (Piggeries) getting two guns into action same night at ANTON'S FARM (the other two guns being at I.O.M. for alteration to take Temple Silencers).	
PLOEGSTRETE	4		Two guns at ANTONS FARM registered on U.9.g.50.10. to U.9.B.10.50. & U.9.6.50.20 to U.9.6.70.80.	
"	10th		2/Lt. D. Rose R.F.A. joined Battery from No 2 Sect 7th D.A.C.	

2449 Wt. W14957/M90 750,000 1/16 J.B.C. & A. Forms/C.2118/12.

Instructions regarding War Diaries and Intelligence Summaries are contained in F. S. Regs., Part II. and the Staff Manual respectively. Title Pages will be prepared in manuscript.

WAR DIARY
or
INTELLIGENCE SUMMARY
(Erase heading not required.)

Army Form C. 2118.

Place	Date	Hour	Summary of Events and Information	Remarks and references to Appendices
PLOEGSTRETE	Oct. 16th		Lt. I. Addis. R.F.A. O.C. of Battery granted leave of absence 2/Lt. W.G. Leckie. R.F.A. taking temporary command.	
— " —	18th		Two guns returned from I.O.M. & taken into action at SEAFORTH FARM.	
— " —	19th		Two guns registered at Seaforth Farm on SNIPERS POST.	
— " —	28th		Gr Foster. S. (killed) to 12388 Sgt G. Selby (wounded) Gr Mummerley (wounded) by a premature at SEAFORTH FARM.	
— " —			Lt. I. Addis. R.F.A. returned from leave taking over command.	

I. Addis
Lt. R.F.A.
Chg 2.7. Im. Bty

2449 Wt. W14957/M90 750,000 1/16 J.B.C. & A. Forms/C.2118/12.

Instructions regarding War Diaries and Intelligence Summaries are contained in F. S. Regs., Part II. and the Staff Manual respectively. Title pages will be prepared in manuscript.

WAR DIARY

20/1, 20/2 Trench Mortar Batteries

~~INTELLIGENCE~~ SUMMARY.

(Erase heading not required.)

Army Form C. 2118.

7

Vols 1 to 5

~~Vol 6~~

Period February – June 1916.

Place	Date	Hour	Summary of Events and Information	Remarks and references to Appendices
	Feb. 1916.		The 20/1 T.M.B. was formed at Valheureux School on Feb. 14th, under the command of 2/Lieut Beddow. The other officer was 2/Lt. Shaw. After eight days training the Battery moved to MEAULTE. Two guns were taken into trenches with 50% of Battery personnel.	
	March 1916		These were relieved by the other half battery after eight days. This continued throughout March	
	April.		On April 20th the Battery was relieved by a Battery of Yorks & Lancs; 2/Lieut. Beddow having reported sick on April 12th & been sent to England. Upon relief the Battery moved to Corbie, where 20/2 Battery joined the Brigade under the command of 2/Lieut Street & 2/Lt. Duff. On the 22nd both batteries moved to Bray & on the 23rd Lieut A.F. Mills took over command of 20/1 T.M.B., 2/Lt. Shaw going on leave. Upon his return, he reported sick, was sent to Base & eventually was struck off the Battery strength.	

T2134. Wt. W708–776. 500000. 4/15. Sir J. C. & S.

Instructions regarding War Diaries and Intelligence Summaries are contained in F. S. Regs., Part II. and the Staff Manual respectively. Title pages will be prepared in manuscript.

WAR DIARY

or

~~INTELLIGENCE SUMMARY.~~

(Erase heading not required.)

Army Form C. 2118.

Place	Date	Hour	Summary of Events and Information	Remarks and references to Appendices
	May 1916.		Both Batteries came out of action & proceeded to Bonnay where they remained for about three weeks. During this time Lieut A.F. Mills attended an advanced course in Stokes' Mortars at the Central ~~st~~ school, Hesdin.	
			Both Batteries then moved to Grovetown & preparations for the July offensive were begun.	
	June 1916.		20/1 & 20/2 TMB. were amalgamated into one Battery, called the 20th T.M.B under the command of Lieut. A.F. Mills, who was ~~calle~~ given the temporary rank of Captain.	

T2134. Wt. W708—776. 500000. 4/15. Sir J. C. & S.

Instructions regarding War Diaries and Intelligence Summaries are contained in F. S. Regs., Part II. and the Staff Manual respectively. Title pages will be prepared in manuscript.

WAR DIARY

or

~~INTELLIGENCE SUMMARY.~~

(Erase heading not required.)

Army Form C. 2118.

20 Tm Bty

Vol. 7

Place	Date	Hour	Summary of Events and Information	Remarks and references to Appendices
			20th Trench Mortar Battery August, 1916	
PICQUIGNY	Aug 1st	9 A.m. to 12 noon	Gun drill. Close order drill. Lecture on Stokes Shell to the twelve men who had just joined the battery.	
		2 P.m.	Gas Helmet inspection	
	2.8.16	9 A.m. to 12 noon	Gun drill. Close order drill. Billets were inspected by the Staff Captain.	
		2 P.m.	Gun drill.	
		3 P.m.	Pay out.	
	3.8.16	9 A.m. to 12 noon	Practice in laying for line & elevation. This took place on a hill just outside of the town where several good targets were available. The new men made good progress and were quick to learn the use of the clinometer and to judge the angle of the gun for a given range. This draft of twelve men is very satisfactory.	
		4 P.m.	Baths.	

T2134. Wt. W708—776. 500000. 4/15. Sir J. C. & S.

Instructions regarding War Diaries and Intelligence Summaries are contained in F. S. Regs., Part II. and the Staff Manual respectively. Title pages will be prepared in manuscript.

WAR DIARY
or
~~INTELLIGENCE SUMMARY.~~
(Erase heading not required.)

Army Form C. 2118.

Place	Date	Hour	Summary of Events and Information	Remarks and references to Appendices
PICQUIGNY	Aug 4th	10 Am	Inspection of Brigade by Army Commander. The men were free in the afternoon for the Brigade Gymkhana.	
	5.8.16	9 Am to 12 noon	Gun laying. Practice in judging the angle of the gun for given ranges. Most of the new men had a very fair idea of an angle of 45° and found the work easy. In this battery laying for line and judging elevation are considered the most important part of the training in view of open fighting.	
	6.8.16	9 Am to 12 noon	Firing practice. This took place in the field on the SOUES road where the bombers trenches were dug. The firing was carried out by the new men. Results were moderate. The ground was extremely hard causing (i) Pistol heads to break off and (ii) Shells to bounce as much as twenty to twenty five feet. As a result, officers of this battery came to the following conclusions:- (i) A mild steel pistol head would	

Instructions regarding War Diaries and Intelligence Summaries are contained in F. S. Regs., Part II. and the Staff Manual respectively. Title pages will be prepared in manuscript.

WAR DIARY
or
~~INTELLIGENCE SUMMARY.~~
(Erase heading not required.)

Army Form C. 2118.

Place	Date	Hour	Summary of Events and Information	Remarks and references to Appendices
PICQUIGNY	6.8.16	9 a.m. to 12 Noon	would be preferable to the present custom [illegible] and (ii) that, on hard ground, graze bursts were necessary for accurate shooting. The remainder of the battery attended church parade. At the request of Brigade H.Q. a report on the handling of Stokes Mortars in an advance was sent in by the O.C. 20th T.M.B.	
	7.8.16	9 a.m. to 12 Noon	Gun drill. Close order drill. The new men were posted to gun teams. Billets were inspected by A.D.M.S.	
	8.8.16	9 a.m. to 12 Noon	Practice at digging in the base plate. Laying for line. Close order drill. Men were free in the afternoon for the Border Regiment sports.	
	9.8.16 10.8.16 11.8.16		Gun drill. Close order drill. Laying for line and elevation.	

T2134. Wt. W708—776. 500000. 4/15. Sir J. C. & S.

Instructions regarding War Diaries and Intelligence Summaries are contained in F. S. Regs., Part II. and the Staff Manual respectively. Title pages will be prepared in manuscript.

WAR DIARY
or
~~INTELLIGENCE SUMMARY.~~
(Erase heading not required.)

Army Form C. 2118.

Place	Date	Hour	Summary of Events and Information	Remarks and references to Appendices
PICQUIGNY	Aug 12th		20th Brigade moved. Parade at 8.20 a.m. marched to HANGEST entrained at 12 Noon and proceeded to MERICOURT. Brigade billeted at BUIRE.	
BUIRE	13.8.16		Two officers and twenty one men forming the 50% reserve joined the battery for training. The officers were:- Lieut D. ELLIOT 2nd Borders 2nd Lieut S.R. GROVER 2nd Gordons. Authority 20/3112. 11 a.m. Church parade	
	14.8.16	9 a.m.	Parade, inspection of 50% reserve. Training of the latter begun. Afternoon wet.	
	15.8.16	9 a.m. to 12 Noon	Gun drill. Close order drill. Training of Reserve carried on. This 50% reserve are not as good on the whole as the twelve men who joined at PICQUIGNY.	
		2 P.m.	Lecture on ammunition to Reserve who then fused shells.	

T2134. Wt. W708—776. 500000. 4/15. Sir J. C. & S.

Instructions regarding War Diaries and Intelligence Summaries are contained in F. S. Regs., Part II. and the Staff Manual respectively. Title pages will be prepared in manuscript.

WAR DIARY
or
~~INTELLIGENCE SUMMARY.~~
(Erase heading not required.)

Army Form C. 2118.

Place	Date	Hour	Summary of Events and Information	Remarks and references to Appendices
BUIRE	Aug 16th	9 Am	Laying for line. Digging in base plate.	
		2 Pm	Firing with dummies by Reserve. Results moderate.	
	17.8.16	9 Am	Laying for line. Gun drill. Close order drill.	
		2 Pm	Fitting guns with new spare parts. Order received that Brigade is on three hours notice.	
	18.8.16	9 Am	Firing with dummies by Reserve. Laying for line. Judging gun angle for a given range. The Reserve did not do as well as the previous draft — having very little idea of angles. Brigade Gymkhana in the afternoon.	
	19.8.16	9 Am	Four guns were taken to the range and dug in. Ranging was carried out with dummy shells. In the afternoon firing was carried out and results were fairly good. None of the guns reached the clinometer range.	

T2134. Wt. W708—776. 500000. 4/15. Sir J. C. & S.

Instructions regarding War Diaries and Intelligence Summaries are contained in F. S. Regs., Part II. and the Staff Manual respectively. Title pages will be prepared in manuscript.

WAR DIARY
or
~~INTELLIGENCE SUMMARY.~~
(Erase heading not required.)

Army Form C. 2118.

Place	Date	Hour	Summary of Events and Information	Remarks and references to Appendices
			range.	
BUIRE	19.8.16		The explanation may be (i) bad cartridges or (ii) old guns the latter reason is probably correct as the guns have been eight months in action and have had plenty of knocking about.	
			Private Smith of the 2nd Borders was wounded by a cartridge container flying back and hitting him in the jaw. He was standing behind the gun at the time. The gun was firing at 270 to 230 yards green cartridges being used. The Brigadier was present and ordered firing to stop.	
			The Divisional General inspected Billets at 5 Pm.	
	20.8.16		Men had baths in the morning. Two officers reconnoitred the CHECK LINE.	
	21.8.16	9 Am	Two gun emplacements and a trench were dug on the range to give cover to the battery when firing.	
		10 Am	Court of Inquiry on the accident of 19.8.16 President Major GREEN, members 2nd Lieut J.G.L. GIRDLESTONE and 2nd Lieut S.R. GROVER, Witnesses	

T2134. Wt. W708—776. 500000. 4/15. Sir J. C. & S.

Instructions regarding War Diaries and Intelligence Summaries are contained in F. S. Regs., Part II. and the Staff Manual respectively. Title pages will be prepared in manuscript.

WAR DIARY
or
INTELLIGENCE SUMMARY.
(Erase heading not required.)

Army Form C. 2118.

Place	Date	Hour	Summary of Events and Information	Remarks and references to Appendices
BUIRE	21.3.16		Witnesses:- Capt. MILLS, 2nd Lieut E. MORRIS, Cpl. SMITH.	
		2 P.m.	The remainder of the shells (32) were fired. Results were much better only one blind. Lieut ELLIOT returned to regimental duty.	
	22.3.16	9 Am to 12 Noon	Laying for line. Close order drill. Gun drill.	
		2 P.m.	Kit inspection. Gas Helmet inspection.	
	23.3.16	9 Am to 12 Noon	2nd Lieut MONTGOMERIE 2nd Borders joined the battery in place of Lieut ELLIOT. Laying for line. Close order drill.	
	24.3.16	9 Am	Route march. Route BUIRE to cross roads I.27.b.3.0 to LAVIÈVILLE to cross roads D11.b.5.4 to BUIRE. Ref: FRANCE 62 D. N.E. On this day orders were received that no more route marches were to take place until further orders	

Instructions regarding War Diaries and Intelligence Summaries are contained in F. S. Regs., Part II. and the Staff Manual respectively. Title pages will be prepared in manuscript.

WAR DIARY
or
~~INTELLIGENCE SUMMARY.~~
(Erase heading not required.)

Army Form C. 2118.

Place	Date	Hour	Summary of Events and Information	Remarks and references to Appendices
BUIRE.	25.8.16	9 AM	Gun drill. Close order drill. Laying for line. Eight men were told off to be trained as signallers. At present T.M. batteries are not equipped with telephones but probably will be in the near future. Arrangements were made for a competition.	
	26.8.16		Close order drill. Laying for line. O.O. 77 received. 7th Division take over the right of 14th Division and the left of the 20th Division. The 20th Brigade remain in present billets. 20/1960/59/1 received ordering the battery to send two mortars to the XVth Corps School.	
	27.8.16	10.30 AM	Baths. Two guns sent to XV Corps School with one man as Store Keeper.	
	28.8.16	9 AM	Gun drill, close order drill. Afternoon wet. Two guns sent for repair on July 2nd. One [illegible] gun + one Mark II gun received this day thus completing establishment of eight guns.	

T2134. Wt. W708—776. 500000. 4/15. Sir J. C. & S.

Instructions regarding War Diaries and Intelligence Summaries are contained in F. S. Regs., Part II. and the Staff Manual respectively. Title pages will be prepared in manuscript.

WAR DIARY
or
~~INTELLIGENCE~~ SUMMARY.
(Erase heading not required.)

Army Form C. 2118.

Place	Date	Hour	Summary of Events and Information	Remarks and references to Appendices
BUIRE	29.8.16	9 Am	Lecture to battery on the new mark II gun. Gun drill and laying for line. Signalling done by eight men.	
		2 Pm	Gun drill. Pay out.	
	30.8.16	9 Am	Battery competition. Two officers 2/Lieut MORRIS, 2nd Lieut GROVER with 11 other ranks detailed for course at XV Corps School. Twelve other ranks are being sent from Battery who will rejoin their units on completion of course.	
	Sep 1st	9 Am	~~Laying for line. Close order drill and signalling.~~	
		2 .		

J. H. Findlestal (?)
2/Lieut OC XV T.M.B

T2134. Wt. W708—776. 500000. 4/15. Sir J. C. & S.

VII

22/2 T M Bhi

Vol. 1

Army Form C. 2118. 7

Instructions regarding War Diaries and Intelligence Summaries are contained in F. S. Regs., Part II. and the Staff Manual respectively. Title Pages will be prepared in manuscript.

WAR DIARY
or
INTELLIGENCE SUMMARY
(Erase heading not required.)

Place	Date	Hour	Summary of Events and Information	Remarks and references to Appendices
			Vol ~~7~~ 5 CONFIDENTIAL WAR DIARY of 22ND TRENCH MORTAR BATTERY VOLUME I	

2449 Wt. W14957/M90 750,000 1/16 J.B.C. & A. Forms/C.2118/12.

Instructions regarding War Diaries and Intelligence Summaries are contained in F. S. Regs., Part II. and the Staff Manual respectively. Title Pages will be prepared in manuscript.

WAR DIARY
or
INTELLIGENCE SUMMARY
(Erase heading not required.)

Army Form C. 2118.

Place	Date	Hour	Summary of Events and Information	Remarks and references to Appendices
BELLOY. s. SOMME [FRANCE]	1916 AUG.			
	1st		Unit at Rest Drill + Training	
	2nd		do	
	3rd		do	
	4th		Inspection by General Sir H. Rawlinson, commanding 4th Army at the CHATEAU at YZEUX in the morning	
	5th		Unit at Rest Drill + Training No. 17024 Pte H. T. WORLAND, 20th MANCHESTER R. att'd this Battery, (now in Hospital) has been awarded D.C.M. for gallantry on JULY 1st	
	6th		Unit at Rest. Church Parade in morning	
	7th		do Drill & Training. Draft of 2 N.C.Os & 13 men selected from various units in Brigade to constitute [illegible] [illegible] and form reserve.	
	8th		Unit at Rest. Drill & Training. Sports held by Brigade M.G. Coy, Brigade [illegible] Coy & this unit in afternoon.	
	9th		Unit at Rest. Drill & Training.	

2449 Wt. W14957/M90 750,000 1/16 J.B.C. & A. Forms/C.2118/12.

Army Form C. 2118.

Instructions regarding War Diaries and Intelligence Summaries are contained in F. S. Regs., Part II. and the Staff Manual respectively. Title Pages will be prepared in manuscript.

WAR DIARY
or
INTELLIGENCE SUMMARY
(Erase heading not required.)

Place	Date	Hour	Summary of Events and Information	Remarks and references to Appendices
	1916 AUGUST			
BELLOY.S. SOMME	10th		Unit at Rest – Drill + Training.	W.R.C.
	11th		do. do. Received orders to move on 12th.	W.R.C.
	12th		Paraded 2.30 am. Marched to HANGEST + entrained at 5.30 am. Arrived at MÉRICOURT 10.45 am + detrained. Marched to DERNANCOURT + were billetted in that village at 12.45 pm.	W.R.C.
DERNANCOURT	13th		Unit in Billets cleaning up the Billets, which were left in very dirty condition by outgoing UNIT. 1 NCO + 3 men + 4 guns lent to XV Corps T.M. School for one week. No. 17783 L/Cpl Wagstaff 20th Manchester R. att. this Battery decorated with Military Medal ~~for~~ won on 19th Apl 1916 by XVth Corps Commander at CHATEAU at HEILLY.	W.R.C.
	14th		Drill + Training. Handcarts + spare kit drawn from D.A.D.O.S at MERICOURT	W.R.C.
	15th		Drill + Training	
	16th		do	
	17th		Drill + Training. One NCO sent to Divisional Gas School at RIBEMONT for instruction. 51 rounds ammunition received for instructional purposes.	
		3.30 pm	22nd Brigade Operation Order No. 82 received. 7th Division is in CORPS RESERVE. Unit to be prepared to move at 1¾ hours notice from 2.40 pm 18th inst. from which time troops may not leave Billet Area	W.R.C.

2449 Wt. W14957/M90 750,000 1/16 J.B.C. & A. Forms/C.2118/12.

Instructions regarding War Diaries and Intelligence Summaries are contained in F. S. Regs., Part II. and the Staff Manual respectively. Title Pages will be prepared in manuscript.

WAR DIARY
or
INTELLIGENCE SUMMARY
(Erase heading not required.)

Army Form C. 2118.

Place	Date	Hour	Summary of Events and Information	Remarks and references to Appendices
	1916 AUGUST			
DERNANCOURT	18th		Unit in Reserve. Drill + Training.	W.C.
	19th		Unit in Reserve. Drill + Training. New men fired dummy rounds in afternoon. N.C.O + 3 men + 4 guns returned from XV Corps T.M. School (see 13th)	W.C.
	20th		Unit in Reserve. Church Parade in morning.	W.C.
	21st		do . Drill, training, firing with dummy rounds.	W.C.
	22nd		do N.C.O. returned from Gas School (see 17th) + another NCO sent on Course	W.C.
	23rd		do . Drill, training, firing with dummy rounds.	W.C.
	24th		do . Drill + training. Men from Battns who have been through Stokes Course were inspected by O.C. + 9 men selected to complete a 50% Reserve + to replace 1 NCO + 2 men who were today returned to duty with their Battns.	W.C.
	25th		Unit in Reserve. Drill + training. C.O's conference at Brigade H.Q. + instructions received re forthcoming attack on GINCHY by Brigade	W.C.
	26th		22nd. Inf. Bde Operation Order No 84 received. Brigade to take over part of line in DELVILLE WOOD. Battery marched from DERNANCOURT at 5.35 pm. to MONTAUBAN where they bivouacked. 2/LT. JONES with 2 guns + their teams marched up to DELVILLE WOOD + relieved	

2449 Wt. W14957/M90 750,000 1/16 J.B.C. & A. Forms/C.2118/12.

Instructions regarding War Diaries and Intelligence Summaries are contained in F. S. Regs., Part II. and the Staff Manual respectively. Title Pages will be prepared in manuscript.

WAR DIARY
or
INTELLIGENCE SUMMARY
(Erase heading not required.)

Army Form C. 2118.

Place	Date 1916	Hour	Summary of Events and Information	Remarks and references to Appendices
	AUGUST 26th	(cont'd)	the 2 guns of 4.121 T.M BATTERY at midnight. 2 NCOs + 1 man left at 'B' Echelon for purposes of supply. Weather bad, heavy rain at intervals.	WRC
MONTAUBAN	27th		2/LT. CHILDE + 2 guns moved up to DELVILLE WOOD at 8 am. Casualties 2 O.R. wounded, 2 shell shock (not sent to hospital). NCO returned from Gas School (see 22nd). Weather bad, heavy rain at intervals.	
	28th		CAPT. HON H.A.J. PRESTON + 2/LT HALL + 4 teams relieved officers + men in line at 7pm. 10 rounds fired (registration). Casualties nil. Weather fine. RUMANIA declares war on AUSTRIA. ITALY declares war on GERMANY.	
	29th		22nd Inf. Bde Operation Order No. 85 received. Brigade to attack GINCHY (date + time to be issued later). 4 Stokes Guns to assist 1st R.W.F. 2 Guns to assist 20th MANCHESTER R. 2 Guns to remain in Reserve. 110 Rounds fired during bombing attacks made by 1st R.W.F. N. of DELVILLE WOOD. CASUALTIES: 3 OR wounded, 1 shell shock (not sent to hospital). Weather dull till 6 pm then continuous rain. GERMANY declares war on RUMANIA.	
	30th		The WOOD bombarded all day by enemy. No firing done. Casualties nil. Weather very bad - continuous rain during 24 hours.	WRC

2449 Wt. W14957/M90 750,000 1/16 J.B.C. & A. Forms/C.2118/12.

Army Form C. 2118.

WAR DIARY
or
INTELLIGENCE SUMMARY
(Erase heading not required.)

Instructions regarding War Diaries and Intelligence Summaries are contained in F. S. Regs., Part II. and the Staff Manual respectively. Title Pages will be prepared in manuscript.

Place	Date 1916	Hour	Summary of Events and Information	Remarks and references to Appendices
	AUGUST.			
MONTAUBAN	31st		2/LTs CHILDE & JENNISON & 4 teams marched up to relieve officers & men in line. 2/LT HALL & 2 teams relieved safely when news came that 91st T.M.B. will relieve this Battery in the line during the day. The enemy, after bombarding heavily for the last 5 days commenced an intense bombardment at 9 am which continued to 1 pm when they attacked, but were repulsed. Intense bombardment recommenced & several attacks by enemy in afternoon all of which were repulsed. At about 5.30 pm a very intense bombardment started & at about 7 pm the enemy attacked & succeeded in entering DELVILLE WOOD. 250 rounds were fired during these attacks & as this was all ammunition left unburied and in order in Wood the guns were then retired to their reserve positions. 2 guns were destroyed by shell fire & 2 baseplates had to be abandoned when the guns were retired. A relief of 91st T.M.B arrived about 7 pm but the teams & guns were immediately almost	

2449 Wt. W14957/M90 750,000 1/16 J.B.C. & A. Forms/C.2118/12.

Army Form C. 2118.

Instructions regarding War Diaries and Intelligence Summaries are contained in F. S. Regs., Part II. and the Staff Manual respectively. Title Pages will be prepared in manuscript.

WAR DIARY
or
INTELLIGENCE SUMMARY
(Erase heading not required.)

Place	Date 1916	Hour	Summary of Events and Information	Remarks and references to Appendices
	AUGUST			
MONTAUBAN	31st	(Contd)	destroyed by shell fire. Orders were then received for 22nd T.M 3 to return to MONTAUBAN + this was done, Capt. PRESTON remaining behind to help reorganise the troops who were holding the enemy in the wood until about 5 am. 1st Sept.	
			Battery moved off to camp near BECORDEL, parties moving off from MONTAUBAN at 7.30 pm., 11.30 pm + finally CAPT. PRESTON + 2/LT. JONES at 6.30 am 1st Sept.	
			Rounds fired 250 Casualties 7 killed, 6 wounded. Weather fine.	
			Gallant service was rendered by No. 17338 Cpl Dow, 20th M/ters R. att? this Battery in rescuing + aiding wounded under very heavy shell fire.	
			TURKEY declares war on RUMANIA.	ERC

Instructions regarding War Diaries and Intelligence Summaries are contained in F. S. Regs., Part II. and the Staff Manual respectively. Title Pages will be prepared in manuscript.

WAR DIARY
or
INTELLIGENCE SUMMARY
(Erase heading not required.)

Army Form C. 2118.

7 Div. T M Brigade

Vol 4

Place	Date	Hour	Summary of Events and Information	Remarks and references to Appendices
PLOEGSTEERT	1916 Nov. 1		X battery engaged in cutting enemy wire	
	2	6 pm + 10 pm	Y battery joined in bombardment of enemy lines, operation [illegible] 38. Both guns were put out of action temporarily through failure of the adapter for [illegible] mechanisms.	
	3		X battery wire cutting, enemy retaliation very heavy, one position rendered useless by direct hit and two others isolated through the communication trenches being shattered	
	6		Z battery engaged during morning in [illegible] Afternoon [illegible] minutes duration	
	7 + 8		All batteries engaged in retaliation. Enemy T.M. fire kept well in hand	
	9		X + Z batteries retaliation. V + Y batteries engaged in operation [illegible]	
	10		Z battery dug new positions at Seaforth farm and afterwards registered for two guns.	
	13		In conjunction with artillery, all batteries joined in bombardment of Ploegsteert front	
	14/15/16		Firing in retaliation and daily subdued enemy T.M.S. [illegible] batteries + heavy [illegible]	
	15		Bombardment by Y.	
	17 to 25		Fired on enemy lines in retaliation.	
	26		Z Y [illegible] positions and moved guns to [illegible] sector	
	27		All batteries engaged in operations in conjunction with the artillery	
	29		X battery relieved by 25th Div. 2 guns in line handed over	
	30		V + Z batteries relieved by 25th Div. 2 guns of each battery being handed over in the line	

2449 Wt. W14957/M90 750,000 1/16 J.B.C. & A. Forms/C.2118/12.

H. C. Atkinson Captain
a/ DTMO

Instructions regarding War Diaries and Intelligence Summaries are contained in F. S. Regs., Part II. and the Staff Manual respectively. Title Pages will be prepared in manuscript.

WAR DIARY
or
INTELLIGENCE SUMMARY

(Erase heading not required.)

Army Form C. 2118.

Vol 5

Place	Date	Hour	Summary of Events and Information	Remarks and references to Appendices
			7th Bn 7th M. Brigade December 1916	

2449 Wt. W14957/M90 750,000 1/16 J.B.C. & A. Forms/C.2118/12.

Instructions regarding War Diaries and Intelligence Summaries are contained in F. S. Regs., Part II. and the Staff Manual respectively. Title Pages will be prepared in manuscript.

WAR DIARY
or
~~INTELLIGENCE~~ SUMMARY
(Erase heading not required.)

7th Div. Trench Mortar Brigade

Army Form C. 2118.

Place	Date	Hour	Summary of Events and Information	Remarks and references to Appendices
1916	Au 1		All 2" Batteries at PONT DE NIEPPE. Heavy battery at PLOEGSTEERT	
	3		Heavy battery moved to PONT DE NIEPPE	
	4		attached to 4 Sec. D.A.C. and moved by road to FLETRE	
	5		Rest at FLETRE.	
	6		By road to STEENBECQUE accomodated in billets	
	7		" " REBY — do —	
	8		Rest in billets at REBY	
	9		By road to MONCHY CAYEUX in billets for the night	
	10		— do — VACQUERIE LE BOUQ — do —	
	11		— do — AUTHIEULE — do —	
	12		— do — ACHEUX — do — All officers billet in BERTRANCOURT.	
	13 to 31.		Brigade attached to D.A.C. to provide fatigues and working parties. V 7 Battery to No 1 Section; X 7 " " 2 "; Y 7 " " 3 "; Z 7 " " 4 "	
	14		Guns in line taken over from 57 Div Trench Mortars	
			3 English and 1 French H.T.M. Taken over by V 7 Battery	
			2 – 2" TMs taken over by Z 7 battery and two guns [illegible]	

2449 Wt. W14957/M90 750,000 1/16 J.B.C. & A. Forms/C.2118/12.

A. G. Smith Capt
DTMO 7th Div.

Instructions regarding War Diaries and Intelligence Summaries are contained in F. S. Regs., Part II. and the Staff Manual respectively. Title Pages will be prepared in manuscript.

WAR DIARY
or
~~INTELLIGENCE SUMMARY~~
(Erase heading not required.)

Army Form C. 2118.

Continued — 7th Div. Trench Mortar Brigade

Place	Date 1916	Hour	Summary of Events and Information	Remarks and references to Appendices
	Dec 14		Guard of six men and 1 N.C.O put in billet in COLINCAMP by Y7 battery and three men and 1 N.C.O — do — HAMEL " Z7 " for the purpose of looking after the guns in the line.	
	18 to 19		Y7 battery removed one of the English Heavy T.M.s from the line. It had been damaged by shell fire and was returned to I.O.M. LOUVENCOURT.	
	19 & 20		Z7 battery removed the 2" mortars from the line and brought them back to ACHEUX.	
	19		T.M. officers transferred to billets in ACHEUX.	
	22		Two 2" mortars placed in position in STATION ALLEY	
	14th to 31st		All men from the batteries at work on fatigues for D.A.C and Town Major of ACHEUX daily.	

A. B. Smith Capt
DTMO 7th Division

2449 Wt. W14957/M90 750,000 1/16 J.B.C. & A. Forms/C.2118/12.

24. 8. 16

To D.A.G.
Base

Herewith War Diary of 20/1 & 20/2 T.M.B. from formation until amalgamation. It is necessarily brief as no records were kept. Further information can be obtained from 20th Brigade War Diary.

A. F. Mills Capt
O.C. 20th T.M.B.

See this for
File to June 2

7th DIVISION.

TRENCH MORTAR BRIGADE.

JANUARY 1917.

Instructions regarding War Diaries and Intelligence Summaries are contained in F. S. Regs., Part II. and the Staff Manual respectively. Title Pages will be prepared in manuscript.

WAR DIARY
or
INTELLIGENCE SUMMARY
(Erase heading not required.)

Army Form C. 2118.

Vol 7

7

Place	Date	Hour	Summary of Events and Information	Remarks and references to Appendices
			Original 7th Trench Mortar Brigade War Diary for January 1917	

2449 Wt. W14957/M90 750,000 1/16 J.B.C. & A. Forms/C.2118/12.

Army Form C. 2118.

Instructions regarding War Diaries and Intelligence Summaries are contained in F. S. Regs., Part II. and the Staff Manual respectively. Title Pages will be prepared in manuscript.

WAR DIARY
or
INTELLIGENCE SUMMARY

(Erase heading not required.) For. T.M. Bde.

Place	Date	Hour	Summary of Events and Information	Remarks and references to Appendices
In the Field	1/1/17		Brigade in Billets (out of action) at Acheux until 24th on fatigues for D.A.C. & Town Major	
	24/1/17		Moved to Billets at Amplier, on fatigues building Horse standings & Huts for 7th D.A. until 31st	
			1.2.17 [signature] Lt. R.F.A. for O.C. T.M. Bde.	

2449 Wt. W14957/M90 750,000 1/16 J.B.C. & A. Forms/C.2118/12.

Army Form C. 2118.

Instructions regarding War Diaries and Intelligence Summaries are contained in F. S. Regs., Part II. and the Staff Manual respectively. Title pages will be prepared in manuscript.

WAR DIARY

or

INTELLIGENCE SUMMARY.

(Erase heading not required.)

Place	Date	Hour	Summary of Events and Information	Remarks and references to Appendices
			Vol 7 Original Trench Mortar Brigade, 1st Division War Diary for February 1917	

A5834 Wt. W4973/M687 750,000 8/16 D. D. & L. Ltd. Forms/C.2118/13.

Army Form C. 2118.

Instructions regarding War Diaries and Intelligence Summaries are contained in F. S. Regs., Part II. and the Staff Manual respectively. Title Pages will be prepared in manuscript.

WAR DIARY
or
~~INTELLIGENCE SUMMARY~~
(Erase heading not required.)

For 7th D.A. Trench Mortars

Place	Date	Hour	Summary of Events and Information	Remarks and references to Appendices
In the Field	1.2.17		Brigade in Billets (out of action) at AMPLIER from 1.2.17 to 27.2.17 on fatigues building huts & horse standings at SARTON for 14th (Army) H.A Brigade and 22nd Bde R.F.A also for Town Major fixing bunks etc in barns.	
	27.2.17		Moved for AMPLIER to FORCEVILLE	

A.C. Smith Capt R.F.A
– D.T.M.O.

2449 Wt. W14957/M90 750,000 1/16 J.B.C. & A. Forms/C.2118/12.

Instructions regarding War Diaries and Intelligence Summaries are contained in F. S. Regs., Part II. and the Staff Manual respectively. Title pages will be prepared in manuscript.

~~WAR DIARY~~ or INTELLIGENCE SUMMARY.

(Erase heading not required.)

Army Form C. 2118.

7 D T M Btys

Vol 8

Place	Date	Hour	Summary of Events and Information	Remarks and references to Appendices
In the field	1-3-17		X. Y & Z. 7. T. M. Batteries in rest Billets at FORCEVILLE.	
	3 -		Batteries moved to MAILLY-MAILLET attached to 7th D.A.C. as working party	
	4 -		Moved up to BEAUCOURT-sur-ANCRE, on road repairs from there to PUISIEUX	
	7 -		Batteries withdrawn from BEAUCOURT to FORCEVILLE	
	8 -		Moved from FORCEVILLE and entrained at ACHEUX for HOUDAIN	
	10 -		Arrived at St. POL and billetted at Rest Camp.	
	11 -		Arrived at HOUDAIN. X. 7. T.M. Bty remaining there awaiting orders until 17th. Y. 7. T.M. Bty marched to Mont St ELOI and were attached to T.M. Group. 2nd Canadian Divn Arty. Z. 7. T.M. Bty marched to AMETTES and were attached to Reserve Divn Arty. remaining there on normal training until 22nd.	
	12 -		Y. 7. T.M. Bty. O.C & NCOs took over 4 Medium Gun emplacements Area A10.B3-6 A4 D4-6	
	14 -		Y. 7. T.M. Bty. Guns taken from MONT. St ELOI up to emplacements	
	15 -		Y. 7. T.M. Bty Guns prepared for action.	
	17 -		Y. 7. T.M. Bty in action wire cutting No of rounds fired 54. No. 46920, Gunner L. C. Ward. wounded accidentally whilst	

A5834 Wt. W4973/M687 750,000 8/16 D. D. & L. Ltd. Forms/C.2118/13.

Army Form C. 2118.

WAR DIARY
or
INTELLIGENCE SUMMARY.
(Erase heading not required.)

Instructions regarding War Diaries and Intelligence Summaries are contained in F. S. Regs., Part II. and the Staff Manual respectively. Title pages will be prepared in manuscript.

Place	Date	Hour	Summary of Events and Information	Remarks and references to Appendices
	17.3.17	(contd)	cleaning his revolver, and removed to Hospital. Owing to scarcity of dug outs, Gun detachments had to return at night to Camp at MONT St ELOI.	
			X. 7. T.M. Bty moved forward from HOUDAIN to ECOIVRES and were attached to T.M. Group 1st Canadian Division Artillery.	
	19.3.17		X. 7. T.M. Bty. commenced work on their gunpits, some of which were partially completed, the frontage of the Bty lying from a point 800 yards N. of ECURIE, 220 yards northwards.	
	19 to 26th		Y. 7. T.M. Bty continued in action. No of rounds fired 107. Dug out being found for two gun detachments.	
	22 to 31		Z. 7. T.M. Bty left AMETTES for BOUVIGNY, were attached to V.R.T.M Bty (Heavy) on fatigues digging gun emplacements.	
	24 to 31		X. 7. T.M. Bty in action, commenced wire-cutting with 2 guns and continued daily with an average rate of about 60 Rds per day. On the 21st suffered 4 casualties on ~~amn~~ ammunition fatigue:- No. 73636. Gr. Arnold. A. No. 66594 Gr Bateman. No. 78133 Gr. Daley. E. No. 14298 Gr. Mann. J. (all wounded)	

A5834 Wt. W4973/M687 750,000 8/16 D. D. & L. Ltd. Forms/C.2118/13.

Army Form C. 2118.

WAR DIARY
or
INTELLIGENCE SUMMARY.
(Erase heading not required.)

Instructions regarding War Diaries and Intelligence Summaries are contained in F. S. Regs., Part II. and the Staff Manual respectively. Title pages will be prepared in manuscript.

Place	Date	Hour	Summary of Events and Information	Remarks and references to Appendices
	29 to 31.		X. 7. T.M. Bty (contd) we suffered two casualties No. 68138 Gr. J. Williams (killed & No 66283 Br Brooks. G. (wounded) caused from a premature which also wrecked gun position. Meanwhile the other two gun pits were completed and guns brought into action. The wire-cutting was quite successful, especially on the right sector where the wire was thin and observation excellent. The Canadians had divided the divisional frontage into two groups for T.M. purposes each under a group commander who was responsible for the firing of his own group, while the ammunition supply was in the hands of two officers, who arranged all carrying parties & the supply of bombs to the gun-pits. No of rounds fired 532.	
	27th		Y. 7. T. M. Bty suffered 5 Casualties No 3305 Sgt. T. Berry No 22552 Bombr. C. Byron (killed) No 74944 Gr Pilcher J. No. 71627 Gr Page. W.R. No 103668 Gr Hayes. R (wounded) owing to a premature explosion at No. 3 Gun Mowcop Trench.	

A5834 Wt. W4973/M687 750,000 8/16 D. D. & L. Ltd. Forms/C.2118/13.

Army Form C. 2118.

WAR DIARY
or
INTELLIGENCE SUMMARY.
(Erase heading not required.)

Instructions regarding War Diaries and Intelligence Summaries are contained in F. S. Regs., Part II. and the Staff Manual respectively. Title pages will be prepared in manuscript.

Place	Date	Hour	Summary of Events and Information	Remarks and references to Appendices
In the Field	28 to 31		Y. 7. T.M. Bty continued wire cutting. No of rounds fired 64. Owing to Rifle Mechanism trouble the battery was constantly put out of action for a time but was remedied by the use of cartridges filled with Black Powder.	
			Total Casualties. Killed. Wounded.	
			X. 7. T.M.B. — 1. 5	
			Y 7 " — 2 4	
			Z 7 " — – –	
			Total Rounds fired	
			X 7. TmB. 532	
			Y 7. T.M.B. 325	
			Z 7 " Nil.	
			A.C. Smith Capt. R.F.A. D.T.M.O 7th D.A	

A5834 Wt. W4973/M687 750,000 8/16 D. D. & L. Ltd. Forms/C.2118/13.

Army Form C. 2118.

Instructions regarding War Diaries and Intelligence Summaries are contained in F. S. Regs., Part II. and the Staff Manual respectively. Title pages will be prepared in manuscript.

WAR DIARY
or
INTELLIGENCE SUMMARY.
(Erase heading not required.)

Place	Date	Hour	Summary of Events and Information	Remarks and references to Appendices
In the Field	1.3.17		V. 7. T.M. Bty in rest Billet at FORCEVILLE	
	3.3.17		Moved to MAILLY-MAILLET attached to D.A.C. as working Party	
	4.3.17		Moved to BEAUCOURT-sur-ANCRE on road repairs from there to PUISIEUX	
	11.3.17		Moved to FORCEVILLE on fatigues Ammunition Dump between BERTRANCOURT & FORCEVILLE	
	23.3.17 to 31.3.17		Moved up to PUISIEUX on fatigues salvaging Ammunition	

A C Smith
Capt. R.F.A.
D.T.M.O.
7th D.A.

A5834 Wt. W4973/M687 750,000 8/16 D. D. & L. Ltd. Forms/C.2118/13.

Instructions regarding War Diaries and Intelligence Summaries are contained in F. S. Regs., Part II. and the Staff Manual respectively. Title pages will be prepared in manuscript.

WAR DIARY
or
INTELLIGENCE SUMMARY.
(Erase heading not required.)

Army Form C. 2118.

Place	Date	Hour	Summary of Events and Information	Remarks and references to Appendices
In the Field	1-4-17 to 8-4/17		X. 7. T. M. Bty continued wire cutting operations in accordance with last months scheme but increased rate of firing the totals for 3rd 4th and 5th exceeding 160 rounds. Another gun was put in action on the left sector to cover wire previously allotted to another Battery. On the 4th a premature occurred at one position and wrecked same, proper precautions since the former premature of last month prevented the loss of more than one N.C.O. No 80888 Cpl G. Lewis (slightly wounded). Fortunately all the wire on this guns frontage had been practically accounted for. We continued firing until 8th (ZERO-1) and then withdrew all personnel that evening. Total number of rounds fired during these 8 days 793. Of the five positions used only one was properly covered in and protected, the rest were open ones, two being with no head cover at all. We had, however two good observations posts and were able to do practically all firing by	

A5834 Wt. W4973/M687 750,000 8/16 D. D. & L. Ltd. Forms/C.2118/13.

Army Form C. 2118.

WAR DIARY
or
INTELLIGENCE SUMMARY.
(Erase heading not required.)

Instructions regarding War Diaries and Intelligence Summaries are contained in F. S. Regs., Part II. and the Staff Manual respectively. Title pages will be prepared in manuscript.

Place	Date	Hour	Summary of Events and Information	Remarks and references to Appendices
In the Field			telephone.	
	1/4/17 to 8/4/17		Withdrawn from trenches to camp at ECOIVRES and remained at rest until 20th	
			Y. 7. T. M. Bty. Continued in action wire cutting, front line area A 10 B 3-6 to A 4. D 4-6. Battery were withdrawn from trenches at 4 P.M. on the 8th prior to coming attack and were encamped at MONT St ELOI at rest until 18th. when guns and all stores were removed from the trenches. Rounds fired 318.	
			Z. 7. T. M. Bty. Attached to V. R (heavy) T. M. Bty. Reserve Division Arty. digging gun emplacements and general fatigues.	
	20/4/17		X. Y. & Z. T. M. Batteries moved to BUSNES and remained at rest until 30th	

A5834 Wt. W4973/M687 750,000 8/16 D. D. & L. Ltd. Forms/C.2118/13.

Instructions regarding War Diaries and Intelligence Summaries are contained in F. S. Regs., Part II. and the Staff Manual respectively. Title pages will be prepared in manuscript.

WAR DIARY
or
INTELLIGENCE SUMMARY.
(Erase heading not required.)

Army Form C. 2118.

Place	Date	Hour	Summary of Events and Information	Remarks and references to Appendices
In the Field	30/4/17		Moved to rejoin Division at ACHIET. le GRAND arriving at FREVENT.	
			Rounds fired. Casualties	
			X. 7. Tm Bty: 793 X. 7. T.M. Bty	
			Y. 7 " 318 1 NCO (Wounded slightly)	
			1/5/17 A. C. Smith Capt. R.F.A. D.T.M.O. 7th D.A.	

A5834 Wt.W4973/M687 750,000 8/16 D. D. & L. Ltd. Forms/C.2118/13.

Instructions regarding War Diaries and Intelligence Summaries are contained in F. S. Regs., Part II. and the Staff Manual respectively. Title pages will be prepared in manuscript.

WAR DIARY

or

INTELLIGENCE SUMMARY.

(Erase heading not required.)

Army Form C. 2118.

Place	Date	Hour	Summary of Events and Information	Remarks and references to Appendices
In the Field	1/4/17 to 16/4/17		V. 7. T. M. Bty at PUISIEUX on fatigues salvaging ammunition	
	17/4/17 to 30/4/17		Moved to ERVILLIERS on fatigues at 7. D.A.C. ammunition Dump	
			1-5-17	
			A.C. Smith Capt. R.F.A. D.T.M.O. 7th D.A.	

A5834 Wt. W4973/M687 750,000 8/16 D. D. & L. Ltd. Forms/C.2118/13.

7th DIVISION.

TRENCH MORTAR BATTERY.

MAY 1917.

Instructions regarding War Diaries and Intelligence Summaries are contained in F. S. Regs., Part II. and the Staff Manual respectively. Title pages will be prepared in manuscript.

WAR DIARY
or
~~INTELLIGENCE SUMMARY.~~

(Erase heading not required.)

Army Form C. 2118.

7 D T M Bty
Vol 10

Place	Date	Hour	Summary of Events and Information	Remarks and references to Appendices
In the Field	1-5-17 to 8-5-17		V. 7. T. M. Bty at ERVILLIERS on fatigues at 7th D.A.C ammunition DUMP	
	1-5-17		X. Y & Z. T.M. Batteries moved from FREVENT by motor transport to ACHIET-le-GRAND.	
	3-5-17 to 8.5-17		X. Y & Z. T.M. Batteries on general fatigues and 7th DAC ammunition dump.	
	2-5-17		V. 7. T. M. Bty. 2 Officers and 22 men to School of Trench Mortars Vth Army on course of 2" T. Ms.	
	9-5-17		V. X. Y & Z. T.M. Batteries moved to Mory. Z. 7. T.M. Bty going into action at BULLECOURT. remainder of Batteries carrying bombs, stores etc	
	10-5-17		V. X & Y. 7. T.M. Bty. fatigues carrying bombs etc for Z 7. T.M. Bty	
	11-5-17		Two casualties Y. 7. T.M. Bty at U. 28 a. 3. 1 No. 11070 Br. A. Morris No. 55742 Gr. A. Hampton. both wounded (H.E.) to Hospital 11/5/17	
	11-5-17		Z. 7. T.M. Bty in action with two guns at U 28. A. 3. 1. Fired on targets U 27. B. 44. U 27. B. 53 Rounds fired 10 Strong retaliation. Morning fairly quiet 2pm - 6pm moderate	

A5834 Wt. W4973/M687 750,000 8/16 D. D. & L. Ltd. Forms/C.2118/13.

Instructions regarding War Diaries and Intelligence Summaries are contained in F. S. Regs., Part II. and the Staff Manual respectively. Title pages will be prepared in manuscript.

WAR DIARY
or
~~INTELLIGENCE SUMMARY.~~
(Erase heading not required.)

Army Form C. 2118.

Place	Date	Hour	Summary of Events and Information	Remarks and references to Appendices
In the Field	12/5/17		Z. 7. T. M. Bty in action at U. 28. a. 3. 1 fired on strong point U 27 b - 60 - 25 also on trench Junction T 27. b. 75. 60. Rounds fired 15	
	13/5/17		Z. 7. T. M. Bty in action fired on strong point U 27. b. 60. 25 as ordered. Rounds fired 20.	
	14/5/17		Z. 7. T. M. Bty in action fired on strong point Rounds fired 10. relieved at night by X. 7. T. M. Bty, who had one casualty No. 790 67 Dr Vale W (Wounded to Hospital)	
	16/5/17		X. 7. T. M. Bty relieved by 58th Divn. T. Ms. V. X. Y & Z. T. M. Btys moved to BAHAGNIES, 2 Officers & 32 men V. 7. T. M. Bty rejoined from School of Mortars & camped at ERVILLERS DUMP.	
	17/5/17 to 31-5-17		V. 7. T. M. Bty on fatigues at ERVILLERS DUMP ~~for~~ 7th D. A. C.	

Instructions regarding War Diaries and Intelligence Summaries are contained in F. S. Regs., Part II. and the Staff Manual respectively. Title pages will be prepared in manuscript.

WAR DIARY
or
~~INTELLIGENCE SUMMARY.~~
(Erase heading not required.)

Army Form C. 2118.

Place	Date	Hour	Summary of Events and Information	Remarks and references to Appendices
In the Field	17/5/17		X.Y & Z. T. M. Bty. on fatigues cleaning guns, stores & camp 2/Lt. J. Addis Z. 7. TMBty proceeded on leave to United Kingdom. Inspected by G.O.C. R.A. 7th D.A.	
	18/5/17		X.Y & Z. T. M. Bs. fatigues and Bath Parades 2/Lt. W.R.H. Downes Y. 7. TMBty with 2 O.Rs V. 7. TMBty to School of Mortars V.th Army.	
	19/5/17 20/5/17 21/5/17		Normal training X.Y & Z TMBs	
	22/5/17 to 24/5/17		X.Y & Z TMBs fatigues for Camp Commandant SAPIGNIES and 7th D.A.C. ERVILLERS DUMP.	
	25/5/17 to 27/5/17		X.Y & Z T.M.Bs fatigues for 7th D.A.C. at ERVILLERS DUMP	

A5834 Wt. W4973/M687 750,000 8/16 D. D. & L. Ltd. Forms/C.2118/13.

Instructions regarding War Diaries and Intelligence Summaries are contained in F. S. Regs., Part II. and the Staff Manual respectively. Title pages will be prepared in manuscript.

WAR DIARY
or
~~INTELLIGENCE~~ SUMMARY.
(Erase heading not required.)

Army Form C. 2118.

Place	Date	Hour	Summary of Events and Information	Remarks and references to Appendices
In the field	28/5/17 to 31/5/17		X. Y & Z. T.M. Bs. Normal Training :- Physical Exercise Marching Drill, Rifle Drill, Gun Drill, Rifle & Revolver Practice, Route Marches etc.	
	28/5/17		Lt. J. Addis Z.7. T.M. Bty appointed Capt & posted to V.7. T.M. Bty.	
			Capt. A. J. Rover V.7. T.M. Bty appointed Lieut & posted to Z.7. T.M. Bty.	
	31/5/17		Capt. J. Addis rejoined from leave	

In the field
31 - 5 - 17

A. C. Smith
Capt. R. F. A.
D. T. M. O
7th D. A.

A5834 Wt. W4973/M687 750,000 8/16 D. D. & L. Ltd. Forms/C.2118/13.

7th DIVISION.

TRENCH MORTAR BATTERY.

JUNE 1917.

Instructions regarding War Diaries and Intelligence Summaries are contained in F. S. Regs., Part II. and the Staff Manual respectively. Title pages will be prepared in manuscript.

WAR DIARY
or
INTELLIGENCE SUMMARY.
(Erase heading not required.)

Army Form C. 2118.

7 D T M Btys
Vol XI

Place	Date	Hour	Summary of Events and Information	Remarks and references to Appendices
In the Field	1/6/17 to 2/6/17		X.Y & Z. 7. T.M. Batteries at BEHAGNIES. Normal training consisting of Physical Training, Marching Drill, Rifle Drill, Rifle & revolver practice, Bomb throwing	
	3/6/17		Capt. A.G. Smith. D.T.M.O. granted leave of absence to United Kingdom.	
	4/6/17		2/Lt. A.M.P. Wilson. X.7. T.M. Bty. to School of Mortars 5th Corps on course for D.T.M.s.	
	4/6/17 to 9/6/17		2/Lt. H.V. Lee and 2/Lt. W.H. Davies on course of instruction at 7th Bde.	
	8/6/17 to 13/6/17		X.Y & Z. T.M. Batteries on fatigues making New Dump BEHAGNIES.	
	15/6/17		Capt. A.G. Smith. D.T.M.O. rejoined from leave.	

A5834 Wt. W4973/M687 750,000 8/16 D. D. & L. Ltd. Forms/C.2118/13.

Army Form C. 2118.

WAR DIARY
or
INTELLIGENCE SUMMARY

(Erase heading not required.)

Instructions regarding War Diaries and Intelligence Summaries are contained in F. S. Regs., Part II. and the Staff Manual respectively. Title Pages will be prepared in manuscript.

Place	Date	Hour	Summary of Events and Information	Remarks and references to Appendices
Battle Field	13.6.17 to 20.6.17		X. Y + Z. 7. T.M. Batteries on fatigues clearing up camp 58th D.A.C. + Town Major ERVILLERS.	
	18/6/17		2/Lt. A.M.P. Wilson. X. 7. T.M. Bty rejoined from course at Vth Army T.M. School	
	11.6.17 to 16.6.17		2/Lt. G. W. C. Parker + 2/Lt. F. Stebington on course of instruction at Hdqtrs. 7th D.A.C.	
	17.6.17		No. 85169 Corpl. C. A. G. Love. Z. 7. T.M. Bty to Infantry School 5th Corps for course of instruction.	
	20/6/17		2/Lt. J. C. Stevens. Y. 7. T.M. Bty granted leave of absence to United Kingdom.	
	18/6/17 to 23/6/17		2/Lt. A.M.P. Wilson + 2/Lt. A. P. Rawes on course of instruction at Headquarters. 7th D.A.C.	

2449 Wt. W14957/M90 750,000 1/16 J.B.C. & A. Forms/C.2118/12.

Army Form C. 2118.

WAR DIARY
or
INTELLIGENCE SUMMARY

(Erase heading not required.)

Instructions regarding War Diaries and Intelligence Summaries are contained in F. S. Regs., Part II. and the Staff Manual respectively. Title Pages will be prepared in manuscript.

Place	Date	Hour	Summary of Events and Information	Remarks and references to Appendices
In the Field	20/6/17 to 22/6/17	–	X Y & Z. 7. Tm Batteries on fatigues clearing old camp for 58th Div ab & on town fatigues ERVILLERS for Town Major	
	1/6/17 to 23/6/17		V. " Tm Bty on fatigues working Ammunition Dump at ERVILLERS for 7th D.A.C.	
	23/6/17		V. 7. T.M. Bty relieved V. 58th T.M. Bty taking over 4. 9.45" T.Ms. 1 in action at U 21. C. 3. 2 (Sheet 51 B) and 3. T.Ms at 58th T.M. Camp near MORY. Ammunition taken over 56 rounds.	
			Z. 7. T.M. Bty relieved 2" T.M. Bty 58 Divn taking over 2 guns in line U 21 D. 6. 0. Ammunition taken over 145 rounds.	
			X. 7. T.M. B'y went into line staying in dug outs at MORT HOMME. CROISELLES ROAD.	
	24/6/17		Remainder of Brigade moved from BEHAGNIES and took over camp occupied by 58th T.M. Bde. near MORY.	
			V. 7. T. M. Bty Two detachments with gun at U. 21. C. 3. 2. Gun was found to be in unsuitable position with no proper bed	

2449 Wt. W14957/M90 750,000 1/16 J.B.C. & A. Forms/C.2118/12.

Army Form C. 2118.

Instructions regarding War Diaries and Intelligence Summaries are contained in F. S. Regs., Part II. and the Staff Manual respectively. Title pages will be prepared in manuscript.

WAR DIARY
or
INTELLIGENCE SUMMARY.

(Erase heading not required.)

Place	Date	Hour	Summary of Events and Information	Remarks and references to Appendices
In the Field	26/6/17		V. 7. T.M. Bty continued also [illegible] [illegible] dug out & shaft had been started by 58th [illegible] this position chosen 30 yds N of old [illegible] [illegible] [illegible] [illegible] gun [illegible] & dug out	
			Two detachments started work on new emplacement and dug outs for position at V. 13. D. 25–18.	
			X. 7. T.M. Bty commenced work on emplacement, dug outs etc for positions at V. 14. C. 2. 9 and V. 14. C. 5. 4	
	24/6/17		Z. 7. T.M. Bty commenced work on emplacements dug outs etc for position at V. 21. D. 6. 0	
	26/6/17 to 28/6/17		V. X + Z. 7. Tm Bty continue work on gun positions etc. No 40932 [illegible] [illegible] V. 7. Tm Bty to hospital wounded 26th inst. No 53773 [illegible] Chater W.H. V. 7. Tm Bty to hospital wounded 27th inst	
	28/6/17		V. X + Z. 7. Tm Batteries continue work on gun positions dug outs etc X. 7 Tm Bty commencing on 3rd position	

A5834 Wt. W4973/M687 750,000 8/16 D. D. & L. Ltd. Forms/C.2118/13.

Army Form C. 2118.

Instructions regarding War Diaries and Intelligence Summaries are contained in F. S. Regs., Part II. and the Staff Manual respectively. Title pages will be prepared in manuscript.

WAR DIARY
or
INTELLIGENCE SUMMARY.

(Erase heading not required.)

Place	Date	Hour	Summary of Events and Information	Remarks and references to Appendices
In the Field	28/6/17		Y. 7. T.M. Bty went into line & commenced digging emergency positions at ECOUST at C. 2. D	
	29/6/17		V. X. Y & Z. 7. T.M. Batteries continue work on gun positions dug outs etc	
	30/6/17		V. X. & Z. 7. T.M. Batteries continue work on gun positions dug outs etc.	
			Y. 7. T.M. Bty took 4 guns into action at Emergency position at ECOUST at C. 2. D	

A. B. [illegible] Capt. R.F.A.
D.T.M.O.

A5834 Wt. W4973/M687 750,000 8/16 D. D. & L. Ltd. Forms/C.2118/13.

7th DIVISION.

TRENCH MORTAR BATTERY.

JULY 1917.

Instructions regarding War Diaries and Intelligence Summaries are contained in F. S. Regs., Part II. and the Staff Manual respectively. Title pages will be prepared in manuscript.

WAR DIARY
or
INTELLIGENCE SUMMARY.
(Erase heading not required.)

Army Form C. 2118.

7 Div TM Btys
Vol 12

Place	Date	Hour	Summary of Events and Information	Remarks and references to Appendices
Shrapnel Field	1/7/17 to 6/7/17		V. 7. T.M. Bty. Work continued on position at U 21. C. 3. 2 Gun pit deepened & timbering commenced. 2nd Entrance complete with 4 frames in position. Work also continued on position U 13. D 25 - 48. Trenches to gun pit and dug out deepened to 6 ft & gun pit to 8 ft. A third position 100 yds N of U 13. D. 25. 48 has been started but been discontinued as there are only 2 guns in possession. Will be proceeded with on completion of other two positions.	
			X. 7. T.M. Bty. Continued work on emplacements, dug outs etc at positions U. 14. C. 2.9. U. 14. C. 5. 4. and U 14. C. 6. 1.	
			Y. 7. T.M. Bty. In action with 4 mortars at C. 2. D. Emergency position 2 guns with bomb stores and 10 rounds per gun.	
			Z. 7. T.M. Bty continued work on emplacements, dug outs at positions at U 21. D. 7. 0. One dug out entrance completed & tunnel advanced at position JOYRIDE. Emplacement completed & ready for gun. Cellar & tunnel to gun position cleared at position in MARE ST	
	6/7/17		V. 7. T.M. Bty. X position (U 21. C. 3. 2.) Work continued. Gun put in action. Casualty. No. 71048. Gr. Lynch. J. wounded. (since died of wounds)	

A5834 Wt. W4973/M687 750,000 8/16 D. D. & L. Ltd. Forms/C.2118/13.

Instructions regarding War Diaries and Intelligence Summaries are contained in F. S. Regs., Part II. and the Staff Manual respectively. Title pages will be prepared in manuscript.

WAR DIARY
or
INTELLIGENCE SUMMARY.
(Erase heading not required.)

Army Form C. 2118.

Place	Date	Hour	Summary of Events and Information	Remarks and references to Appendices
In the Field	6/7/17		X.7. T.M. Bty. Work continued on E + F positions, Guns in action ready to fire. G + H positions.	
			Y.7. T.M. Bty. One gun taken out of action at Emergency position ECOUST to be put in X position (V. 7. T. M. Bty)	
			Z.7. T. M. Bty. Work continued on A + B. positions	
	7/7/17 to 13/7/17		V.7. T.M. Bty. X position. Gun taken out of action and 2" put in to replace by Y.7. T.M. Bty ready to fire with 30 rounds ammunition. Work continued on Dug Outs. Z. position work continued on gun pit, dug outs etc.	
			X.7. T.M. Bty. E and F positions. Ammunition recesses completed to hold 40 and 70 bombs. G and H position Guns in action with 30 bombs each ready to fire when ordered. Work continued on dug outs.	
			Y.7. T.M. Bty. 1 Gun in action at X position ready to fire when required. 3 guns in action ECOUST emergency position.	

A5834 Wt. W4973/M687 750,000 8/16 D. D. & L. Ltd. Forms/C.2118/13.

Instructions regarding War Diaries and Intelligence Summaries are contained in F. S. Regs., Part II. and the Staff Manual respectively. Title pages will be prepared in manuscript.

WAR DIARY
or
INTELLIGENCE SUMMARY.
(Erase heading not required.)

Army Form C. 2118.

Place	Date	Hour	Summary of Events and Information	Remarks and references to Appendices
In the Field	7/7/17 to 13/7/17		Z.7. Tm Bty. Work continued in A & B position. Guns in action ready to fire.	
	14/7/17 to 15/7/17		Z.7. T.M. Bty. Two 2" T.Ms in action, in conjunction with Infty Raid, forming a block on BOYS TRENCH on the left of the GORDONS raid. These two guns only fired 20 rounds, being greatly hampered by faulty ammunition taken over from 58th Divn. Both the charges and explosives were damp but as far as could be observed all the Bombs burst. One round failed to clear the parapet but fortunately did not explode. When the bomb was taken out it was found that the charge was only smouldering.	
			Y.7. T.M. Bty. The 2" T.M in X (heavy) position fired 40 rounds with good results, as far as could be seen, on MEBUS U21.A.3.1 and MEBUS U21.A.4.1.	

A5834 Wt. W4973/M687 750,000 8/16 D. D. & L. Ltd. Forms/C.2118/13.

Instructions regarding War Diaries and Intelligence Summaries are contained in F. S. Regs., Part II. and the Staff Manual respectively. Title pages will be prepared in manuscript.

WAR DIARY
or
INTELLIGENCE SUMMARY.
(Erase heading not required.)

Army Form C. 2118.

Place	Date	Hour	Summary of Events and Information	Remarks and references to Appendices
In the field	14/7/17 to 15/7/17		X. 7. T. M. Bty. G position fired 26 rounds in conjunction with raid by S. STAFFORDS. the 26th round being a premature which put the gun out of action, but fortunately no casualties. H. position fired 30 rounds in conjunction with same raid. Both guns came in for enemy barrage which blew in trenches and greatly hindered them keeping up a good rate of fire. A report of the premature of "G" position was forwarded.	
	17/7/17		V. 7. T. M. Bty (X position) 2" in action) Work continued on dug out. An 8" enemy shell landed beside gun pit, blowing in trenches leading to it. Z. position. Dug out completed. Recess to hold ammunition for 50 - 9.45 bombs, completed. X. 7. T. M. Bty. Worked on relaying beds, clearing and revetting the trenches smashed in by enemy barrage.	

Army Form C. 2118.

Instructions regarding War Diaries and Intelligence Summaries are contained in F. S. Regs., Part II. and the Staff Manual respectively. Title pages will be prepared in manuscript.

WAR DIARY
or
INTELLIGENCE SUMMARY.

(Erase heading not required.)

Place	Date	Hour	Summary of Events and Information	Remarks and references to Appendices
In the field	17/1/17		X. 7. T.M. Bty. (contd) and premature 14/15th inst.	
			Y. 7. T.M. Bty. 1 gun in action in x position (Hy) and 3 guns in emergency position ECOUST.	
			Z. 7. T.M. Bty. Second gun put in action at B. position in other end of cellar.	
	18/1/17		V. X Y + Z. T.M. Batteries continued work on dug outs etc.	
	19/1/17		Z. 7. T.M. Bty fired 10 rounds with silencer at BOVIS TRENCH at U 21. D. 5. 6.	
	20/1/17		V. X. Y + Z. T. M. Batteries continued work on dug outs etc.	
			Z. 7. T. M. Bty fired 10 rounds with silencer at U 21. D. 5. 6 and along BOVIS TRENCH.	
			Y. 7. T. M. Bty. took out gun from x position also 3 guns from emergency position at ECOUST and battery returned to T.M. Camp. MORY COPSE.	

A5834 Wt. W4973/M687 750,000 8/16 D. D. & L. Ltd. Forms/C.2118/13.

Army Form C. 2118.

Instructions regarding War Diaries and Intelligence Summaries are contained in F. S. Regs., Part II. and the Staff Manual respectively. Title pages will be prepared in manuscript.

WAR DIARY
or
INTELLIGENCE SUMMARY.
(Erase heading not required.)

Place	Date	Hour	Summary of Events and Information	Remarks and references to Appendices
In the Field	20/7/17		V. 7. T.M. Bty replaced 9.45" gun in X position	
	21/7/17		All batteries continued work on dug outs etc	
			X. 7. Tm Bty. fired 10 rounds from G position on V.14.C.9.9. two direct hits being observed on junction of FAG ALLEY and TUNNEL TRENCH.	
			Z. 7. Tm Bty fired 4 rounds on V 14. D. 4. 7 and 6 rounds on V 21. D. 5. 6 and along BOVIS TRENCH.	
	22/7/17		V. + X. 7. T.M. Bty. Continued work on dug outs etc.	
			Y. 7. Tm Bty at MORY COPSE on Camp and Brigade fatigues getting material and ammunition to guns.	
			Z. 7. Tm Bty fired 40 rounds, in conjunction with Infantry raid on V 21. D. 6. 0 and V 21. D. 4. 7.	
	23/7/17		V. X. + Z. Tm Batteries. Continued work on dug outs etc	

A5834 Wt. W4973/M687 750,000 8/16 D. D. & L. Ltd. Forms/C.2118/13.

Army Form C. 2118.

Instructions regarding War Diaries and Intelligence Summaries are contained in F. S. Regs., Part II. and the Staff Manual respectively. Title pages will be prepared in manuscript.

WAR DIARY
or
INTELLIGENCE SUMMARY.

(Erase heading not required.)

Place	Date	Hour	Summary of Events and Information	Remarks and references to Appendices
In the field	23/7/17		X. 7. T. M. Bty. fired 13 rounds on V 14. C. 95. 70. Rounds were observed to drop on parapet or in TRENCH.	
			Z. 7. Tm Bty fired 10 rounds with Silencer on V 14. D. 5. 6 and along BOVIS TRENCH.	
	24/7/17		V. 7. T. M. Bty. fired for registration on MEBUS at V 14. D. 98. 00 also fired on suspected "MINENWERFER" at V 20. B. 80. 70. and obtained 2 direct hits on enemy front line. 6 Rounds fired	
			Z. 7. Tm Bty fired with silencer from "B" position on V 21. D 5. 6. and along BOVIS TRENCH.	
	25/7/17		V. X+Z 7. Tm Bty continued work on dug outs etc	
			Z. 7. Tm Bty fired 10 rounds with silencer on V 21. D. 5. 6. Enemy had one direct hit on B position doing little damage.	
	26/7/17		V. X + Z. 7. T. M. Batteries continued work on dug outs etc.	

A5834 Wt. W4973/M687 750,000 8/16 D. D. & L. Ltd. Forms/C.2118/13.

Instructions regarding War Diaries and Intelligence Summaries are contained in F. S. Regs., Part II. and the Staff Manual respectively. Title pages will be prepared in manuscript.

WAR DIARY
or
INTELLIGENCE SUMMARY.
(Erase heading not required.)

Army Form C. 2118.

Place	Date	Hour	Summary of Events and Information	Remarks and references to Appendices
In the Field	16/7/17		Z. 7. Tm Bty 10 Rounds were fired from B. position on BOVIS TRENCH at U 21. D. 4. 7. and U 21. D. 70. 55. Infantry reported that cries were heard after one round.	
	27/7/17		V X & Z. 7. Tm Batteries continued work on dug outs etc	
		2.40pm to 7.10pm	X. 7. Tm Battery fired 30 rounds on TUNNEL TRENCH & MEBUS at U 14. C. 95. 55. MEBUS U 14. D. 1. 5 and machine gun at U 20. B. 20. 85. 9 direct hits on TUNNEL TRENCH were observed.	
	27/7/17		Z. 7. T. M. Bty fired 10 rounds on BOVIS TRENCH at U 21. D 4. 7 and U 21. D. 70. 55.	
	27/7/17		V. 7. T. M. Bty fired 6 rounds on MEBUS at U 21. A. 60. 35. One round dropped near the MEBUS and one direct hit on trench 30 yards in rear	
	28/7/17		V, X. Y & Z. 7. Tm Batteries. continued work on dug outs etc.	

A5834 Wt. W4973/M687 750,000 8/16 D. D. & L. Ltd. Forms/C.2118/13.

Instructions regarding War Diaries and Intelligence Summaries are contained in F. S. Regs., Part II. and the Staff Manual respectively. Title pages will be prepared in manuscript.

WAR DIARY
or
INTELLIGENCE SUMMARY.
(Erase heading not required.)

Army Form C. 2118.

Place	Date	Hour	Summary of Events and Information	Remarks and references to Appendices
In the Field	29/7/17.		V. & Z. 7. T.M.Bs continued work on dug outs	
			X. 7. T.M. Battery relieved in the trenches by Y. 7 & returned to T.M. camp at MORY COPSE.	
			Y. 7. T.M. Battery fired 10 rounds from G position on junction of FAG ALLEY and TUNNEL TRENCH and dispersed enemy wiring party. H. position fired 10 rounds at MEBUS U 14. D. 00. 50.	
			Z. 7. T.M. Bty fired 10 rounds from B. position at U 21. D. 4. 5 and U 21. D. 7. 5.	
	30/7/17		V. 7. T.M. Bty. fired 5 rounds from X position on TUNNEL TRENCH at U 20. B. 7. 8. Two rounds hit trench but both were blind.	
			X. 7. T.M. Bty fired 10 rounds from F. position on MEBUS at U 14. 0. 5. 10 rounds from G position on junction of FAG ALLEY and TUNNEL TRENCH at U 14. C. 8. 9. 9 rounds from H. position on junction of FAG ALLEY and TUNNEL TRENCH.	

A5834 Wt. W4973/M687 750,000 8/16 D. D. & L. Ltd. Forms/C.2118/13.

Instructions regarding War Diaries and Intelligence Summaries are contained in F. S. Regs., Part II. and the Staff Manual respectively. Title pages will be prepared in manuscript.

WAR DIARY
or
INTELLIGENCE SUMMARY.
(Erase heading not required.)

Army Form C. 2118.

Place	Date	Hour	Summary of Events and Information	Remarks and references to Appendices
In the field	30/7/17	4 am	Y. 7. T.M. Bty (contd) The ninth round being a premature which put the gun temporarily out of action and wounded the No. 1. No. 54362. Corpl Dow. H J to Hospital (wounded)	
		8pm	G position fired 6 rounds on U 14. C. 95. 60 in retaliation for enemy pineapple	
	31/7/17		V. 7. T.M. Bty. fired 7 rounds at 7.30pm to 8.5pm on TUNNEL TRENCH with good effect. 3 direct hits were observed at U 20. B. 7. 8 and one at U 20. B. 85. 70.	
			Y. 7. T. M. Bty. fired 30 rounds from F & G positions on TUNNEL TRENCH at U 14. B. 90. 90 and U 14. D 00. 65.	
			Z. 7. T. M. Bty. fired 10 rounds with silencer on BOVIS TRENCH at U 21. D. 4. 5 and U 21. D. 7. 5	
	29/7/17 to 31/7/17		X. 7. T. M. Bty. on fatigues supplying ammunition & material to other batteries in action	

A5834 Wt. W4973/M687 750,000 8/16 D. D. & L. Ltd. Forms/C.2118/13.

Instructions regarding War Diaries and Intelligence Summaries are contained in F. S. Regs., Part II. and the Staff Manual respectively. Title pages will be prepared in manuscript.

WAR DIARY
or
INTELLIGENCE SUMMARY.
(Erase heading not required.)

Army Form C. 2118.

Place	Date	Hour	Summary of Events and Information	Remarks and references to Appendices
In the Field	31/7/17		T. M. Bde camp moved from MOR COPSE to point B. 16. D. 5. 4.	
			The batteries have been greatly hampered with the unsatisfactory state of ammunition taken over from 58th Divn and also received in first batch supplied from DUMP. Two prematures occurred one destroying the mortar and the other wounding a most valuable NCO and temporarily putting gun out of action. On two occasions the bomb fell on parapet of gun emplacement and on two other occasions fell back onto the muzzle. In addition we have had about 100 misfires, on one occasion 13 in succession and of 280 rounds observed 10% were blinds. Most of dates of ammunition were Spring 1916 and appeared to have been lying about, not always under cover, most of last winter. Before commencing firing 14/15 July I personally inspected all Component Part boxes and had to condemn all Exploders and 21 boxes complete.	

A5834 Wt. W4973/M687 750,000 8/16 D. D. & L. Ltd. Forms/C.2118/13.

Army Form C. 2118.

Instructions regarding War Diaries and Intelligence Summaries are contained in F. S. Regs., Part II. and the Staff Manual respectively. Title pages will be prepared in manuscript.

WAR DIARY
or
INTELLIGENCE SUMMARY.

(Erase heading not required.)

Place	Date	Hour	Summary of Events and Information	Remarks and references to Appendices
In the [illegible]			Casualties. 1 O.R. wounded (since died of wounds) V.7. 2 m.R.G.	
			1 O.R. — Y. 7. "	
			Ammunition expended.	
			9.45" T.M. 2" T.M.	
			24 rounds. 409 rounds.	
			A.G. Smith Capt. R.F.A. D.T.M.O.	
			1. 8. 17.	

A5834 Wt. W4973/M687 750,000 8/16 D. D. & L. Ltd. Forms/C.2118/13.

7th DIVISION.

TRENCH MORTAR BATTERY.

AUGUST 1917.

18

WAR DIARY
or
INTELLIGENCE SUMMARY.
(Erase heading not required.)

Army Form C. 2118.

Instructions regarding War Diaries and Intelligence Summaries are contained in F. S. Regs., Part II. and the Staff Manual respectively. Title pages will be prepared in manuscript.

7 D TM Bty
Vol 13

Place	Date	Hour	Summary of Events and Information	Remarks and references to Appendices
In the field	1/8/17		V. 7. T. M. Bty. X position. Work continued. No firing owing to Infantry relieving. Z position work continued on dug outs, gun pit etc.	
			Y. 7. T.M. Bty. E. F & G. positions fired 30 rounds on TUNNEL TRENCH at U 14. D. 25. 00. to U 14. C. 9. 9.	
			X. 7. T.M. Bty. Out of action, in camp at MORY COPSE on General fatigues.	
			Z. 7. T.M. Bty. Work continued on B position also on third position in FOX TROT.	
	2/8/17	12 Noon	V. 7. T.M. Bty. X position Heavy T.M. fired 5 rounds on TUNNEL TRENCH from U 21. A. 65. 30 to U 21. A. 1. 3. Two good bursts on each side of WILLOW TREE, one air burst and 2 blinds. Z position continued work on gun pit etc.	

A5834 Wt. W4973/M687 750,000 8/16 D. D. & L. Ltd. Forms/C.2118/13.

Instructions regarding War Diaries and Intelligence Summaries are contained in F. S. Regs., Part II. and the Staff Manual respectively. Title pages will be prepared in manuscript.

WAR DIARY
or
INTELLIGENCE SUMMARY.
(Erase heading not required.)

Army Form C. 2118.

Place	Date	Hour	Summary of Events and Information	Remarks and references to Appendices
In the Field	2/8/17		Y. 7. Tm Bty. fired 30 rounds on TUNNEL TRENCH at V 14. D. 00. 25 to V 14. C. 9. 9	
			X. 7. Tm Bty out of action on general fatigues	
			Z. 7. Tm Bty fired 7 rounds on BOVIS TRENCH V 21. D. 4. 5 to V 21. D. 7. 5.	
	3/8/17		V. 7. T. M. Bty. X & Z positions continued work on dug outs, gun pits etc.	
			X. 7. Tm Bty Out of action on general fatigues	
			Y. 7. Tm Bty E. F & G. positions fired 30 rounds on TUNNEL TRENCH. on V 14. D. 25. 00 to V 14. C. 9. 9.	
			Z. 7. Tm Bty. B. position fired 8 rounds on BOVIS TRENCH at V 21. D. 4. 5 – V 21. D. 7. 5.	
	4/8/17	10 AM	V. 7. Tm Bty X position. fired 6 rounds on Sunken Road	

A5834 Wt. W4973/M687 750,000 8/16 D. D. & L. Ltd. Forms/C.2118/13.

Army Form C. 2118.

Instructions regarding War Diaries and Intelligence Summaries are contained in F. S. Regs., Part II. and the Staff Manual respectively. Title pages will be prepared in manuscript.

WAR DIARY
or
INTELLIGENCE SUMMARY.
(Erase heading not required.)

Place	Date	Hour	Summary of Events and Information	Remarks and references to Appendices
In the Field	4/8/17	10 AM.	V. 7. TmBty. (X pos. contd) at V 21. A. 1. 3 and 5 rounds at U 20. B. 8. 8.	
			X. 7. TmBty relieved Y. 7. TmBty at E. F. G & H. positions fired 22 rounds from E & F positions on U 14. D. 2. 1.	
			Y. 7. TmBty relieved by X. 7. TmBty and returned to Tm Camp.	
			Z. 7. TmBty. fired from B. position 16 rounds on BOVIS TRENCH at U 21. D. 4. 5 – U 21. D. 7. 5.	
	5/8/17.		V. 7. TmBty. X & Z positions continued work on gun pits etc.	
			X. 7. TmBty. E. F & G. positions fired 16 rounds on U 14. D. 25. 00. to U 14. C. 9. 9 in retaliation to enemy light mortar.	
			Y. 7. TmBty. out of action on general fatigues.	

A5834 Wt. W4973/M687 750,000 8/16 D. D. & L. Ltd. Forms/C.2118/13.

WAR DIARY
or
INTELLIGENCE SUMMARY.
(Erase heading not required.)

Instructions regarding War Diaries and Intelligence Summaries are contained in F. S. Regs., Part II. and the Staff Manual respectively. Title pages will be prepared in manuscript.

Place	Date	Hour	Summary of Events and Information	Remarks and references to Appendices
In the Field	5/8/17		Z. 7. Tm Bty Fired 14 rounds from B position on BORIS TRENCH at V14.D.0.5 to V14.D.7.5. Several direct hits in trench being observed.	
	6/8/17		V. 7. Tm Bty X + Z positions continued work on dug outs. ~~the~~ second guns put in action in X position 10 yards to right of other gun.	
			X. 7. Tm Bty. G. position 10 rounds fired on V14.D.25.00 to V.14.C.9.9 in retaliation.	
			Y. 7. Tm Bty. Out of action on general fatigues.	
			Z. 7. Tm Bty. B. position fired 33 rounds on V21.D.5.6. on new work that had been done by enemy also in retaliation to enemy MINENWERFER.	
	7/8/17		V. 7. Tm Bty. Z. position fired 4 rounds registration on	

A5834 Wt. W4973/M687 750,000 8/16 D. D. & L. Ltd. Forms/C.2118/13.

Instructions regarding War Diaries and Intelligence Summaries are contained in F. S. Regs., Part II. and the Staff Manual respectively. Title pages will be prepared in manuscript.

WAR DIARY
or
INTELLIGENCE SUMMARY.
(Erase heading not required.)

Army Form C. 2118.

Place	Date	Hour	Summary of Events and Information	Remarks and references to Appendices
In the Field.	7/8/17		V.7. TmBty (contd) TUNNEL TRENCH at U 14. D. 1. 4. Four excellent bursts observed.	
			X.7. TmBty. E.F.G + H. positions did not fire on account of Infantry relieving	
			Y.7. TmBty. out of action on general fatigues.	
			Z.7. TmBty fired 10 rounds on BOVIS TRENCH. U 21. D. 5. 6	
	8/8/17		V.7. T.M. Bty. fired 21 rounds on TUNNEL TRENCH. at U 14. D. 1. 4	
			X.7. T.M. Bty fired 30 rounds on U 14. D. 25 00 to U 14. C. 9. 9.	
			Z.7. T.M. Bty fired 30 rounds on BOVIS TRENCH at U 21. D. 5. 6	
			V.7. T.M. Bty handed over 3 - 9.45. T.Ms, one to 62nd Divn in the line and 2 to 21st Divn in the line	

A5834 Wt. W4973/M687 750,000 8/16 D. D. & L. Ltd. Forms/C.2118/13.

Army Form C. 2118.

Instructions regarding War Diaries and Intelligence Summaries are contained in F. S. Regs., Part II. and the Staff Manual respectively. Title pages will be prepared in manuscript.

WAR DIARY
or
INTELLIGENCE SUMMARY.
(Erase heading not required.)

Place	Date	Hour	Summary of Events and Information	Remarks and references to Appendices
	8/8/17		V. 7. T.M.Bty (contd) personnel still being found for 2 mortars	
			X. 7. T.M.Bty handed over 4 guns in E. F. G & H. positions to 21st Divn. T.M. Bde.	
			Z. 7. T.M.Bty handed over 3 guns in B. positions to 62 Divn. T.M.Bde.	
	9/8/17 to 14/8/17		T.M.Bde on general fatigues for pioneer Officer & 9th Divn Arty Bdes.	
	14/8/17		Z. 7. T.M.Bty 2 Officers & 23 men to School of Mortars on refresher course.	
	14/8/17 to 31/8/17		T.M. Bde on general fatigues for Pioneer Officer	

A5834 Wt. W4973/M687 750,000 8/16 D. D. & L. Ltd. Forms/C.2118/13.

Instructions regarding War Diaries and Intelligence Summaries are contained in F. S. Regs., Part II. and the Staff Manual respectively. Title pages will be prepared in manuscript.

WAR DIARY
or
INTELLIGENCE SUMMARY.
(Erase heading not required.)

Army Form C. 2118.

Place	Date	Hour	Summary of Events and Information	Remarks and references to Appendices
	14/8/17 to 31/8/17		and Divn Arty Brigades.	
	28/8/17		Z. 7 T.M.Bty. rejoined from School of Mortars	
			G W C Parker Capt. R.F.A. actg. D.T.M.O.	
			31. 8. 17.	

7th DIVISION.

TRENCH MORTAR BATTERY.

SEPTEMBER. 1917.

Army Form C. 2118.

Instructions regarding War Diaries and Intelligence Summaries are contained in F. S. Regs., Part II. and the Staff Manual respectively. Title pages will be prepared in manuscript.

WAR DIARY
or
INTELLIGENCE SUMMARY.
(Erase heading not required.)

Trench Mortar Brigade RFA

Vol 14

Place	Date	Hour	Summary of Events and Information	Remarks and references to Appendices
	1/9/17		March from Mory Dumps to Behagnies	
	2/9/17		Proceed to Bucourt entrained for Castre	
	3/9/17		Arrived at Castre disentrained proceed to St Johns Cappel rest 5 days	
	8/9/17		Proceed to Kemmel General fatigues [illegible] (Ammunition supply)	
	22/9/17		Leave Kemmel march to [illegible] rest 5 days	
	27/9/17		Proceed to Dickebush General fatigues [illegible] (Ammunition supply)	
	30/9/17		Fatigues [illegible] Ammn	

H C Atkinson
Capt RFA
for DTMO [illegible]

A5834 Wt. W4973/M687 750,000 8/16 D. D. & L. Ltd. Forms/C.2118/13.

7th DIVISION

TRENCH MORTAR BATTERY.

OCTOBER 1917.

17

Instructions regarding War Diaries and Intelligence Summaries are contained in F. S. Regs., Part II. and the Staff Manual respectively. Title pages will be prepared in manuscript.

WAR DIARY
or
INTELLIGENCE SUMMARY.
(Erase heading not required.)

Army Form C. 2118.

7 D T M B [illegible]

Vol 15

Place	Date	Hour	Summary of Events and Information	Remarks and references to Appendices
	1-10-17	7 AM	Preparing positions for 7th Div Arty	
	2-10-17		" " Ammunition Supply 7th Div Arty	
	3-10-17		Fatigues H Q 7th [illegible] Ammunition Supply " " etc	
	4-10-17		Fatigues	
	5-10-17		"	
	6-10-17		Fatigues H. Q. 7th D A	
	7-10-17		— Signal Office + [illegible] all watches put back 1 hour at 1. AM.	
	8-10-17		Ammunition Supply etc 7th D Arty	
	9-10-17		" "	
	10-10-17		Fatigues etc 7th Div Arty	
	11-10-17		" " "	
	12-10-17		" " "	
	13-10-17		" " "	
	14-10-17		" " "	
	15-10-17		" " "	
	16-10-17		" " "	
	17-10-17		" " "	
	18-10-17		" " "	
	19-10-17		" " "	
	20-10-17		" " "	
	21-10-17		25 N.C.O's & men attached [illegible] batteries to reinforce during operations	
	22-10-17		Fatigues 7th DA	

A5834 Wt. W4973/M687 750,000 8/16 D. D. & L. Ltd. Forms/C.2118/13.

Army Form C. 2118.

Instructions regarding War Diaries and Intelligence Summaries are contained in F. S. Regs., Part II. and the Staff Manual respectively. Title pages will be prepared in manuscript.

WAR DIARY
or
INTELLIGENCE SUMMARY.

(Erase heading not required.)

Place	Date	Hour	Summary of Events and Information	Remarks and references to Appendices
	23-10-17		Fatigues 4th Div. Arty	
	24-10-17		" "	
	25-10-17		" & assisting to get the guns in action	
	26-10-17		Fatigues 4th Div Arty	
	27-10-17		" & Salvaging 12" B.L. guns	
	28-10-17		" & " " " "	
	29-10-17		" " H.V. A[illegible]	
	30-10-17		" " " "	
	31-10-17		" " " "	

A. B. Smith. Capt RFA
DTMO 4th Div

A5834 Wt. W4973/M687 750,000 8/16 D. D. & L. Ltd. Forms/C.2118/13.

7th DIVISION

TRENCH MORTAR BATTERY.

NOVEMBER 1917.

Army Form C. 2118.

7 D T M Bty

Vol 16

Instructions regarding War Diaries and Intelligence Summaries are contained in F. S. Regs., Part II. and the Staff Manual respectively. Title pages will be prepared in manuscript.

WAR DIARY
or
INTELLIGENCE SUMMARY.
(Erase heading not required.)

Place	Date	Hour	Summary of Events and Information	Remarks and references to Appendices
DICKEBUSH	1/11/17. to 9/11/17		Fatigues for 7th Div: Arty.	
	10/11/17.		Moved to BOESCHEPE	
BOESCHEPE	11/11/17		Inspected by X Corps General.	
"	12/11/17		V/7. Heavy T. M. Battery disbanded 27 N.C.O's & men posted to 35th Brigade R.F.A	
	13/11/17.		Moved to EECKE	
	14/11/17.		Moved to RENESCURE	
RENESCURE	15/11/17 to 17/11/17.		Fatigues at ARQUES Station loading up trains	
	18/11/17		Moved to ARQUES	
ARQUES.	19/11/17 to 20/11/17		Fatigues at ARQUES station	
	21/11/17.		Entrained at ARQUES station for Italy	
	21/11/17 to 30/11/17		In train	
ITALY.	30/11/17.		Detrained at PIANO. & marched to EAARLESEGA. for the night	

A. G. Smith Capt
D.T.M.O.

A5834 Wt. W4973/M687 750,000 8/16 D. D. & L. Ltd. Forms/C.2118/13.

7TH DIVISION

7TH DIVL AMMN COLUMN

SEP 1914-~~MAR 1919~~ 1917 NOV

TO ITALY

Index..............................

SUBJECT.

No.	Contents.	Date.
	7TH DIV.	
	AMMUNITION COLUMN	
	~~JAN - DEC 1915~~	
	1914 SEP – 1915 DEC	

(56,425). Wt.24,741—161. 2000. 11/20. **Gp.164.** A.&E.W.

7th Divisional Artillery.

7th DIVISIONAL AMMUNITION COLUMN R.F.A.

8th SEPTEMBER - 9th DECEMBER 1914.

Mar 1919

ORIGINAL.

CONFIDENTIAL.

WAR DIARY.

OF

7TH DIVISIONAL AMMUNITION COLUMN.

FROM 8TH SEPTEMBER 1914 TO 9.12.14.

(Volume. I)

Page 1

Army Form C. 2118.

Instructions regarding War Diaries and Intelligence Summaries are contained in F. S. Regs., Part II. and the Staff Manual respectively. Title pages will be prepared in manuscript.

WAR DIARY

~~or~~

~~INTELLIGENCE SUMMARY.~~

(*Erase heading not required.*)

7th Divisional Ammunition Column.

Hour, Date, Place	Summary of Events and Information	Remarks and references to Appendices
8th September 1914. SOUTHAMPTON.	Captain the Honble D.A. FORBES. R.F.A. joined from 67th Battery R.F.A. on posting as Adjutant.	
" " " "	Lieut N. THIELE. R.F.A. joined on posting to No. 1. Section.	[initials]
9th " " "	Major T.C.W. MOLONY. D.S.O. joined from 5.B. Reserve Bde R.F.A. to command the column.	
" " " "	Captain. H. SPENCER. R.F.A. (R. of O.) joined on posting as O.C. No 2. Sec:	
" " " "	2 Lieuts W. McGEE. and M.A. MOTION. Special Reserve R.F.A. joined from 5A. Reserve Bde R.F.A. on posting to No 3. Section.	[initials]
10th " " "	Lieut R.H. RADFORD. Special Reserve R.F.A. joined on posting to No. 2. Section.	
" " " "	2 Lieut L.B. THOMAS. Special reserve R.F.A. joined on posting to No 2. Sec.	
" " " "	Capt: H. OSTLER. Special reserve. R.F.A. joined on posting to No 4. Sec:	
" " " "	2 Lieut S.P. HANNAM. Special reserve. R.F.A. joined on posting to Base Details.	[initials]
10th Sept: 14. "	Officers of the Column moved to CAMBRIDGE. BKS. PORTSMOUTH.	[initials]
12th " " PORTSMOUTH.	N.C.O.s and men commenced to join the column.	[initials]

(9 29 6) W 2794 100,000 8/14 H W V Forms/C. 2118/11

Army Form C. 2118.

Instructions regarding War Diaries and Intelligence Summaries are contained in F. S. Regs., Part II. and the Staff Manual respectively. Title pages will be prepared in manuscript.

WAR DIARY

~~or~~

~~INTELLIGENCE SUMMARY.~~

(*Erase heading not required.*)

7th Divisional Ammunition Column.

Hour, Date, Place	Summary of Events and Information	Remarks and references to Appendices
15th September. 1914. PORTSMOUTH.	2Lieut J.F. FORD. Special Reserve R.G.A. joined on posting to No. 4. Section.	
" " " "	Lieut HENDERSON. ~~RAMC~~ [illegible] Medical officer - and Lieut W. S. MORTON. Veterinary officer. joined on posting to the column.	[initials]
17th " " "	The column commenced to draw equipment from Ordnance.	[initials]
18th " " "	Horses commenced to arrive from Remounts. WOOLWICH.	
" " " "	Temporary Lieut. W.E. HEYDEMAN. RFA. joined on posting to No. 1. Section.	[initials]
19th " " "	Major. L.B. MONTRESOR. joined and took over command of No. 1 Section	
" " " "	Personnel of No. 4 Section changed from R.F.A. to R.G.A.	
" " " "	Captain. C.S.S. CURTEIS. R.G.A. (R. of O.) joined on posting to No. 4 Section.	[initials]
20th " " "	Captain. R.W. LAMB. R.F.A. (R. of O.) joined and took over command of No. 3. Section.	[initials]
22nd " " "	2Lieut J.F. FORD. S.R. RGA. left for WOOLWICH. on posting to Heavy Brigade.	[initials]
24th " " "	The column was brought up to full establishment of vehicles.	[initials]
25th " " "	Major MOLONY. D.S.O. left the column to join 104th Battery R.F.A.	[initials]

(9 29 6) W 2794 100,000 8/14 H W V Forms/C. 2118/11

Army Form C. 2118.

Instructions regarding War Diaries and Intelligence Summaries are contained in F. S. Regs., Part II. and the Staff Manual respectively. Title pages will be prepared in manuscript.

WAR DIARY
or
~~INTELLIGENCE SUMMARY.~~
(Erase heading not required.)

7th Divisional Ammunition Column.

Hour, Date, Place	Summary of Events and Information	Remarks and references to Appendices
25th Sept: 1914. PORTSMOUTH.	Major MONTRESOR left the column.	
" " " "	Major G. J. HENDERSON. R.F.A. (R. of O.) joined from 4. B. Reserve Brigade R.F.A. to command No. 1. Section.	
" " " ".	Lieut-Col: H.A. LAKE. R.F.A. joined from 104th Battery R.F.A. to command the column.	
~~[illegible]~~ " " "	2nd Lieut. F.D. WISEMAN joined on posting to column as Interpreter.	[initials]
2nd October. " "	Reported to Head Qrs 7th Divisional Artillery that column was ready to move.	[initials]
5th October. " "	The column marched from PORTSMOUTH to SOUTHAMPTON.	
" " " "	2nd Lieut. S.P. HANNAM. S.R. R.F.A. and Base details left at PORTSMOUTH.	
" " " SOUTHAMPTON.	Embarked at SOUTHAMPTON as follows:- 1st Section on "NOVIAN" and "PANCRAS." 2nd Section on "AUSTRALIND." and "NOVIAN." 3rd Section. 4th Section and Hd Qrs on "PANCRAS."	
" " " "	Major HENDERSON and ½ No. 1. Section, Capt: SPENCER. Lieut: THOMAS. and ½ No. 2. Section sailed from SOUTHAMPTON in "NOVIAN."	[initials]

Army Form C. 2118.

Instructions regarding War Diaries and Intelligence Summaries are contained in F. S. Regs., Part II. and the Staff Manual respectively. Title pages will be prepared in manuscript.

WAR DIARY
~~or~~
~~INTELLIGENCE SUMMARY.~~ 7th Divisional Ammunition Column.
(Erase heading not required.)

Hour, Date, Place	Summary of Events and Information	Remarks and references to Appendices
7th October. 1914. OSTEND	and disembarked at OSTEND on 7th October, and marched	[initials]
9th " " "	on 9th October to BRUGES and joined remainder of column.	[initials]
5th " " SOUTHAMPTON	Lieut. RADFORD. and ½ No 2 Section sailed from SOUTHAMPTON in "AUSTRALIND."	[initials]
7th " " ZEEBRUGGE	and disembarked at ZEEBRUGGE on 7th October and marched to BRUGES.	[initials]
8th " " BRUGES.	and marched to OSTEND on 8th October and joined remainder of section.	[initials]
9th " " OSTEND.	and marched to BRUGES on 9th October + joined remainder of column.	[initials]
7th " " SOUTHAMPTON.	3rd Section, 4th Section and Hd Qrs sailed in "PANCRAS" from SOUTHAMPTON	[initials]
8th " " ZEEBRUGGE	and disembarked at ZEEBRUGGE on 8th Oct. and	[initials]
9th " "	marched to BRUGES. via BLANKENBERGH.	[initials]
10th " " BRUGES	Whole column marched to AKKERSTRAET.	[initials]
12th " " AKKERSTRAET.	marched to SVEVEZEELE with 21st Infantry Brigade.	[initials]

(9 29 6) W2794 100,000 8/14 H W V Forms/C. 2118/11

Page 5.

Army Form C. 2118.

Instructions regarding War Diaries and Intelligence Summaries are contained in F. S. Regs., Part II. and the Staff Manual respectively. Title pages will be prepared in manuscript.

WAR DIARY

~~or~~

~~INTELLIGENCE SUMMARY.~~

(*Erase heading not required.*)

7th Divisional Ammunition Column.

Hour, Date, Place	Summary of Events and Information	Remarks and references to Appendices
13th October 1914. SVEVEZEELE.	Marched to ROULERS and joined remainder of 7th Division.	[illegible]
14th " " ROULERS.	Marched to YPRES with 7th Division and billetted on PLAINE D'AMOUR.	[illegible]
17th " " YPRES.	Moved into the Cavalry Barracks.	[illegible]
18th " " "	Returned to PLAINE D'AMOUR.	[illegible]
15th " " "	7th Division in cooperation with the French 87th Division ordered to entrench a position covering YPRES from E and S.E.	
" " " "	7th Division ordered to advance on 16th Oct: and occupy a line covering villages of ZANDVOORDE - GHELUVELT - ZONNEBEKE - St JULIEN.	[illegible]
16th " " "	7th Division ordered to halt in its present position.	[illegible]
17th " " "	7th Division ordered to move forward to a general line KORTEWILDE - KRUISEIK - TERHAND - WATERDAMHOEK on 18th Oct.	[illegible]
18th " " "	7th Division ordered to carry out an attack on MENIN on 19th Oct.	[illegible]
19th " " "	7th Division ordered to continue to hold its present line on 20th Oct: and improve existing trenches.	[illegible]

Army Form C. 2118.

WAR DIARY
or
~~INTELLIGENCE SUMMARY.~~
(Erase heading not required.)

7th Divisional Ammunition Column

Instructions regarding War Diaries and Intelligence Summaries are contained in F. S. Regs., Part II. and the Staff Manual respectively. Title pages will be prepared in manuscript.

Hour, Date, Place	Summary of Events and Information	Remarks and references to Appendices
20th October 1914. YPRES.	Enemy's attack successfully repulsed to-day all along the line. 7th Division remains in present position and ordered to improve entrenchments.	[initials]
21st " " "	Large quantities of Gun and S.A. Amn supplied to Bde Am: Columns	[initials]
25th " " "	7th Division ordered to advance in conjunction with 1st Army, by swinging forward its left using KRUISEIK as a pivot.	[initials]
27th " " "	7th Division attached to 1st Corps and ordered to occupy defensive line while 1st and 2nd Divisions continue advance.	[initials]
28th " " "	Left PLAINE D'AMOUR and went into billets about one mile S.E. of the town, near KLEIN ZILLEBEKE.	
" " " Nr YPRES.	7th Division ordered to remain within defensive line, but to be prepared to cooperate with 1st and 2nd Division who are continuing their attack.	[initials]
31st " " " "	The Column moved to MILLEKRUIS.	[initials]
2nd Nov: " MILLEKRUIS.	The Column moved to WESTOUTRE.	[initials]
3rd " " WESTOUTRE.	The infantry brigades of 7th Division ordered to be relieved in the firing line.	[initials]

(9 29 6) W2794 100,000 8/14 H W V Forms/C. 2118/11

Army Form C. 2118.

Instructions regarding War Diaries and Intelligence Summaries are contained in F. S. Regs., Part II. and the Staff Manual respectively. Title pages will be prepared in manuscript.

WAR DIARY
~~or~~
~~INTELLIGENCE SUMMARY.~~

(*Erase heading not required.*)

7th Divisional Ammunition Column.

Hour, Date, Place	Summary of Events and Information	Remarks and references to Appendices
4th Nov: 1914. WESTOUTRE.	Lieut. N.W. THIELE. R.F.A. left column on posting to 22nd Bde Am: Col.	
" " " "	The column moved to OUDERDOM.	
" " " OUDERDOM.	Lieu HENDERSON. Medical officer left the column on posting to South Staffordshire Regiment.	[initials]
5th " " "	Lieut. P. D. WARBURTON. R.A.M.C. joined the column on posting from South Staffordshire Regiment.	[initials]
13th " " "	Hd Qrs Nos 1. 2 & 3. Sections moved to billets near BAILLEUL. No 4 Section being left at OUDERDOM and attached to 1st Divisional Ammunition Column.	
" " " ~~[struck out]~~ " [initials]	Notification received that decision given to allow 2 Heavy Draught Horses to every 4 Light Draught Horses. This will allow 2 Light and 2 Heavy Draught horses per wagon.	
" " " "	No 3. Section had a wagon destroyed near YPRES on being hit by a shell when returning from supplying ammunition, Six men being wounded and 3 horses killed and 3 horses wounded.	[initials]

Page. 8

Army Form C. 2118.

Instructions regarding War Diaries and Intelligence Summaries are contained in F. S. Regs., Part II. and the Staff Manual respectively. Title pages will be prepared in manuscript.

WAR DIARY

or

~~INTELLIGENCE SUMMARY.~~

(*Erase heading not required.*)

7th Divisional Ammunition Column.

Hour, Date, Place	Summary of Events and Information	Remarks and references to Appendices
15th November 1914. Nr. BAILLEUL.	Personnel of 4th Amn. Coln. posted to column as reinforcements.	
" " " OUDERDOM.	No. 4 Section left OUDERDOM and moved to 2 miles S. of POPERINGHE.	H.L.
16th " " Nr. BAILLEUL.	2nd Lieut. N. BOLTON and 2Lieut. A.R TABOR joined from the base and posted to No. 1 Section.	
" " " "	The column left Nr. BAILLEUL and moved to DOULIEU.	H.L.
17th " " DOULIEU.	2Lieut. W.E. HEYDEMAN left the column on posting to 104th Battery. R.F.A.	H.L.
18th " " "	2Lieut. A.R. TABOR left the column on posting to 35th Bde. R.F.A.	H.L.
20th " " "	Notification received that Hale's Rifle bombs now available for issue and are to be drawn.	H.L.
22nd " " Nr. POPERINGHE.	No. 4 Section rejoined column at DOULIEU.	H.L.
24th " " DOULIEU.	6 wagons with men and horses to supply "C" Battery R.H.A. posted from No. 1 Section to 3rd Cavalry Divn. Amn. Column.	H.L.
25th " " "	Notification received that a supply of High explosive 18pr shell now available and is to be drawn.	H.L.

Army Form C. 2118.

WAR DIARY
or
~~INTELLIGENCE SUMMARY.~~
(Erase heading not required.)

7th Divisional Ammunition Column.

Instructions regarding War Diaries and Intelligence Summaries are contained in F. S. Regs., Part II. and the Staff Manual respectively. Title pages will be prepared in manuscript.

Hour, Date, Place	Summary of Events and Information	Remarks and references to Appendices
28th Nov: 1914. DOULIEU.	4. G.S wagons with men and horses attached to No1. Section. to supply 4.5. Amn: to 55th Battery. R.F.A. (How:) attached to 14th Bde R.H.A.	H.L.C.
30th " " "	2Lieut: N. BOLTON left the column on posting to 104th Bat. R.F.A.	H.L.C.
4th Dec: " "	2Lieut: L.B. THOMAS left the Column on posting to 58th Bat: R.F.A.	H.L.C.
5th " " "	2Lieut: J. SELWYN. joined the column on posting from No1 Gen: Base.	H.L.C.
8th " " "	Capt: H.L. COTTINGHAM. RFA (R. of O) joined the Column on posting from No1. Gen: Base.	
" " "	First supply of Very pistols and cartridges received.	
" " "	First supply of Grenades Hand bombs, and Grenades Lyddite Hand bombs received.	H.L.C.
9th " " "	2Lieut: R.W. CORBETT. on obtaining commission from R.S.M. (W.O.) left the Column on posting to the base.	
" " " "	Lieut: P.D. WARBURTON. ~~Medical officer~~ RAMC left the Column on posting to Base. BOULOGNE.	
" " " "	Lieut: H.F. MARRIS. Medical officer joined the column on posting from Base. BOULOGNE.	H.L.C.

nil

121/4262

Ab. 6.

7th Divisional Amm^n Col^n

Vol II. 16.12.14 — 26.7.15

Army Form C. 2118.

Instructions regarding War Diaries and Intelligence Summaries are contained in F. S. Regs., Part II. and the Staff Manual respectively. Title pages will be prepared in manuscript.

WAR DIARY
~~or~~
~~INTELLIGENCE SUMMARY.~~
(Erase heading not required.)

7th Divisional Ammunition Column.

Hour, Date, Place	Summary of Events and Information	Remarks and references to Appendices
16th Dec: 1914. DOULIEU.	The column moved to near TROU BAYARD.	HaK
17th " " Nr TROU BAYARD.	First supply of French hand bombs & slings received.	HaK.
20th " " "	Owing to reduction of Pom Pom Section, the column ceased to carry ammunition for that gun.	HaK
3rd Jan: 1915. "	Lieut W. E. HEYDEMAN joined on reposting to Column from 22 B^de Am. Col. & posted to No 2. Sec:	HaK
7th " " "	First supply of grenades of local pattern received.	HaK
" " " "	3 Trench Mortars and Ammunition drawn from MERVILLE and handed over to 55th Battery R.F.A.	HaK
" " " "	2 Lieut M J R. WOOD. R.F.A. joined on posting to column from No 1. General Base & posted to No 3. Sec:	HaK
8th " " "	2 Lieut W. R. McGEE. SR. R.F.A. left the column on posting to 22nd Brigade R.F.A.	HaK
9th " " "	Notification received that 2 Lieut ~~S~~ J. SELWYN. SR. R.F.A. from Cambridge University is granted a permanent commission in R.F.A. Regular Army. Authority. W.O. 28616/1. dated 5th January 1915.	HaK
11th " " "	2 Lieut S. F. SHINGLETON. R.F.A. joined from the Base and posted to No 1. Section.	HaK

Page.

Army Form C. 2118.

WAR DIARY

~~or~~

~~INTELLIGENCE SUMMARY~~.

(Erase heading not required.)

7th Divisional Ammunition Column

Instructions regarding War Diaries and Intelligence Summaries are contained in F. S. Regs., Part II. and the Staff Manual respectively. Title pages will be prepared in manuscript.

Hour, Date, Place	Summary of Events and Information	Remarks and references to Appendices
16th Jan: 1915. Nr. TROUBAYARD	2nd Lieut. J. SELWYN. R.F.A. left the column on posting to 35th Brigade R.F.A.	H.a.k.
17th " " "	2nd Lieut. A. BURROWS. R.F.A. joined the column from No 2 General Base and posted to No 2 Section.	H.a.k.
" " " "	2nd Lieut. A. DANN. R.F.A. joined the column from No 2 General Base and posted to No 3. Section.	H.a.k.
18th " " "	Temporary Lieut. W.E. HEYDEMAN. R.F.A., admitted to hospital, struck off the strength of the column. Authority H.d Qrs 7th D.A.	H.a.k.
" " " "	2nd Lieut. M.A. MOTION. S.R. R.F.A., sick leave, struck off the strength of the column. Authority Hd. Qrs 7th D.A.	H.a.k.
22nd " " "	First supply of "AASEN" Hand Grenades received.	
" " " "	First supply of "double cylinder" Hand Grenades received	H.a.k.
25th " " "	First supply of "hand grenades without handles" received.	H.a.k.
26th " " "	The column moved to billets at DOULIEU.	H.a.k.

121
4530

7th Divisional Ammn Coln

Vol III. 3.2 — 4.3.15

Nil

Army Form. C. 2118.

Instructions regarding War Diaries and Intelligence Summaries are contained in F. S. Regs., Part II. and the Staff Manual respectively. Title pages will be prepared in manuscript.

WAR DIARY
or
~~INTELLIGENCE SUMMARY.~~
(*Erase heading not required.*)

7th Divisional Ammunition Column

Hour, Date, Place	Summary of Events and Information	Remarks and references to Appendices
3rd February 1915. DOULIEU.	First supply of "TROTYL" Hand Grenades received.	H.a.k.
25th January 1915. TROUBAYARD.	First supply of "Waterpipe" ~~[illegible]~~ Grenades received.	H.a.k.
3rd February 1915. DOULIEU.	Captain. R.W. LAMB. RFA. (R of O) posted to 58th Battery R.F.A. and left	H.a.k.
" " " "	the column on 5th Feb: 15. 7th Div: Art: Routine order No 24 3rd Feb. 15.	
5th " " "	Captain C.C.S. CURTEIS. R.G.A. (R of O.) ordered to proceed to ENGLAND,	
" " " "	and left the column on 5th Feb: 15. A.G. No 1165. 4th Corps. No 769 (A)	H.a.k.
5th " " "	Captain H.L. COTTINGHAM. took over command of No 3. Section.	
" " " "	Captain. H. OSTLER. took over command of No 4 Section.	H.a.k.
6th " " "	No RFA 20325. Regt Sergt Major (W.O) W.G. CORNFORD. posted, on	
	promotion. authority. H.Q. D.A. No 523. of 2.2.15.	H.a.k.
11th " " "	2 Lieut M.J.R. WOOD. RFA. posted to 7th Div: Am: Park &	
	Struck off Strength of the column.	H.a.k.
14th " " "	Major The Honble D.A. FORBES. RFA. ordered to proceed to	
	England and report to War Office. Left the column on 18 Feb: 1915.	H.a.k.
~~14~~ 16th " " "	2 Lieutenant G. BEVERIDGE. joined the column from 7th	
	Divisional Ammunition Park & posted to No 3. Section.	H.a.k.

(9 29 6) W2794 100,000 8/14 H W V Forms/C. 2118/11

Instructions regarding War Diaries and Intelligence Summaries are contained in F. S. Regs., Part II. and the Staff Manual respectively. Title pages will be prepared in manuscript.

WAR DIARY ~~or~~ ~~INTELLIGENCE~~ SUMMARY.

(*Erase heading not required.*)

Army Form C. 2118.

7th Divisional Ammunition Column.

Hour, Date, Place	Summary of Events and Information	Remarks and references to Appendices
16th February 1915. DOULIEU.	Lieut. Colonel H. A. LAKE. RFA ordered to proceed to	
"	England and report to War Office. Left the column on 20th Feb. 15.	HALe
18th " "	Captain H. L. COTTINGHAM RFA took over duties of Adjutant vice	
"	Major Hon DA FORBES posted to Home Establishment. 17.2.15.	HC
20th " "	Major G. J. HENDERSON RFA (R of O) assumed command of the	
"	Column vice Lieut Col H. A. LAKE left for England	HC
1st MARCH 1915 "	MAJOR G. J. HENDERSON. RFA posted to 8th Division Artillery Authority GOC IV Corps	HC
" " " "	A GS Wagon added to Establishment of Column to carry 25% Explosives	
" " "	for 3 Field Companies RE. Auth: IV Corps OS 9/29 26th Feb. 1915	HC
2nd " "	The Column moved to billets in VIEUX BERQUIN.	HC
3rd " " VIEUX BERQUIN	Major G. J HENDERSON. RFA (R of O) left to join 3rd Battery RFA	
" " "	8th Divisional Artillery. Auth: GOC IV Corps.	HC
" "	Captain H. L COTTINGHAM RFA assumed command of the Column	
" " "	vice Major HENDERSON. RFA	HC
" " "	Illuminating Fireworks (Rockets) 17 Sets received.	HC
4th " "	Reinforcements arrived from Base consisting of two	HC

121/4576

7th Div[l] Amm[n] Col[n]

Vol IV 4 — 30.3.15

Instructions regarding War Diaries and Intelligence Summaries are contained in F. S. Regs., Part II. and the Staff Manual respectively. Title pages will be prepared in manuscript.

WAR DIARY
or
~~INTELLIGENCE SUMMARY.~~
(Erase heading not required.)

7th Divn Ammn Column

Army Form C. 2118.

Page 14

Hour, Date, Place	Summary of Events and Information	Remarks and references to Appendices
1915		
4th MARCH. VIEUX BERQUIN.	Two specially enlisted Farrier Q.M. Sergts & 5 Gunners and 11 Gunners Drivers	HC
" " " "	Howitzer Section 4th Div. Ammn Column, attached No 1 Section 7 D.A.C. detached to join 8th Divl Artillery. Author S.C. 7 D.A.	
6 " " "	Colonel H. MONTGOMERY CAMPBELL. RFA. arrived from base and assumed command of the Column from Capt COTTINGHAM. RFA	HC
" " " "	Two 4 inch rifled Howitzers sent up to the trenches under 2nd Lt A. DANN. RFA with detachment from No 3. Section 7. D.A.C	HC
8th "COURANT. METTEREN BEC	The Column moved into billets, COURANT. METTEREN-BECQUE	HML
9th " " " "	Captain CARWITHEN. RGA. joined from 22 B.A.C. posted to command No 3. Section.	HML
	S.A.A. · 18 Pr. · 13 Pr.	HML
9 " " " "	Ammunition supplied to Column during action at & about NEUVE CHAPELLE. · 1.254.250 · 2140 · –	HML
10 " " " "	146.600 · 3806 · 1387	HML
11 " " " "	190100 · 2954 · 328	HML
12 " " "	294400 · 3423 · 1080	HML
13 " " "	410050 · 2484 · 914	HML
	Total. 2.295.400 · 14807 · 2709	

(9 29 6) W 2794 100,000 8/14 H W V Forms/C. 2118/11.

Instructions regarding War Diaries and Intelligence Summaries are contained in F. S. Regs., Part II. and the Staff Manual respectively. Title pages will be prepared in manuscript.

WAR DIARY

or

~~INTELLIGENCE SUMMARY.~~

(Erase heading not required.)

7 Divl Amm Column

Army Form C. 2118.

Hour, Date, Place	Summary of Events and Information	Remarks and references to Appendices
1915.		
11 MARCH. METTEREN.BEC	Authority received for appointment of Captain H. L. COTTINGHAM to be ADJUTANT from 18.2.15.	HWL
15 " " "	60 light draught horses & 2 riding horses joined column	HWL
" " "	2/Lt J.R.H. STROYAN joined from 22 Bde RFA	
17 " " "	Section 4.5 Howitzer Bty (43) attached to column.	
18 " " "	2 Sections D.A.C. MEERUT DIVn attached to column.	
21 " " "	8 3.7 Mortars received from Park.	
23 " "	Column moved into billets at LE SART.	
" " LE. SART.	Major C.E. BERLY. posted to Column and took over command of No I Section	
28 " " "	No 4 Section detached posted to No 3 Heavy Brigade Strength 1 officer 39 other ranks, 42 horses, 10 wagons	
29 " " "	1 Section 4.5 Howitzer 4 D.A.C attached to column (No I Section) Strength 0 officer, 22 other ranks, 32 horses, 6 wagons.	
30 " " "	2/Lt M STEWART. joined the column from Special Reserve attached No 3 Section	

(9 29 6) W 2794 100,000 8/14 H W V Forms/C. 2118/11.

121/5254

Divl: Ammn Coln. 7th Division

Vol V 4 — 28.4.15

B 2

Army Form C. 2118.

WAR DIARY
or
INTELLIGENCE SUMMARY.
(Erase heading not required.)

Instructions regarding War Diaries and Intelligence Summaries are contained in F. S. Regs., Part II. and the Staff Manual respectively. Title pages will be prepared in manuscript.

Page 16

Hour, Date, Place	Summary of Events and Information	Remarks and references to Appendices
1915		
4th April, LE SART	No 1 Section MEERUT D.A.C left the column	[illegible]
5 " "	No 3 " " " " "	[illegible]
	Section 4.5 43rd Howitzer Bde left the column	[illegible]
6 " "	Captain H. B. Ostler admitted to hospital and	
	subsequently sent to ENGLAND.	[illegible]
12 " "	Column moved to fresh billets at MEURILLON	[illegible]
13 " MEURILLON	20 new pattern R.L. hand grenades received: passed	
	to 22nd Infantry Bde for experiment	[illegible]
20 " "	Section 4.5 Howitzer Bde joined 8 D.A.C.	[illegible]
24 " "	Received orders to hold column in readiness to	
~~25~~ "	march at 2 hours notice	[illegible]
25 " "	2 Wagons 4.5 How. Section attached from 8 D.A.C	[illegible]
27 " "	" " " " "	[illegible]
" "	4 " " "	
" "	Captain S CARMITHEN admitted to hospital	
2[illegible] "	Column moved to new billets at VIEUX BERQUIN.	

(9 29 6) W 2794 100,000 8/14 H W V Forms/C. 2118/11

121/5556

7th Div: Ammn Coln

Vol VI 4 — 22.5.15

Instructions regarding War Diaries and Intelligence Summaries are contained in F. S. Regs., Part II. and the Staff Manual respectively. Title pages will be prepared in manuscript.

WAR DIARY
or
INTELLIGENCE SUMMARY.
(Erase heading not required.)

Army Form C. 2118.

Page 17.

Hour, Date, Place	Summary of Events and Information	Remarks and references to Appendices
1915		
4th May VIEUX BERQUIN	Column returned [illegible] at MEURILLON	HM
5 " MEURILLON	No. 1 Section [illegible] from 8th D.A.C.	HM
	4.5 Howitzer Section [illegible] 8 D.A.C.	HM
[illegible]	[illegible] at 4 a.m. to NOUVEAU MONDE	HM
	Battle of FROMELLES.	HM
10 " NOUVEAU MONDE	4.5 Howitzer Section [illegible] 8 D.A.C.	
	41 N.C.O.s & men [illegible]	HM
11 " "	[illegible] ANNEZIN LES BETHUNE	HM
11 " ANNEZIN	[illegible]	HM
14 " "	[illegible] DAVIES [illegible]	
" " "	[illegible] at ANNEZIN.	HM
15 " "	Captain S. CARWITHEN [illegible] ENGLAND and	
	[illegible] 22.5.15.	HM
20 "	7 Gunners exchanged for 7 Gunners 106th Battery 22nd Bde	HM
22 " "	Authority received that Captain H. B. OSTLER [illegible] transferred to ENGLAND (Head Quarters 7 D.A. [illegible] 22.5.15)	HM

(29 6) W 2794 100,000 8/14 H W V Forms/C. 2118/11

7th Division

121/6015

7th Divl: Ammn Coln

Vol VII 23.5. — ~~30~~ 23.6.15.

A2
a96

Instructions regarding War Diaries and Intelligence Summaries are contained in F. S. Regs., Part II. and the Staff Manual respectively. Title pages will be prepared in manuscript.

WAR DIARY
or
INTELLIGENCE SUMMARY.
(Erase heading not required.)

Army Form C. 2118.

Page 18.

Hour, Date, Place	Summary of Events and Information	Remarks and references to Appendices
1915		
23. MAY. ANNEZIN	No 46126 "B" J H KEARNEY wounded in trenches.	Hml
25 " "	Authority received for release of unsentenced prisoners	
	No 96666 Gunner J PEARSON. } Date of release	
	No 96846 Driver P CONNOR. } 23.5.15	Hml
26 " "	2/Lieut STEWART 1 NCO 3 men despatched for instruction	
~~29~~ " "	to Trench Mortar School.	Hml
29 " "	Lieut. RADFORD attached to 22^d B^de R.F.A.	Hml
31. " "	Column moved billets to LES. CHOQUIAUX.	Hml
5. JUNE LES. CHOQUIAUX.	Howitzer Section 43 B^de attached to 7. D.A.C.	
	1 Officer, 58 Men. 69 Horses. 13 Wagons.	Hml
10. " " "	LIEUT. A.L. CHRISTIE. assumes medical charge of Column	Hml
18 " " "	2/LIEUT. M. STEWART. posted to No 3. Trench Mortar battery.	Hml
" " " "	2/LIEUT. A. DANN attached to anti aircraft Gun Section	Hml
23 " " "	Howitzer Section 43. B^de left the Column.	
25 " " "	4.5 Howitzer Section taken on strength of Column	
	Authority H.Q. D.A. 564 dated 23.6.15.	

(9 29 6) W2794 100,000 8/14 H W V Forms/C. 2118/11

7th Division

181/6214

7th Div: A. Column.

Vol: VIII

[illegible] 25-6 - 30.7.15

Instructions regarding War Diaries and Intelligence Summaries are contained in F. S. Regs., Part II. and the Staff Manual respectively. Title pages will be prepared in manuscript.

WAR DIARY
or
INTELLIGENCE SUMMARY.
(Erase heading not required.)

7th Div. A.C.

Army Form C. 2118.

Page 19

Hour, Date, Place	Summary of Events and Information	Remarks and references to Appendices
1915		
25 JUNE. LES.CHOQUIAUX.	Reinforcement of 10 drivers arrived from base.	HmL
27. " "	12 Horses H.D. transferred to VII Divl Train.	HmL
30 " "	Major C.E. BERLY attached 22nd Brigade RFA for instruction in duties of Battery Commander	HmL
" " "	12 heavy draught horses posted from base.	HmL
1 JULY "	Major BERLY rejoined column.	HmL
2 " "	Column moved billet to CANTRAINNE.	HmL
4. " CANTRAINNE.	12 horses LD & 6 drivers arrived from base.	HmL
5 " "	12 horses L.D transferred to 14 Bde RHA	HmL
6 " "	11 drivers & 3 gunners arrived from base	HmL
14 " "	Major W.W. IRWIN arrived from base posted to command 37 Bde Howitzer Section. D.A.C	HmL
18 " "	2/Lt A. DANN. rejoined from anti-aircraft section	HmL
20 " "	216 L.D. horses received from Remount Depot	HmL
20 " "	104 H.D horses evacuated to Remount Depot.	HmL

(9 29 6) W2794 100,000 8/14 H W V Forms/C. 2118/11

Instructions regarding War Diaries and Intelligence Summaries are contained in F. S. Regs., Part II. and the Staff Manual respectively. Title pages will be prepared in manuscript.

WAR DIARY
or
INTELLIGENCE SUMMARY.
(Erase heading not required.)

Army Form C. 2118.

Page 20

Hour, Date, Place	Summary of Events and Information	Remarks and references to Appendices
1915 JULY 22. CONTRAINNE	6 [illegible] arrived from No 2 General base	[illegible]
22 " "	4 H.D. horses evacuated to Remount Depot.	[illegible]
" " "	Lieut J. H. A. STROYAN attached for duty to 35th Brigade RFA.	[illegible]
" " "	A portion of No 3 Section and 4.5 Howitzer Section detached for duty	[illegible]
" " "	Strength 1 officer 82 other ranks 119 horses	[illegible]
26 " "	2 [illegible] arrived from No 2 Base	[illegible]
28 " "	Gunner CLAYTON posted to 35 Bde RFA	[illegible]
" " "	Tr WARREN posted to 22 Bde RFA.	[illegible]
29 " "	Temp 2Lt W J RALPH posted to Column	[illegible]
" " "	Temp 2Lt D B HOWARD posted to Column.	[illegible]
30 " "	2Lt A BURROWS posted to 14 Bde R.H.A. (Authority S.C. 157 dated 29.7.15)	[illegible]

8

7th Division

7th Divl: Ammn Coln

Vol IX

From 5 - 28. 8. 15

Instructions regarding War Diaries and Intelligence Summaries are contained in F. S. Regs., Part II. and the Staff Manual respectively. Title pages will be prepared in manuscript.

WAR DIARY
or
INTELLIGENCE SUMMARY.
(Erase heading not required.)

Army Form C. 2118.

Page 21.

Hour, Date, Place	Summary of Events and Information	Remarks and references to Appendices
1915		
5 August CANTRAINNE	2/Lt ROBERTON, H.G. joined from 35th Bde R.F.A.	HMM
" " "	Temp Lt RALPHS, W.J. posted to 35th Bde R.F.A. Authority H.Q. 7.D.A. 4.8.15.	HMM
14 " "	Sergt HATTON posted to 31st Battery R.F.A. on probation as B.Q.M.S.	HMM
" " "	Captain BEVERIDGE posted to 37th Bde R.F.A.	HMM
" " "	2/Lt DANN, A assumed command of No 3 Section.	HMM
" " "	2/Lt ROBERTON admitted to hospital	HMM
15 " "	Column moved billets to RIEZ-DU-VINAGE.	HMM
17 " RIEZ-DU-VINAGE	4 Gunners employed with Trench Mortar Battery struck off strength of column (H.Q. 7 D.A. 16.8.15)	HMM
18 " "	Column moved billets to PARADIS.	HMM
20 " PARADIS	Major IRWIN assumed command of No II Section.	HMM
" " "	Lt RADFORD assumed command of Howitzer Section on arrival posted from Base	HMM

Instructions regarding War Diaries and Intelligence Summaries are contained in F. S. Regs., Part II. and the Staff Manual respectively. Title pages will be prepared in manuscript.

WAR DIARY
or
INTELLIGENCE SUMMARY.
(Erase heading not required.)

Army Form C. 2118.

PAGE 22

Hour, Date, Place	Summary of Events and Information	Remarks and references to Appendices
1915		
22 AUGUST - PARADIS	Authority received for promotion to 2 Lieut with effect from 16.8.15 of No 20325 RSM CORNFORD W.G and No 11676 BSM HOUGHTON A	
23 " "	2 Lt PHEAR H.J. posted from Base	
27 " "	Column moved billets to RIEZ DU VINAGE	
" " RIEZ DU VINAGE	No 29734 BQMS MOXHAM promoted BSM vice HOUGHTON	
" " "	Two specially enlisted Farrier QM Sergeants posted as under No 52314 TROWBRIDGE F.W to 37 Bde RFA No 52317 LUSH T.H to 35 Bde RFA.	
28 " "	No 19750 Sergt WILLIAMS E posted as BQMS from 37 Bde vice MOXHAM	
" " "	RMS (W.O) BULL T.H posted as RSM vice CORNFORD commissioned.	
" " "	No 3145 Dr TERRY J rejoined from 27 DAC	
" " "	6 L.D. horses arrived from Remount Depot	

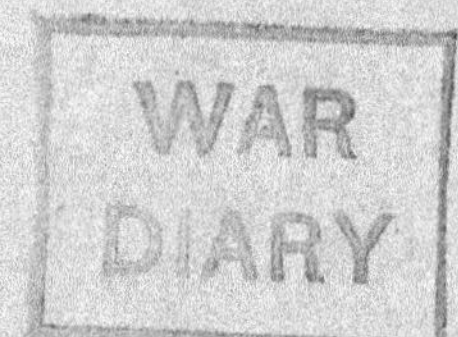

DIVISIONAL AMMUNITION COLOUMN.

7TH DIVISION.

S E P T E M B E R

1 9 1 5

Instructions regarding War Diaries and Intelligence Summaries are contained in F. S. Regs., Part II. and the Staff Manual respectively. Title pages will be prepared in manuscript.

or

INTELLIGENCE SUMMARY. 4th D.A.C. PAGE 23.

(Erase heading not required.)

Hour, Date, Place	Summary of Events and Information	Remarks and references to Appendices
1915		
2 Sept. RIEZ DU VINAGE	Column moved [illegible] to FOUQUIERS	[illegible]
3 " FOUQUIERS	Bomb. TAYLOR [illegible]	[illegible]
6 " "	Temp. Capt. G. BEVERIDGE [illegible]	[illegible]
6	Captain H. L. [illegible] posted to [illegible] R.F.A.	[illegible]
8	[illegible] (	
18	G. A. YOUNG ([illegible] from [illegible]	[illegible]
15	[illegible] of 4th D.A.C. [illegible]	[illegible]
15	MAJOR C. E. BERLY [illegible]	[illegible]
16	[illegible] R. S. ADAMS (	
	J. E. WALKER ([illegible]	[illegible]
	[illegible]	[illegible]
	[illegible] G. A. YOUNG [illegible]	[illegible]
21	[illegible] H. Q. D. [illegible]	[illegible]
22	[illegible] P. R. B[illegible] posted from [illegible]	
	[illegible]	
24	[illegible] posted [illegible] R.H.A.	[illegible]

(9 29 6) W2794 100,000 8/14 H W V Forms/C. 2118/11

Instructions regarding War Diaries and Intelligence Summaries are contained in F. S. Regs., Part II. and the Staff Manual respectively. Title pages will be prepared in manuscript.

INTELLIGENCE SUMMARY. 4th D.A.C. PAGE 24

or

(*Erase heading not required.*)

Hour, Date, Place	Summary of Events and Information	Remarks and references to Appendices
1915		
25 September FOUQUIERS	Captain H SPENCER 2/Lt H.Q. ROBERTSON [illegible]	
	strength of column [illegible] 22.9.15	[illegible]
	[illegible] LABOURSE	[illegible]
26 " LABOURSE	[illegible] D.A.C. [illegible]	[illegible]
	[illegible] of Drivers [illegible] L D [illegible] 22nd Bde	[illegible]
28 " "	2 Lieut J.E WALKER posted to 22nd Bde R.F.A.	[illegible]
" " "	" H.G BOON posted to 35th Bde R.F.A.	[illegible]
" " "	" J.R.A STROYAN posted to 37th Bde R.F.A.	[illegible]
29 " "	Column moved billets to BÉTHUNE	[illegible]
30 " BÉTHUNE	2 Lieut G.J TOBIN } Joined from [illegible]	
	" G.W. ARMSTRONG }	[illegible]
	" E H BECKETT }	
"	8 L D horses arrived from [illegible] Depot	[illegible]

(9 29 6) W 2794 100,000 8/14 H W V Forms/C. 2118/11

7th Division

121/7435

7th Divl. Ammn. Col.

Oct 15

Vol XI

Army Form C. 2118.

Instructions regarding War Diaries and Intelligence Summaries are contained in F. S. Regs., Part II. and the Staff Manual respectively. Title pages will be prepared in manuscript.

WAR DIARY
or
INTELLIGENCE SUMMARY. 47th D.A.C.

(*Erase heading not required.*)

PAGE 25.

Hour, Date, Place	Summary of Events and Information	Remarks and references to Appendices
1915		
1 October 1915 BETHUNE	2/Lieut C MORLEY posted to 22nd Brigade R.F.A.	
" "	" G.J. TOBIN posted to 35th " "	
" "	" E.H. BECKETT posted to 37 " "	
2 "	Lieut L.T. DAY joined from Base	
" "	2/Lieut F.C. NAUMANN " " "	
" "	" H BONNY " " "	
" "	" H.S. MACNEIL " " "	
" "	" C GOULD " " "	
5 "	Lieut L.T. DAY posted to 14 Brigade R.H.A.	
5 "	2/Lieut NAUMANN " " "	
8 "	2/Lieut McCORQUODALE joined from base	
" "	" T.N. ROBINSON " " "	
11 "	13 Gunners & 23 Drivers received from base	
12 "	2/Lieut H.S. MACNEIL posted to 14th Brigade R.H.Q.	
	No 4 Section 46 Bde joined D.A.C.	
	1 Officer 42 other ranks, 43 horses.	

(9 29 6) W2794 100,000 8/14 H W V Forms/C. 2118/11

Army Form C. 2118.

Instructions regarding War Diaries and Intelligence Summaries are contained in F. S. Regs., Part II. and the Staff Manual respectively. Title pages will be prepared in manuscript.

WAR DIARY
or
INTELLIGENCE SUMMARY. 7th D.A.C.
(Erase heading not required.)

PAGE. 26.

Hour, Date, Place	Summary of Events and Information	Remarks and references to Appendices
1915		
14 October BETHUNE	10 Gunners posted to 37 Brigade to replace casualties	[illegible]
16 " "	Column moved billets to ANNEZIN	[illegible]
" " "	2/Lieut ADAMS admitted to hospital	[illegible]
" " "	13 L.D. horses arrived from Remount Depot	[illegible]
" " "	2/Lieut J. PERRY joined from base	[illegible]
18 " ANNEZIN	4 Section 46 D.A.C. rejoined 46 Division	[illegible]
19 " "	Column moved billets to MOLINGHEM	[illegible]
20 " MOLINGHEM	202 L.D. horses handed over to 28 Division	[illegible]
" " "	103 H.D. horses received from 28 Division	[illegible]
24 " Vendin Lez Bethune	Column moved billets from MOLINGHEM	[illegible]
26 " "	A.D.V.S. 7th DIV. inspected heavy draught horses rec'd from 28th DIV.	[illegible]
" " "	and ordered 12 to be transferred to Mobile Vet. Sec. 7 DIV., and 6 to be	[illegible]
" " "	classified as Light Draught	[illegible]
30 "	11 Gunners 1 Driver joined as reinforcements from No 2 Gen. Base	
" " "	Depot Havre.	[illegible]
30 " "	2/Lt C. GOULD posted to 35 Bde R.F.A.	[illegible]

(9 29 6) W 2794 100,000 8/14 H W V Forms/C. 2118/11.

7th Div. Ammn. Col.

Nov

Vol XII

121/7655

Army Form C. 2118.

WAR DIARY
~~or~~
~~INTELLIGENCE SUMMARY.~~
(*Erase heading not required.*)

4/1st D.A.C. SHEET. 24

Instructions regarding War Diaries and Intelligence Summaries are contained in F. S. Regs., Part II. and the Staff Manual respectively. Title pages will be prepared in manuscript.

Hour, Date, Place		Summary of Events and Information	Remarks and references to Appendices
1915			
[illegible]0 Oct	VENDIN-LEZ-BETHUNE	2/Lt J. CAVE-BIGLEY posted from 35th Bde R.F.A.	[illegible]
31 "	"	2/Lt H.S. MACNEIL posted from 14 Bde R.F.A.	[illegible]
[illegible] Nov.	"	2/Lt D.B. HOWARD posted to 35th Bde R.F.A.	[illegible]
[illegible]5 "	"	2 Lt H. BONNY } posted to 37th Bde R.F.A.	[illegible]
"	"	2 Lt J. PERRY }	
[illegible] "	"	2 Lt T.N. ROBINSON posted to 22 Bde R.F.A.	[illegible]
[illegible] "	"	Captain H. GOLDIE posted from 9th Bde A.C.	[illegible]
[illegible]6 "	"	Captain L. CHRISTIE R.A.M.C. posted to 37 Bde R.F.A.	[illegible]
"	"	Captain C.F. STEPHEN posted from Base	[illegible]
17 "	"	198 L.D. horses received from Remounts	[illegible]
"	"	57 H.D. horses evacuated to Remounts	[illegible]
"	"	12 H.D. horses sent to Mobile Section	[illegible]
20 "	"	20 H.D. horses transferred to XII Div Train	[illegible]
24 "	"	2/Lt E. CROFT posted from Base	[illegible]
" "	"	9 Drivers joined from No 2 Gen. Base	[illegible]
25 "	"	2 Lt D.M. ROOKE posted from Base	[illegible]
26 "	"	2 Lt F.D. WISEMAN temporarily proceeded to BOULOGNE to form Supply School of Instruction	[illegible]

7th Divl Ammn Col.

Dec.

Vol. XIII

121
7939

Army Form C. 2118.

Instructions regarding War Diaries and Intelligence Summaries are contained in F. S. Regs., Part II. and the Staff Manual respectively. Title pages will be prepared in manuscript.

WAR DIARY
or
INTELLIGENCE SUMMARY.
(Erase heading not required.)

7th D.A.C.

SHEET. 28.

Hour, Date, Place	Summary of Events and Information	Remarks and references to Appendices
1915		
30 Nov. VENDIN	~~2/Lt J CAVE-BIGLEY posted from 35 Bde RFA~~	[illegible]
3 Dec. "	Column moved billets to LA GOULÉE	[illegible]
7 " LAGOULEE	Column proceeded by train from LILLERS & BERGUETTE to new billets in III Army area forming part of XIII Corps.	[illegible]
8 " LE QUESNOY	Column arrived and in billets at LE QUESNOY LE GARD and CROUY.	[illegible]
10 " "	2/Lt ADAMS posted to 35 Brigade RFA	[illegible]
" " "	2/Lt CROFT & 2/Lt ROOKE posted to 22 Bde RFA	[illegible]
" " "	2/Lt SHINGLETON reposted from 22 Bde RFA	[illegible]
12 " "	1 Corpl & 12 drivers arrived from Base	[illegible]
16 " "	17 LD horses & 20 mules arrived from Remount Dep[ot]	[illegible]
22 " "	Colonel H MONTGOMERY CAMPBELL [illegible] command of column on transfer to ENGLAND	[illegible]
		RHR.
23 " "	Lieut McCORQUODALE posted to 11 Section Anti-Aircraft guns 10 Corps	RHR.
26 " "	Major C E BERLY sick to England 12/12/15.	
31 " "	Lieut CAVE-BIGLEY J. struck [off] strength of column.	RHR.

R H Radford Lieut RFA Adjt 7 DAC
for O.C. 7 DAC
31/12/15

4 Div Amm Col

Jan

Vol XIV

Instructions regarding War Diaries and Intelligence Summaries are contained in F. S. Regs., Part II. and the Staff Manual respectively. Title pages will be prepared in manuscript.

WAR DIARY
or
INTELLIGENCE SUMMARY.
(Erase heading not required.)

7th D.A.C.
SHEET 29.

Army Form C. 2118.

Hour, Date, Place	Summary of Events and Information	Remarks and references to Appendices
1916		
1 Jan. Le Lucorne	Lieut S.F. Shingleton proceeded to Trench Mortar School Valhuon to undergo course of instruction in Medium Trench Mortar	
6 " " "	10 Drivers joined from No 2 General Base Depot, Havre.	
10 " " "	Lt Col H.H. Rogers R.F.A. assumed command of 7th DAC	
13 " " "	4 Drivers joined from No 2 Gen. Base Depot Havre	
17 " " "	Lt J.R.A. Strogan rejoined 7th DAC from 37th Bde R.F.A. (Authority A/C/34 of 13.1.16 DAA & QMG 7th Div.)	
20 " " "	2 Lieut Duncan R.A., " Mitchell C.D., " Valle-Pope E.L., " Mackenzie A.K., " Gaylard A.W. — Joined from No 2 General Base Depot Havre. Authority H.Q. 7 DA of 19th	
20 " " "	2 Lieut Valle-Pope posted to 37th Bde R.F.A. " Gaylard A.W. posted to 22nd Bde R.F.A.	
21 " " "	3 Gunners joined from No 2 Gen. Base Depot Havre	
22 " " "	6 Drivers joined " " " "	
24 " " "	Lieut Gaylard A.W. rejoined 7th DAC from 22nd Bde R.F.A.	
27 " " "	19 Gunners & 2 Drivers joined from No 2 Gen. Base Depot Havre	
28 " " "	2 Riding Horses & 7 Mules received from Remount Depot	
29 " " "	Temp. Capt J.G. Miller R.F.A. joined 7th DAC from Kite Balloon Section	H.H. Rogers Lt Col. R.F.A. Cdr 7th DAC 31/1/16

Instructions regarding War Diaries and Intelligence Summaries are contained in F. S. Regs., Part II. and the Staff Manual respectively. Title pages will be prepared in manuscript.

WAR DIARY
or
INTELLIGENCE SUMMARY.
(Erase heading not required.)

7th D.A.C.
SHEET. No. 30

Army Form C. 2118.

Hour, Date, Place		Summary of Events and Information	Remarks and references to Appendices
1916			
2nd Feby.	LE QESNOT.	Reinforcements 2 drivers joined from No 2 General Base Depot	
5 "		Column moved from LE QUESNOT to St GRATIEN	
6 "		Column moved from St GRATIEN to BONNAY.	
" "	BONNAY	2 Lieut McKENZIE. A.K admitted to Hospital.	
10 "	"	T Captn H.M. GOLDIE attached as A.P.M. to 13th Corps.	
12 "	"	T Captn J.P. LEGGOTT R.F.A posted to 7th D.A.C from 14th R.H.A, B.A.C.	
14 "	"	" " " " joined 7th D.A.C. & assumed command of No 1 Section 7th D.A.C.	
15 "	"	Reinforcements 1 Driver joined from No 2 Genl Base Depot	
19 "	"	12 mules received from Remount Depot.	
23 "	"	1 Sergt, 1 Corpl & 6 Gunners posted to 3rd Army Trench Mortar School to form Medium Trench Mortar Battery.	
24 "	"	Reinforcements 1 Gunner from Military Prison in the Field on remission of unexpired portion of sentence.	
25 "	"	Reinforcements 13 Gunners & 3 Drivers from No 2 Genl Base Depot.	H M Rogers Lt Col R.F.A. Comdg 7th DAC

(9 29 6) W 2794 100,000 8/14 H W V Forms/C. 2118/11.

Confidential

Subject
War Diary.

HEADQUARTER OFFICE
No. C 998/1
Date 29.2.16
7th DIVISIONAL AMMN. COLN.

To The Officer In Charge of
R.A. Branch A. General's Office.
(3rd Echelon)

I forward herewith the War Diary (Original) page 36 of the 7th Divisional Ammunition Column, Royal Field Artillery in accordance with Field Service Regulations part II, Section 140, para: (2).

Kindly acknowledge receipt hereon.

In the Field
29th February 1916

H.W. Rogers Lieut Colonel R.F.A.
Commanding 7th Divisional Ammn Coln

Original

Army Form C. 2118.

WAR DIARY
or
INTELLIGENCE SUMMARY.
(Erase heading not required.)

4th D.A.C.
SHEET. NO. 31.

Instructions regarding War Diaries and Intelligence Summaries are contained in F. S. Regs., Part II. and the Staff Manual respectively. Title pages will be prepared in manuscript.

Hour, Date, Place		Summary of Events and Information	Remarks and references to Appendices
1916			
2nd March	BONNAY	4 Gunners joined from No 2 Gen Base Depot.	
6 "	"	Column moved billets from BONNAY to BUIRE	
8 "	"	Lieut J R.A. STROYAN R.F.A. proceeded to England & was struck off strength.	
9 "	BUIRE	Captn J.G MILLER posted to Trench Mortar Battery & struck off.	
13 "	"	MAJOR W. IRWIN R.F.A. posted to 38th Divn Arty.	
14 "	"	2 LIEUTT G.W. ARMSTRONG R.F.A. assumed command No 2 Section	
16 "	"	8 Drivers joined from No 2 Gen Base Depot.	
	"	2 LIEUTT H.S. McNEIL posted to Royal Flying Corps & struck off.	
30 "	"	6 Drivers joined from No 2 Gen Base Depot.	
31 "	"	Column moved from BUIRE to MERICOURT	
23 April	MERICOURT	CAPTN H.M. GOLDIE invalided to England & struck off.	
26 "	"	4 Gunners & 3 Drivers joined from No 2 Gen Base Depot	

H.H. Rogers Lt Col R.F.A.
Comdg 7th D.A.C.

Instructions regarding War Diaries and Intelligence Summaries are contained in F. S. Regs., Part II. and the Staff Manual respectively. Title pages will be prepared in manuscript.

WAR DIARY
or
INTELLIGENCE SUMMARY.
(Erase heading not required.)

Army Form C. 2118.

7th D.A.C.
SHEET 31 (a)
Vol 18 19 20

Hour, Date, Place		Summary of Events and Information	Remarks and references to Appendices
1916			
1st May	MERICOURT	Column moves billets to BONNAY	
16 "	BONNAY	" was reorganised into Head Quarters, A & B Echelons.	
		B Echelon moved from BONNAY to TREUX.	
19 "	"	Section details from 37th Bde R.F.A. BAC joined H.Q.	
		7th DAC at BONNAY.	
25 "	"	Surplus details, horses, mules & vehicles left for ABBEVILLE	
26	TREUX	H.Q. moved from BONNAY to TREUX.	
to 12 June	"	The Column was working hard night & day preparing	
to		for Pontoons, Trench work & other Fatigues.	
25 "	"	Large ammunition dumps were put in to Battery	
		positions of 1000 rounds per gun.	
30 "	MORLANCOURT	B Echelon moved to MORLANCOURT	[illegible] Lt Col R.F.A. Comdg 7th DAC

(9 29 6) W 2794 100,000 8/14 H W V Forms/C. 2118/11.

Instructions regarding War Diaries and Intelligence Summaries are contained in F. S. Regs., Part II. and the Staff Manual respectively. Title pages will be prepared in manuscript.

WAR DIARY
or
~~INTELLIGENCE SUMMARY~~.
(Erase heading not required.)

7th D.A.C.
Sheet 32.

Army Form C. 2118.

Hour, Date, Place		Summary of Events and Information	Remarks and references to Appendices
1916			
1 July.	MORLANCOURT	A. Echelon moved to Bois-de-Tailles; also the Section of 17th D.A.C. attached to us.	
4th	MÉAULTE	The whole column moved to MEAULTE	
7th	"	A portion of the 38th D.A.C. was attached to us in addition to 2, 3 & 4 Sections 17th D.A.C. A limber of No. 2 Section 7th DAC disabled by shell fire.	
9th	"	Lieut W. J. S. ANDERSON RFA wounded at MAMETZ dump, one saddler killed and 3 gunners wounded same time. The dump was afterwards discontinued. Two men working in the dump have been missing since this date	
20th	"	Lieut. R. A. RADFORD RFA was transferred with Trench [illegible]	
	HEILLY	The column moved back to HEILLY at 9 p.m.	
		The turnover of ammunition during the operations was very large. Between the 29th June & 15th July we handled the following ammunition: A 185,818 rounds, AX 76,078, BX 36086	H M Rogers Lt Col RFA Comdg 7th D.A.C.

(9 29 6) W2794 100,000 8/14 H W V Forms/C. 2118/11

7th Divisional Artillery.

7th DIVISIONAL AMMUNITION COLUMN R.F.A.

AUGUST 1 9 1 6

Instructions regarding War Diaries and Intelligence Summaries are contained in F. S. Regs., Part II. and the Staff Manual respectively. Title pages will be prepared in manuscript.

WAR DIARY
or
INTELLIGENCE SUMMARY.
(Erase heading not required.)

Army Form C. 2118.

1/7th D.A.C. SHEET 33. Vol 19

Hour, Date, Place		Summary of Events and Information	Remarks and references to Appendices
15 Augt	HEILLY	Lieut R.H. RADFORD Adjt struck off the strength, sick and invalided to ENGLAND.	
20 "	MEAULTE	Column moved to MEAULTE into action with 7th D.A.	
23 "	"	Undermentioned details placed under orders of O.C. 7th D.A.C. No 3 Section 5th D.A.C complete, as well as the ammn wagons 4.5 How. of No 2 Section 5th D.A.C 20 G.S wagons of No 4 Section 5th D.A.C; No 3 Section 1st Indian Cavalry D.A.C (complete); No 1 Section A Echelon 33rd D.A.C complete; No 4 Section B Echelon 33rd D.A.C (15 wagons)	
28 "	"	Four men of No 3 Section wounded by Enemy shell fire.	
31	"	5 N.C.O's & men wounded by enemy shell fire and 1 man killed. 6 horses wounded and 1 killed.	

H.H. Rogers Lieut R.F.A.
Comdg 7th D.A.C.

(9 29 6) W2794 100,000 8/14 H W V Forms/C. 2118/11

Confidential

Army Form C. 2118.

Instructions regarding War Diaries and Intelligence Summaries are contained in F. S. Regs., Part II. and the Staff Manual respectively. Title pages will be prepared in manuscript.

WAR DIARY
or
INTELLIGENCE SUMMARY.
(Erase heading not required.)

7th D.A.C.
SHEET. 34.
Vol 20

Hour, Date, Place		Summary of Events and Information	Remarks and references to Appendices
3 Sept/16	MEAULTE.	Vicinity of Camp shelled from 8.30 am to 10.30 am. Delivery of ammunition to gun positions very difficult, 3 men died of wounds 6 L.D. Horses wounded, 5 mules killed.	
4 Sept.	"	4 men wounded, 1 horse & 2 mules killed, 6 mules wounded. Vicinity of Camp shelled nearly every day.	
17 "	MONTAUBAN	Column moved to MONTAUBAN to be near Ammunition Railhead, but owing to Enemy shelling no ammunition was forthcoming there.	
18 "	BECORDEL & FRICOURT.	The column moved to FRICOURT & BECORDEL temporary ammunition railhead. Teams & wagons from A Echelon were sent to supplement Battery Wagon Lines at MONTAUBAN & remained there till 28th.	
28th	BONNAY	Column moved back from the line to BONNAY & bivouaced.	
30/1 Oct.	LONGEAU	Column entrained & detrained at CAESTRE and marched to SCHAEKSKEN.	H H Rogers Lt Col RFA Comd. 7th DAC

(9 29 6) W 2794 100,000 8/14 H W V Forms/C. 2118/11.

Army Form C. 2118.

Instructions regarding War Diaries and Intelligence Summaries are contained in F. S. Regs., Part II. and the Staff Manual respectively. Title pages will be prepared in manuscript.

WAR DIARY
or
INTELLIGENCE SUMMARY.
(Erase heading not required.)

7th D.A.C.
SHEET. 35.
Vol 21 20

Hour, Date, Place		Summary of Events and Information	Remarks and references to Appendices
1916			
Oct 2	SCHAEKSKEN	Column marched from SCHAEKSKEN to NIEPPE	
6	NIEPPE	S.A.A. Section of 509th Batt.n posted to 7th DAC. A great deal of work was done throughout the month making brick standings for horses, putting up roofs to cover same, & linking of stables and huts for men, with trench boards & cinder paths.	
10	NIEPPE	7 N.C.O's & men awarded Military Medal.	
12	"	2 " " " " " for Operations on the Somme. Ammunition supply very light throughout the month.	

W H Rogers Lt Col RFA
Comd 7th DAC

(9 29 6) W 2791 100,000 8/14 H W V Forms/C. 2118/11.

Army Form C. 2118.

Instructions regarding War Diaries and Intelligence Summaries are contained in F. S. Regs., Part II. and the Staff Manual respectively. Title pages will be prepared in manuscript.

WAR DIARY or INTELLIGENCE SUMMARY. 7th DAC Sheet 36

(Erase heading not required.)

Vol 22

Hour, Date, Place	Summary of Events and Information	Remarks and references to Appendices
1916 Nov. 5th NIEPPE	Corps Commander presented ribbons of military medal to Eleven N.C.O's & men 7th DAC.	
7 "	14 reinforcements arrived from the base Depot Havre.	
23 "	2 Lieut A. J PREVOST R.F.A posted to 35th Bde R.F.A.	
	Ammunition supply during the month very small	

A H Rogers Lt Col RFA
Comd 7th DAC.

(9 29 6) W2794 100,000 8/14 H W V Forms/C. 2118/11

Army Form C. 2118.

Instructions regarding War Diaries and Intelligence Summaries are contained in F. S. Regs., Part II. and the Staff Manual respectively. Title pages will be prepared in manuscript.

WAR DIARY
or
INTELLIGENCE SUMMARY.

(Erase heading not required.)

7th D.A.C.
Sheet 37. Vol 23

Hour, Date, Place	Summary of Events and Information	Remarks and references to Appendices
1916		
Decr. 4 FLETRE.	Column moved to FLETRE.	
5 "	Halted at FLETRE.	
6 STERN BECQUE	Column moved to STERN BECQUE.	
7 RELY	" " " RELY	
8 MONCHY CAYEUX	" " " MONCHY CAYEUX.	
9	halted at " "	
10 VACQUERIE	" moved to VACQUERIE.	
	The Secretary to Lord Kitchener Memorial Fund acknowledged receipt of £69 – subscribed by the Column	
11th AUTHIEULE	Column moved to AUTHIEULE.	
12th ACHEUX	" " " ACHEUX	
to	Took over ammunition & grenade dumps from	
31st	3rd & 37th Divisions and continued normal work in the Line to end of month.	
		H H Rogers Lt Col R F A Comd 7th D.A.C.

(9 29 6) W 2791 160,000 8/14 H W V Forms/C. 2118/11.

7th DIVISION.

DIVISIONAL AMMUNITION COLUMN.

JANUARY 1917.

Original

Instructions regarding War Diaries and Intelligence Summaries are contained in F. S. Regs., Part II. and the Staff Manual respectively. Title pages will be prepared in manuscript.

WAR DIARY
or
INTELLIGENCE SUMMARY.
(Erase heading not required.)

7 Div Col

Army Form C. 2118.

Vol 23

Hour, Date, Place	Summary of Events and Information	Remarks and references to Appendices
1917 Jan 1 ACHEUX to 31st ACHEUX.	The supply of ammunition to gun positions was made under very difficult conditions. The first part of the month was distinguished by water & deep mud in roads & lines, and the last half by snow & hard frosts which made transportation very hard & tended to great discomfort as regards the men. A large number were put out of action, and the wastage in animals was still more pronounced. The reduction in animals since our arrival here amounts to 250 in evacuations and deaths from exposure.	W H Rogers Lt Col RFA Comd 7th DAC 4/2/17

(9 29 6) W 2794 100,000 8/14 H W V Forms/C. 2118/11.

Instructions regarding War Diaries and Intelligence Summaries are contained in F. S. Regs., Part II. and the Staff Manual respectively. Title pages will be prepared in manuscript.

WAR DIARY
or
INTELLIGENCE SUMMARY.
(Erase heading not required.)

Army Form C. 2118.

7 D Am Col

Sheet 39

Vol 25

Hour, Date, Place	Summary of Events and Information	Remarks and references to Appendices
1917. Feby 1st to 4th Acheux.	Normal ammunition supply	
5th Amplier	Column moved to Amplier	
7 "	Column reorganized, formed 14th Bde. H.A.B.A.C.	
8 " "	17 NCO's & men Trench Mortar Course Talkeweux	
8 " "	15 " " " reinforcements	
12 " "	1 officer, 5 O.R. Signal School. La HALE FARM	
14 " "	B.S.M. Moxham H. commissioned posted to 62nd Division	
19 " "	32 men, reinforcements arrived	
24 " "	114 " " "	
25 Arqueves.	Column moved to ARQUEVES.	
26 ACHEUX.	" " " ACHEUX wood.	
26 to 28 "	Took over Ammunition Dumps from 62nd D.A.C.	

Capt. [signature]
Comnds 7 D.A.C.
R.F.A.

5/3/17.

(9 29 6) W4141—463 100,000 9/14 H W V Forms/C. 2118/10

Instructions regarding War Diaries and Intelligence Summaries are contained in F. S. Regs., Part II. and the Staff Manual respectively. Title pages will be prepared in manuscript.

WAR DIARY
or
INTELLIGENCE SUMMARY.
(Erase heading not required.)

Sheet 40

Army Form C. 2118.

Hour, Date, Place	Summary of Events and Information	Remarks and references to Appendices
1917		Vol 25
March 1. ACHEUX	Column engaged chiefly in road and other Fatigues.	
" 3	No 2 Section moved to Sucrerie MAILLY	
" 6 MAILLY	Remainder of Column moved to MAILLY. Ammunition supply commenced, mostly carried out by pack animals	
" 20 "	2 Lieut D.A. LARDER was taken on the strength from 13th	
" 26 ABLAZENVILLE to	Column moved to PUISSIEUX & ABLAZENVILLE No 2 Section engaged in collecting ammunition from old gun positions.	
" 31 "	Remainder ordinary supply of ammunition.	

W H Rogers Lt Col RFA
Comd 7 DAC

7th DIVISION.

DIVISIONAL AMMUNITION COLUMN.

M A Y. 1917.

Instructions regarding War Diaries and Intelligence Summaries are contained in F. S. Regs., Part II. and the Staff Manual respectively. Title pages will be prepared in manuscript.

WAR DIARY
or
INTELLIGENCE SUMMARY.
(Erase heading not required.)

Army Form C. 2118.

Sheet 42

7 D Amn Col

Vol 27

Hour, Date, Place	Summary of Events and Information	Remarks and references to Appendices
1917. May 1 to May 15th ACHIET-LE-GRAND	Usual ammunition to guns; 2Lieut. J H Roberts was wounded when in charge of wagons on special work near BULLECOURT. 6th May.	
" BEHAGNIES	Hd. Qrs. & Nos. 2 & 3 Section moved up and camped close to No. 1 Section.	
23rd "	The military medal was awarded to No. 2899 Farrier Sergt. R. James 7th DAC in connection with the work done near BULLECOURT on 6th May.	
to		
" 31st "	Usual ammunition to guns at night	

W H Rogers Lt Col RFA
Comdg 7th DAC

7th DIVISION.

DIVISIONAL AMMUNITION COLUMN.

J U N E. 1917.

Instructions regarding War Diaries and Intelligence Summaries are contained in F. S. Regs., Part II. and the Staff Manual respectively. Title pages will be prepared in manuscript.

WAR DIARY
or
INTELLIGENCE SUMMARY.
(Erase heading not required.)

Army Form C. 2118.

Vol 28

Place	Date	Hour	Summary of Events and Information	Remarks and references to Appendices
			Original	
			7 Divisional Ammunition Column	
			War Diary for June 1917	

A5834 Wt. W4973/M687 750,000 8/16 D. D. & L. Ltd. Forms/C.2118/13.

Instructions regarding War Diaries and Intelligence Summaries are contained in F. S. Regs., Part II. and the Staff Manual respectively. Title pages will be prepared in manuscript.

7th D.A.C.
Sheet 43

Army Form C. 2118.

WAR DIARY
or
INTELLIGENCE SUMMARY.
(Erase heading not required.)

Hour, Date, Place	Summary of Events and Information	Remarks and references to Appendices
1917		
June 21st BEHAGNIES	Advance (Grenade) Section moved to MORY	
" 24th "	Took over Nos 1 & 2 Tramway dumps of ammunition from 58th Division; removed	
" 25th	all ammunition from ERVILLERS dump and abolished it.	
to		
"	Supply of ammunition to the guns very easy throughout the month, the line being very quiet. Filled up to establishment in animals after being from 100 to 200 down	
30th "	for some months.	
		H R Rogers Lt Col RFA Comdg 7th D.A.C.

(9 29 6) W4141—463 100,000 9/14 H W V Forms/C. 2118/10

7th DIVISION.

DIVISIONAL AMMUNITION COLUMN.

J U L Y. 1917.

Instructions regarding War Diaries and Intelligence Summaries are contained in F. S. Regs., Part II. and the Staff Manual respectively. Title pages will be prepared in manuscript.

WAR DIARY
or
INTELLIGENCE SUMMARY.
(Erase heading not required.)

Sheet No. 44

7 Div. Am Col

Army Form C. 2118.

Hour, Date, Place	Summary of Events and Information	Remarks and references to Appendices
1917 July		VIII 29
5 BEHAGNIES	Salvage operations were commenced on a map area	
10th "	Leave allotment was increased, allowing of over 100 men being away in England at a time.	
15th "	All horse blankets were disinfected at ACHIET-LE-PETIT.	
21st "	Up to this date the following ammunition was salved damaged ammunition (live) 18 Pr. 12994 rounds 4.5 How. 3975 " Empty cases 18 Pr. 96611 cases 4.5 How. 18680 " as well as large quantities of equipment & stores. The G.O.C RA VIth Corps inspected the 7th D.A.C and expressed his satisfaction with the turn out.	
24th "	The Army Commander expressed in orders his appreciation of an act of courage (stopping runaway team & cart) of No. 11431 Dr. Shelton No. 3 Section 7th DAC	31/7/17
31st "	Light ammn. supply, heavy fatigues during month	H H Rogers Lt Col RFA Comdg 7th DAC

(9 29 6) W 2794 100,000 8/14 H W V Forms/C. 2118/11.

7th DIVISION.

DIVISIONAL AMMUNITION COLUMN.

AUGUST 1917.

18 7 DAC Sheet 45 Vol 30

Army Form C. 2118.

Instructions regarding War Diaries and Intelligence Summaries are contained in F. S. Regs., Part II. and the Staff Manual respectively. Title pages will be prepared in manuscript.

WAR DIARY
or
INTELLIGENCE SUMMARY.
(Erase heading not required.)

Hour, Date, Place	Summary of Events and Information	Remarks and references to Appendices
1917 August 11 BEHAGNIES	Turn-out competition for 7th D.A. took place; No. 1 Section 1st, 104th Batt. 2nd, Nos 2 & 3 Section bracketed 3rd.	
14th "	Winter brick Horse Lines commenced.	
24th/25th "	7th D.A. withdrawn from the Line.	
25th to 30th	Preparation for move; everything overhauled and ordered to be ready by midnight 31st/1st Sept. preparatory to entraining	

4/9/17

[signature] Lt Col RFA
Comd. 7th DAC

7th DIVISION.

DIVISIONAL AMMUNITION COLUMN.

SEPTEMBER 1917.

Instructions regarding War Diaries and Intelligence Summaries are contained in F. S. Regs., Part II. and the Staff Manual respectively. Title pages will be prepared in manuscript.

WAR DIARY
or
INTELLIGENCE SUMMARY.
(Erase heading not required.)

Army Form C. 2118.

~~Sheet 46.~~ 7th Div Amm: Column

Vol 31

Place	Date	Hour	Summary of Events and Information	Remarks and references to Appendices
	1917 Sept.			
BEHAGNIES	1		Column moved off for new area, half entraining at MIRAMONT. Remainder at BEACOURT. The 1st half detrained at HOPOUTRE, remainder at GODEWAERSVELDE. Marched to billets at RENINGHELST. Stayed there the night.	
METEREN ~~RENINGHELST~~	2		Moved to METEREN artillery area.	
	4		Advance (grenade) Section moved to STAPLE.	
	6		Party of 80 NCO and men moved to PARRET FARM under Lieut Ingram, Bryce & Rose ?/c as a working party to build new gun positions.	
			Lieut Cook took over Ammunition Office in forward area.	
	6 15 11		Capt Burrows moved up to BEAVER CORNER with 40 GS wagons teams and personnel, to help in carting materials for new gun positions	
STRAZEELE	12		Moved to new area.	
	14		Lieut Addis joined from hospital	
	21		Working parties under Capt Burrows & Lt Ingram returned from forward area	
WESTOUTRE	27		Moved to new area.	
DICKEBUSCH	28		Capt Armstrong with 40 GS wagons, teams, & personnel moved up as a working party	
	15		Three officers & 600 O.R also went up as a working party. Lieut Cook took over Ammunition Dump	
	30		General supply of ammunition in wagons, & on pack animals.	[illegible] Anderson Capt RFA for Lt Col Commanding 7 D.A.C.

D. D. & L., London, E.C. (A8c04) Wt W1771/M2031 750,000 5/17 Sch. 52 Forms/C2118/14

7th DIVISION.

DIVISIONAL AMMUNITION COLUMN.

OCTOBER 1917.

19

WAR DIARY
or
INTELLIGENCE SUMMARY.
(Erase heading not required.)

Army Form C. 2118.

Instructions regarding War Diaries and Intelligence Summaries are contained in F. S. Regs., Part II. and the Staff Manual respectively. Title pages will be prepared in manuscript.

Sheet 47. 9th Divisional Ammunition Column.

VOL 32

Place	Date	Hour	Summary of Events and Information	Remarks and references to Appendices
DICKEBUSCH	October 1914.			
	1st		Column moved from WESTOUTRE Area to DICKEBUSCH.	
			No 94409. Dr A. J. McDowell (Wounded). Since died.	
			" 19583. Dr J. E. Dodgson (Wounded).	
— " —	2nd		No 96630. Dr J. B. Bushby (Wounded).	
— " —	3rd		No 36355. Gr S. Hartshorne (Wounded).	
			2nd Lt J. J. Gordon taken on Strength.	
— " —	4th		No 78242. Dr Scowcroft. (Wounded).	
— " —	8th		No 9611 Dr G. Day. (Wounded).	
			" 211327 Dr E. Williamson Reported Missing. Since reported Wounded and to Hospital	
— " —	12th		No 150332 Gr R.T. Perry (Wounded).	
— " —	16th		No 631337 Dr A. Morris (Wounded).	

D. D. & L., London, E.C.
(A8c04) Wt W1771/M2031 750,000 5/17 Sch. 52 Forms/C2118/14

Instructions regarding War Diaries and Intelligence Summaries are contained in F. S. Regs., Part II. and the Staff Manual respectively. Title pages will be prepared in manuscript.

WAR DIARY
or
INTELLIGENCE SUMMARY.
(Erase heading not required.)

Army Form C. 2118.

Sheet 47 Contd.

Place	October Date 1914.	Hour	Summary of Events and Information	Remarks and references to Appendices
DICKEBUSCH.	18th		No 149293. Dr A Horocks (Killed in Action). No 76258 Dr V. E. B. Page (Wounded). No 94104 Dr Richardson (Wounded) remained at duty.	
— " —	19th		Major K. M. Agnew. M. C. Attached D. A. C.	
— " —	20th		Colonel H. H. Rogers D. S. O. to Home establishment	
— " —	21st		No 21193 Dr W. H. Langton (Killed in Action) No 77817 Dr E. Truett (Seriously wounded). No 69563 Dr J. Lay (Wounded).	
— " —	22nd		No 88320 Dr A. Gibson (Wounded). remained at duty.	
— " —	23rd		No L/34385 Dr W. Hatch (Wounded). No 60185 Dr G. Watkins (Reported Missing).	
— " —	24th		No 68107 Dr J. Duncan. No 34430. Dr Mattock G. Awarded Military Medal.	
— " —	30th		No [illegible] Dr W. Cavanagh (Wounded). Major K. M. Agnew M. C. to 106th Battery	
			During the month General Ammunition Supply and Fatigues	
			[signature] Capt. R. F. A. Commanding 47th D. A. C.	

D. D. & L., London, E.C.
(A8c04) Wt W1771/M2031 750,000 5/17 Sch. 52 Forms/C2118/14

7th DIVISION.

DIVISIONAL AMMUNITION COLUMN.

NOVEMBER 1917.

Instructions regarding War Diaries and Intelligence Summaries are contained in F. S. Regs., Part II. and the Staff Manual respectively. Title pages will be prepared in manuscript.

WAR DIARY
or
INTELLIGENCE SUMMARY. Sheet 48
(Erase heading not required.)

Army Form C. 2118.

Vol 33

7 Div: Amn: Column

Place	Date	Hour	Summary of Events and Information	Remarks and references to Appendices
	Nov 1917			
Dickebusch	4		30 gunners posted from D.A.C. to 35th Bty. R.F.A. and 22nd Bde. R.F.A. to replace casualties.	
—"—	7	✓	56 O.R's joined from Base – 10 reported to 22nd Bde R.F.A. and rest to 35th Bde. R.F.A. 18 O.R's arrived late at night from Base of these on the	
—"—	8	✓	6 were reported to 22nd Bde. R.F.A. 12 " " " 35th " "	
			No. 19827 Sergt. R.C. Ruth. No. 2. Sec. D.A.C. awarded the Military Medal – date of award 2/10/17 Auth: 7th D.A. 248/21 d/ 6-11-17	
Boeschepe	10	✓	D.A.C. moved from Dickebusch to Boeschepe	
—"—	11	✓	3 O.R's from Base – Reinforcements for 22nd Bde	
—"—	12	✓	Inspection of D.A.C. by Corps Commander X Corps 98 O.Rs joined from Base – reinforcements for D.A.C. & Bdes.	

Ang. [illegible] Major
Commdg – D.A.C. 7th Div

D. D. & L., London, E.C.
(A8c04) Wt W1771/M2031 750,000 5/17 Sch. 52 Forms/C2118/14

Instructions regarding War Diaries and Intelligence Summaries are contained in F. S. Regs., Part II. and the Staff Manual respectively. Title pages will be prepared in manuscript.

WAR DIARY
or
INTELLIGENCE SUMMARY.
(Erase heading not required.)

Army Form C. 2118.

Sheet 48 Continued
7th Div Ammn Column

Place	Date	Hour	Summary of Events and Information	Remarks and references to Appendices
Boschepe	Nov 12	✓	2nd Lieut. Ross struck off strength effect from 11.10.17 on account of Medical Board in England while on leave. Auth. X Corps No. 024 [illegible] 11.10.17.	
RENESCURE	13	✓	D.A.C. moved by road from Boschepe to Renescure.	
—"—	14	✓	Major A.W. LYLE-KIDD joined & commanded D.A.C. and posted with effect from 6.11.17 vice Lt. Col. H.H. Rogers D.S.O. to England. Auth. 7 D.A. R.O. No. 236 of 7.11.17	
—"—	17	✓	109 O.R. joined from base as reinforcements	
—"—	18	✓	2nd Lieut. M. MacLean and 2nd Lieut. J.H. Roberts reported their arrival from base and posted to No 2 & 3 Sections respectively.	
—"—	19	✓	Inspection of D.A.C. and billets by C.R.A.	
ARQUES	20	✓	D.A.C. moved to Arques for purpose of entraining to Ventimiglia.	

[illegible] Lt Col
Comdg D.A.C. 7th Div

D. D. & L., London, E.C.
(A8c04) Wt W1771/M2031 750,000 5/17 Sch. 52 Forms/C2118/14

Army Form C. 2118.

Instructions regarding War Diaries and Intelligence Summaries are contained in F. S. Regs., Part II. and the Staff Manual respectively. Title pages will be prepared in manuscript.

WAR DIARY
or
INTELLIGENCE SUMMARY.

Sect 48. Confined
7 Div Amm Column

(Erase heading not required.)

Place	Date	Hour	Summary of Events and Information	Remarks and references to Appendices
Arques	21	✓	Entrained and departed from ARQUES.	
CEREA. (ITALY)	27	✓	arrived CEREA. ITALY detrained and marched to PRESCANO.	
ABOSLIAR	29	✓	Column marched to ABOSLIAR	
CERVARESSE S. CROCE	30		Column marched to CERVARESSE. S. CROCE.	

[signature]
Cmdg.
Comdg. D.A.C.
7. DIV.

D. D. & L., London, E.C.
(A8c04) Wt W1771/M2031 750,000 5/17 Sch. 52 Forms/C2118/14

7 DIVISION. H.Q. TROOPS

37 BRIGADE. R.F.A.

1915 MAR TO 1916 MAY.

7 DIVISION TRENCH
MORTAR BATTERIES
(X,Y, & Z)

1916 FEB TO 1917 NOV.

DIVISION AMMUNITION
COLUMN.

1914 SEPT TO 1917 NOV.

7 DIVISION. H.Q. TROOPS

37 BRIGADE. R.F.A.

1915 MAR TO 1916 MAY.

7 DIVISION TRENCH MORTAR BATTERIES (X, Y, & Z)

1916 FEB TO 1917 NOV.

DIVISION AMMUNITION COLUMN.

1914 SEPT TO 1917 NOV.

7 DIVISION. H.Q. TROOPS

37 BRIGADE. R.F.A.
1915 MAR TO 1916 MAY.

7 DIVISION TRENCH
MORTAR BATTERIES
(X, Y, & Z)
1916 FEB TO 1917 NOV

DIVISION AMMUNITION
COLUMN.
1914 SEPT TO 1917 NOV.

www.ingramcontent.com/pod-product-compliance
Lightning Source LLC
Chambersburg PA
CBHW080917230426
43668CB00014B/2144
* 9 7 8 1 4 7 4 5 0 6 4 4 1 *